HISTORY

A WORKBOOK OF SKILL DEVELOPMENT

HISTORY

A WORKBOOK OF SKILL DEVELOPMENT

Conal Furay and Michael J. Salevouris

NEW VIEWPOINTS
A Division of Franklin Watts
New York/London/1979

New Viewpoints
A Division of Franklin Watts
730 Fifth Avenue
New York, New York 10019

**To our parents
Guy and Marguerite,
Mike and Gretchen**

Cover design by Ginger Giles

Book design by Rafael Hernandez

Library of Congress Cataloging in Publication Data

Furay, Conal.
  History, a workbook of skill development.

  Bibliography: p.
  1. History—Examinations, questions, etc. I. Sale-
vouris, Michael J., joint author. II. Title.
D21.F947   907'.6   78-31324
ISBN 0-531-05620-1 Workbook
ISBN 0-531-05622-8 Teacher's Manual

Preface

Two recent trends in American education have been instrumental in moving us to write this book. First, there has been a drift away from traditional forms of history in many high schools and colleges in favor of "relevant" topic courses in the social sciences. Valuable though they may be, such courses often leave students aware of many contemporary problems but tragically ignorant of the historical antecedents to those problems. Further, these courses do little to encourage students to develop the conceptual tools to think historically. Second, there has been of late an exodus from "liberal arts" curricula to professional and preprofessional training programs. The unstated (and often stated) assumption is that courses in the liberal arts cannot prepare one adequately for a career in the "real world."

A basic premise of this book is that a good liberal-arts education can often provide better all-round career preparation than many narrowly vocational programs. It is a further premise of this book that, within the context of a liberal-arts education, the development of basic historical literacy is essential. Not only can history give one a perspective on the world that no other discipline can provide, but the serious study of history will help the student develop skills that *are* highly relevant and applicable to the world of work.

This matter of skill development requires further comment. In their otherwise admirable concern with assisting students to rise above the here and now through history, too many teachers fail to give sufficient voice to history's other advertisement: that it promotes development of certain highly transferable (and highly marketable) intellectual skills. Such skills have been variously described in educational literature, including, notably, the well-known Bloom taxonomy of educational goals (1956), and, more recently, the works defining the "competencies" that emerge from training in each discipline. In this work we focus on five skills that reach not only into all sub-fields of history, but also across all disciplinary lines, and across the major seam that separates the academic and occupational worlds. These skills are:

1. the skill of systematic questioning,
2. the skill of evaluation of evidence,
3. the skill of synthesizing complex materials,

4. the skill of orderly presentation of thought in writing, and

5. the skill of efficient analysis of a written communication.

There are few students who would not benefit from further development of these skills, and there are few professional and managerial occupations that do not put a high premium upon them.

In this book we have tried to combine theory and practice, with the balance leaning in the direction of the latter. In each chapter we provide a brief introductory overview of the topic in question, but it is the exercises that constitute the essential core of the book. The aim of the essays and exercises is not to teach sophisticated research skills to prospective graduate students in history, but to make the study of history more meaningful for the countless students who major in history, take history courses, or simply read history, without any intent other than to profit from the experience. It is our hope that this workbook will enhance students' appreciation of history on a purely intellectual level and at the same time help them develop skills that have applicability both to other academic subjects and to the outside world of work.

The exercises in this book range from the relatively simple to the complex. Many of the exercises (but not all) have two sets of questions—Set A and Set B. Few instructors will want to assign every exercise to every student, but in instances where the instructor feels that the repetition of an exercise might be beneficial to a student, a second set of materials is provided. Although most of the exercises call for written responses, ideally students should have the opportunity to discuss their answers in a classroom setting. History is not like arithmetic where one, and only one, answer is "correct," and the value of many exercises will be greatly enhanced by general debate and discussion.

This book can also be used as a programmed text for individual students if circumstances so dictate. The programmed approach may be especially valuable for students with family and work responsibilities who find it difficult to conform to class schedules designed for the resident nonworking student. It is also quite conceivable that a teacher might wish to assign certain exercises to individual students in a "content" course so that they might bolster their skills in a particular area—for example, writing book reviews, reading secondary sources, and so on.

We might also note here that many of the quoted extracts from historical literature reveal a bias toward the more traditional narrative varieties of history. This may seem peculiarly old-fashioned at a time when so many researchers have abandoned the narrative "storytelling" approach to history in favor of analytical social-scientific approaches (see Chapter Two). But we have our reasons: (1) First, for a person to think historically, he or she must, before all else, be able to see events as part of an organic continuum linking past ages and experiences to our own. In our opinion, narrative, chronological history facilitates the development of this sense of historical continuity better than many purely analytical studies. (2) Furthermore, narrative histories still constitute the bulk of most library collections, and such histories are a logical place for students to begin. Moreover, the critical skills needed to interpret and evaluate narrative histories are equally applicable to analytical histories. (3) Finally, the authors share the belief that when history is true to its intellectual heritage it *does* tell a story. A sense of chronological development—one thing happening after another—is one of the basic characteristics that distinguishes history from the other academic disciplines.

We wish to express our gratitude to the many colleagues, students, and friends who have helped us in putting together this book. We extend special thanks to our colleagues in the Department of History–Political Science at Webster College—as always they have been full of encouragement and helpful in practical ways; to Professor Neil George, department chairman, political scientist, and friend of historians—through his determined efforts we secured extra funds to print the experimental copies of this workbook; to Ms. Karen Luebbert and Mrs. Anne Moedritzer of the Eden-Webster Library—their critique of our chapter on library usage has measurably improved its usefulness; to Professor Richard Birdsall of Connecticut College—his willingness to go out of his way helped us at a crucial moment; and to Marie Durbin, Mary Fechner, and Michael Lindsay, thoughtful students and occasionally severe critics—we trust they realize how highly we have valued their suggestions. We owe a special debt of gratitude to Ms. Bridget McGrath, whose proofreading, editing, and typing skills were invaluable, and to Mrs. Ruth Southern, who typed the final copy of the manuscript. Finally, who can write a book such as this and fail to thank the many scholars from whose works we have sought counsel? Indeed, we stand on their shoulders.

Contents

The Meanings and Nature of History

Exposure to the "past" for the average American begins very early, perhaps at that point when the child's mother first follows the ideas on child care given to her by her mother. As the child grows he or she is increasingly exposed to family traditions, religious traditions, and cultural traditions, all survivors of the past, each "separated out" from common experience and thus given a special value. At age five or six a child hears folk tales set somewhere in a vague past; at perhaps seven or eight the youngster learns of heroes who lived somewhere "back there," and at age nine or ten the study of the national past is introduced. None of these experiences may yet have involved the word history, but the term now begins to be used, and the study of it becomes increasingly sophisticated as past events are presented in a systematic way. History becomes one of the "givens" that one must learn, if only to satisfy school requirements. Very soon a student begins to regard "the past" as whatever is written down in history books, much to the detriment of that living reality that was the past.

Already, in just one paragraph, the term history has been used several times, and before it is bandied about any further it is crucial that we (the authors) and you (the reader) establish a common ground of understanding as to its meaning. It has a fuzziness, especially in the English language, that frequently muddles clear discussion and leads to a distortion of what the school subject "history" really is.

The main difficulty is that "history" has two distinct meanings. First, it can refer to the sum total of all that has actually happened in the past—that vast accumulation of millions of years, billions of people, and untold trillions of occurrences. Used in this sense "history" is surely one of the broadest concepts of human intellectual experience. But broad as it is, its use is indispensable in separating the first fundamental reality of human existence, the past, from the second, the present. *This meaning—things that happened in the past—is what most people have in mind when, in day-to-day conversation, they use the term history.*

On to the other meaning, the crucial one so far as study of the past is concerned, that is, history as an *account* of some portion of that past reality. We ask you to visualize yourself walking away from a lofty mountain range, its peaks and valleys hidden in a sort of purple mist. Now a companion turns a searchlight back upon the mountain range, and asks you to watch with him as his beam lights some of the shapes and promontories and recesses of the range. Momentarily your interest is caught by a glimpse of the contours of the landscape from which you are drawing away. But alas! your companion's beam is transient and imperfect, and it soon fades away. Yet the mountain range is still there, and remains there, perhaps awaiting other beams, projected from other angles, to further illumine its mysteries.

In this allegory the mountain range is "the past," history in its first meaning. The man with the searchlight is the historian who by using the beam of his intelligence reveals some of the outlines of that mountain range that towers in the distance. Essentially he "lights up" some segment of what lies behind us. If his beam is strong enough and focused correctly he shows us a certain past—its shape, its peculiarities, its color and texture. In short he gives an account of it, he gives us a history—*his* history. This is of course history in its second meaning: *an account or story of some part of the past.*

Granted that the analogy is imperfect, leaving too many questions unanswered, still, it serves to express a most fundamental distinction: that on the one hand there is this enormous *reality* called the past; on the other hand there is this here-and-now *account* of some aspect of that reality. Both are called "history," yet are really distinct. It is unfortunate that the English language, ordinarily so resourceful in showing variations of meaning, fails to provide us two distinct terms in this matter. By way of contrast, the French have an effective way of showing the difference: in speaking of the real, total past, they use a capital—*l'Histoire*; in speaking of *accounts* of the past they use the lower case—*l'histoire*. American and British historians must find other ways to show the distinction, using "history-as-actuality" to designate the past in its full reality and using "history-as-written" or "subjective history" to designate accounts of the past.

The difference between the two meanings is not just another unimportant textbook distinction called forth to pester students with subtleties. Rather, it is essential to any true understanding of what history as a school subject or discipline is. When one clearly perceives the distinction he comes to know what an *account* is and must be: an inherently *subjective*, individualized view of some segment of past reality; one particular vision of that past reality; a personal rendering of one's understanding of some past. The history we read in books and articles is *always* in the form of a communication that attempts to re-create a past in some way. It is *never* anything more than the merest smattering of some full-blown past reality, and thus represents an effort to depict rather than picture completely. Fundamentally, *any* written (or spoken) piece of history ought to be treated as an individual creation, respectable insofar as it calls forth in the reader a clear image or understanding of some past. This is not a "putdown"; rather, it is a description of the essential nature of this school subject called history.

We need not look far to see why written history can be only a pale reflection of the past reality it attempts to represent. In one respect the earlier analogy is misleading, for the historian cannot even shine a weak beam of light on the real past as if it were a mountain range. The real past, unlike the mountain range, is gone forever. Instead, the historian must construct an account of the past on the basis of surviving *records*—that is, all the written and non-written materials that the past has left. (The use of such records is discussed in Chapter Four.)

It is obvious that surviving records, compared to the real past they reflect, are like a very few drops of water in a very large bucket. For instance, most past events left no records at all! Think of the number of events in your own life for which there is no record but your own memory. Multiply those unrecorded events in your own life by the billions of human beings who inhabit the earth and you get some idea of the number of "events" each day that go unrecorded. Moreover, of the past events that *were observed and recorded*, the correspondence between the reality and the record is often slight. After all, much of what was observed in the past was not remembered, only a part of what was remembered was recorded, some of what was recorded has been lost or destroyed, and part of what remains is not totally trustworthy. In the words of one historian:

> Before the past is set forth by the historian, it is likely to have gone
> through eight separate steps at each of which some of it has been lost;
> and there is no guarantee that what remains is the most important, the
> largest, the most valuable, the most representative, or the most
> enduring part. In other words the "object" that the historian studies is
> not only incomplete; it is markedly variable as records are lost or
> recovered.[1]

Thus the historian can never get the full truth about a given past; the best he or she can deliver, even under the best of conditions, is a sketch of a vanished past. Noted historian Bruce Catton put it this way: "Even the best history is not much better than a mist through which we see shapes dimly moving." Or, in the words of W. S. Holt, "History is a damn dim candle over a damn dark abyss." Small wonder that written history is "subjective."

If written history—the account—is inherently subjective, then where does that leave us so far as "truth" is concerned? The answer is that there is no necessary opposition between the terms *subjective* and *truth*. Shakespeare's works are subjective, yet there is much truth in them; Rembrandt's portraits are subjective, yet reveal character with great accuracy. And the view of Christopher Columbus's voyages presented by historian Samuel Eliot Morison in *Admiral of the Ocean Sea* is subjective, yet is acknowledged to be a clear depiction of the discoverer's great adventure. Morison's account is "true" because of his extensive research, careful analysis of available evidence, and superb synthesizing ability.

An overview of a historian's procedure in re-creating some segment of the past will give deeper insight of history as an account. At the very outset every historian approaches his work with an approximate model of human life, or better, a model of the way human affairs typically work. His starting point is some past event (or condition); his procedure is to *work backward* from that event, examining the traces (evidence) left by it; his purpose is to show that event as part and parcel of a larger whole. In other words, the historian wants to place the event in a setting so that after the story is told a reader (or listener) will respond

---

[1]Louis Gottschalk, *Understanding History* (New York: Knopf, 1950), p. 46.

with something like, "Yeah, the whole thing makes sense." Such is the substance of the historian's task. In summary, he has taken assorted bits of evidence, perceived in them a certain set of relationships, and expressed these relationships in an account.

It is obvious that no event is ever a unique and isolated phenomenon. No one is satisfied by a list like the following, in which all items are unrelated "bits of evidence":

—The Citizens' National Bank was robbed on August 20, 1952.
—A total eclipse of the sun occurred on the same day.
—John Smith was admitted to City Hospital suffering from gunshot wounds.

Such a list, called a chronicle, immediately sets one's mind to speculating about connections between the events, but given the scarcity of evidence, no relationships can be clearly drawn. Equally unsatisfying is the placement of an event as the culmination of a seemingly infinite series of antecedent occurrences such as the following: the election of Franklin Roosevelt in 1932, which took place in a setting of depression desperation, which was preceded by reduced farmer purchasing power, which was influenced by overproduction, which was possible through development of farm technology, which was furthered by American inventiveness, which was necessitated by the nineteenth-century labor shortage, and so on. Such an approach to history, remarked Mark Twain wryly, always seems to make any given event depend ultimately on Julius Caesar's decision to cross the Rubicon into Italy!

What the reader of history wants is not mention of isolated facts or an endless string of antecedents. Nor does the reader want anything so cryptic as a World War II American flyer's account of his morning patrol: "Sighted sub, sank same." Nor does he want an account so complicated that he "can't see the forest for the trees." What is needed is a description and elaboration of the crucial linkages, a story one can follow. Good history is quite comparable to ordinary explanation in real life, or, as one writer put it, "a journalist's account of the decision to bomb North Vietnam and a cocktail-party tale of wife swapping in Scarsdale" both entail tracing the "intrinsic relations" between events and locating each of them in a setting.

Earlier on, mention was made of the fact that a historian comes to the work of reconstruction with a sort of flexible model of how human affairs work. He has something of a theory of how things typically happen, and, once he begins to explore what might lie behind a given event, that theory leads him to read the evidence with certain questions in mind. These "starter questions" will be discussed in detail in a later chapter; for the present it is sufficient to indicate their general lines: What individuals crucially influenced the situation? Were certain ideas and attitudes of vital importance? Economic considerations? Institutional forces? Group pressures? Technological developments? Environmental conditions? As the historian asks these questions, he becomes increasingly familiar with the main elements of the real past under consideration. His speculations and hypotheses become less tentative. Gradually he identifies a cluster of antecedent events, influences, and components that, by their linkages, make the end event a logical development. As the historian completes the patterning of the various influences that culminated in the event, he very likely singles out one (or perhaps more) of them as having been pivotal, thus giving his account a distinctive flavor or "interpretation." In summary, what the historian has done with some segment of the past is to show the meaningful interconnections between an event and particular aspects of the situation in which it was contained, with some of those aspects having a relatively greater explanatory value.

After the historian has completed the first half of his task—asked his questions, evaluated the evidence, and identified a pattern of interrelated events and conditions—his effort is culminated by the telling of the story. The telling of it has its own special requirements. Basically, though the historian is going to give an account of a sequence of events through time, it cannot be simply a matter of "this happened, then this happened, then this happened," and so on. Pure narrative or the "then, then, meanwhile, afterward" format does an injustice to the reader, who, in order to comprehend, needs chunks of analysis sandwiched between the flow of events. In fact, there is a form of history that is called analytical in contrast to narrative.

Narrative history tells a story in more or less chronological order. *Analytical history*, on the other hand, puts the chronological movement of events into the background. Analytical history either (1) attempts to describe and analyze the characteristics of a specific period, event, or situation at a given time; or (2) attempts to *compare and contrast* events, periods, or situations in order to uncover general features that transcend the immediate particulars of a given place or time. An example of the first type of analytical history is Peter Laslett's *The World We Have Lost* (1965). In this study Laslett examines the social and economic structure of preindustrial England without concerning himself with the day-to-day movement of events. He draws examples from many places and years in order to show, in general terms, what English life was like during the century or so before the industrial revolution. An example of the second type of analytical history (comparative history) is Crane Brinton's *Anatomy of Revolution* (1938, 1952) in which Brinton compares four revolutions separated by more than two hundred years. In this book Brinton is not so much concerned with writing the history of, say, the French Revolution or the Russian Revolution, but he *is* interested in pointing out what past revolutions *in general* have had in common. Thus, in this second type, the traditional historical concern with the unique, concrete event takes a back seat to comparative analysis and generalization.

It is to be emphasized that both analytical approaches still qualify as history. Each analytical approach depends ultimately on a careful reconstruction of concrete realities and leads to a better understanding of them. However, in practice, the distinction between "narration" and "analysis" tends to blur, as it is impossible to narrate events of a period without analyzing certain of its aspects. Likewise, analysis must be firmly based on the concrete events that constitute the backbone of all history. The typical way in which narrative and analysis are combined in a piece of written history is illustrated in the passage below, which discusses the end of World War II in 1945. Note our bracketed remarks:

On August 6, after an ultimatum to surrender, the first atomic bomb destroyed rather more than four square miles of Hiroshima and killed upward of seventy thousand persons. [A narrative sentence—note the action verbs.] Since the Japanese high command still ignored the ultimatum, a second and more powerful bomb was dropped three days later on Nagasaki, destroying six square miles and killing an unknown number. [Again, part of the basic narrative flow.] These two holocausts were on about the same scale as an Anglo-American triple air raid on Dresden, which had been undertaken in support of the Russian winter offensive in February, 1945. [This is a bit of comparative analysis enabling the reader to appreciate the destructive force of just two bombs.] The new bomb was, however, decisive because it appeared capable of limitless, pitiless, irresistible repetition. [Again, analysis—of the threat the bomb posed.] The Japanese government resolved to submit before a third bomb fell, leaving the conquerors to wrestle with the problem of atomic weapons which still darkens the thoughts of mankind. [Basically narrative, though the latter part of the sentence does briefly describe the long-term menace of the bomb.][2]

This chapter would be incomplete without a discussion of several ways in which the historian gives a sense of coherence to his re-creation of some segment of the past. It is especially important to keep in mind this principle of re-creation. The historian knows he cannot bring back the full past reality. The historian knows too that the sequence of events cannot be presented in the same helter-skelter way in which they originally occurred. And so, to achieve coherence, he uses several *conventions,* some of which are various forms of analysis, others of which are specifically narrative techniques. It is important to be aware of these conventions because they reveal how important the individual historian is in the process of reconstructing the past. Some of the most important conventions are as follows: (1) The historian manipulates time. He reaches back from the event being studied, sometimes way back in time, to specify earlier developments or traditions; he looks forward from the event, discussing its significance; he condenses time, often presenting in a staccato way a series of separate actions or "briefing" a time period by a summary characterization. (2) He characterizes individuals, analyzes strengths and weaknesses of major figures, and provides a glimpse of their perceptions, motivations, and attitudes. (3) The historian surveys the basic conditions that generated or intensified problems. (4) He sharpens oppositions. Aware that coherence will sometimes be advanced by clear-cut rivalries, he makes oppositions more unequivocal and single-minded perhaps than they were in reality. (5) The historian shifts scenes, thus conveying a sense of the whole. (6) He editorializes, offering his own value judgments by choice of words or sometimes by a sort of "voice offstage" technique. (7) He analyzes the significance of certain developments or their short- or long-term effects. This is not an exhaustive list, but it suffices to delineate some of the major conventions. Note our bracketed comments in the following excerpt discussing military operations during the Revolutionary War:

The year 1778 was one of incompetence and failure on all sides, redeemed only by the indomitable patriotism of Washington. [The author opens with a summary of the entire year, but note also his characterization and opinion of Washington.] While Washington's troops suffered in frigid Valley Forge, Sir William Howe's men reveled in Philadelphia. [Note shift of scene, also author's choice of the word *revel.*] But Howe was recalled in the spring of 1778, and his successor, Sir Henry Clinton, was ordered to evacuate the city and to concentrate on New York in preparation for a

---

[2]Ernest J. Knapton and Thomas J. Derry, *Europe and the World Since 1914* (New York: Scribner, 1966), p. 289.

new campaign. On 28 June, Washington attacked Clinton's retiring army at Monmouth Court House, New Jersey: a confused battle in which an American disaster was barely averted by Washington's sending Charles Lee off the field, and saving the day himself. Clinton's army reached New York safely; and all that Washington could do was to encamp at White Plains, fortify West Point, and look on. [These three sentences are simply a continuation of narrative flow, though note the quick summary of separate actions—"encamp...fortify...look on."]

The only successful American campaign of 1778 was that of George Rogers Clark, acting for the state of Virginia. He shot the rapids of the Ohio, and, undismayed by a total eclipse which frightened his men, led his little force across the wilderness to take the British post of Kaskaskia in Illinois, first in a series of bloodless victories. [Note again a quick summary of actions.] When the British struck back and threatened to recapture each of the posts he had taken, the intrepid Clark in February 1779 marched his men 180 miles in the dead of winter through icy floods, sometimes shoulder-high, until sick, sodden and weary they arrived at Vincennes to surprise the disbelieving British. [Note characterization of Clark; also note author's description of the environmental conditions that Clark confronted]. Clark is often credited with saving the West for his country; but if the peace negotiators in 1782 were aware of his exploits, they did not allude to them in a single one of their numerous notes and dispatches. [A manipulation of time, as the author looks forward in time to 1782.]

The war had now reached the nasty stage common to many wars, when one side or the other, unable to reach a military decision, resorts to desultory and haphazard operations that have no useful military result but arouse bitterness and hatred. [The author here makes a value judgment on the progress of the war, using something of a generalization to do so— "...the nasty stage common to many wars."][3]

The foregoing passage is too short to illustrate all of the conventions described earlier, but it gives you at least some idea of the technique of re-creation. Viewed in terms of a common American experience, the historian's presentation is not so very different from that of an announcer in a press box broadcasting an athletic event. Just as the announcer is at a distance from the action so that he can see things panoramically, so too is the historian. Just as the announcer spends time between "plays" analyzing the strategy, tactics, and people that make things work, so too does the historian. Just as the announcer evaluates the performances of the main figures he sees, so too does the historian. Just as the announcer immerses himself in the flow of the action and then steps back from it, so too does the historian. Just as the announcer tries to make his account colorful and personal, so too does the historian. And just as some announcers show obvious favoritism toward one side or another, so too do some historians. There are these evident parallels, but of course the historian's task is measurably more difficult. He must picture something he cannot see except through evidence and recount something that is far more complex than an athletic contest. This difficulty suggests that there is a bit of truth in Oscar Wilde's witty observation that "Any fool can make history, but it takes a genius to write it."

---

[3]S. E. Morison, H. S. Commager, W. E. Leuchtenburg, *The Growth of the American Republic* (New York: Oxford University Press, 1969), pp. 195–97. Reprinted by permission.

EXERCISES

**SET A
Exercise 1**

The following statements use "history" in one or the other of its two crucial meanings, referring either to the *reality* that is the past or to an *account* of the past (someone's version of the reality). Your task here is to decide which meaning of history the author of each statement intended. Use "R" to refer to its usage as "reality" and "A" to refer to its usage as "account."[4]

_____ **1.** "History is not the accumulation of facts, but the relation of them." (Giles Lytton Strachey)

_____ **2.** "In its amplest meaning History includes every trace and vestige of everything that man has done or thought since first he appeared on the earth." (James Harvey Robinson)

_____ **3.** "A page of history is worth a volume of logic." (Oliver Wendell Holmes)

_____ **4.** "History itself touches only a small part of a nation's life. Most of the activities and sufferings of the people...have been and will remain without written record." (E. L. Woodward)

_____ **5.** "History is baroque. It smiles at all attempts to force its flow into theoretical patterns or logical grooves; it plays havoc with our generalizations, breaks all our rules." (Will Durant)

_____ **6.** "History without politics descends to mere literature." (Sir John Robert Seeley)

_____ **7.** "History is not melodrama, even if it usually reads like that." (Robert Penn Warren)

_____ **8.** "We cannot escape history and neither can we escape a desire to understand it." (Anonymous)

_____ **9.** "History, as the study of the past, makes the coherence of what happened comprehensible by reducing events to a dramatic pattern and seeing them in a simple form." (Johann Huizinga)

_____ **10.** "Inertia is the first law of history, as it is of physics." (Morris R. Cohen)

**SET A
Exercise 2**

The second exercise is intended to deepen your understanding of the essentially *re-creative* character of history. As we have seen, historians use various conventions in trying to make the past comprehensible. We would like you to identify several such conventions in the passage that follows. More specifically, we want you to find specific usage of the following conventions, citing the point in the passage or the sentence in which you see the convention exemplified.

1. Characterization of an individual: _____

_____

[4]Nearly all of the particular quotations in this exercise, and in Set B, Exercise 1, were drawn from an extensive list compiled by Ferenc M. Szasz and printed in the following issues of *The History Teacher*, a quarterly periodical published by the Society for History Education, California State University, Long Beach, California: Vol. VII, No. 4 (August 1974), pp. 552-63; Vol. VIII, No. 1 (November 1974), pp. 54-63; Vol. VIII, No. 2 (February 1975), pp. 208-16; Vol. IX, No. 2 (February 1976), pp. 217-27.

2. Description of perceptions, motivations, etc.:_____

_____

_____

3. Shift of scene:_____

_____

4. Value judgment of author: _____

_____

5. Analysis of significance of a development:_____

_____

_____

6. Manipulation of time (two examples of this, please—check the description of this convention given in our discussion earlier)

    a. _____

    _____

    b. _____

    _____

The passage is taken from William L. Shirer's *The Rise and Fall of the Third Reich*.[5] It provides a description of Adolf Hitler's aggressive moves in the years just before the outbreak of World War II in 1939.

The First Steps: 1934–37

¶ 1 On May 2, 1936, Italian forces entered the Abyssinian capital, Addis Ababa, and on July 4 the League of Nations formally capitulated and called off its sanctions against Italy. Two weeks later, on July 16, Franco staged a military revolt in Spain and civil war broke out.

¶ 2 Hitler, as was his custom at that time of year, was taking in the opera at the Wagner Festival at Bayreuth. On the night of July 22, after he had returned from the theater, a German businessman from Morocco, accompanied by the local Nazi leader, arrived in Bayreuth with an urgent letter from Franco. The rebel leader needed planes and other assistance. Hitler immediately summoned Goering and General von Blomberg, who happened to be in Bayreuth, and that very evening the decision was taken to give support to the Spanish rebellion.

¶ 3 Though German aid to Franco never equaled that given by Italy...it paid handsome dividends to Hitler.

¶ 4 It gave France a third unfriendly fascist power on its borders. It exacerbated the internal strife in France between Right and Left and thus

---

[5](New York: Simon & Schuster, 1960, pp. 297-9. Reprinted by permission of Simon & Schuster, a Division of Gulf and Western Corporation.

weakened Germany's principal rival in the West. Above all it rendered impossible a *rapprochement* of Britain and France with Italy, which the Paris and London governments had hoped for after the termination of the Abyssinian War, and thus drove Mussolini into the arms of Hitler.

¶ 5   From the very beginning the Fuehrer's Spanish policy was shrewd, calculated and far-seeing. A perusal of the captured German documents makes plain that one of Hitler's purposes was to *prolong* the Spanish Civil War in order to keep the Western democracies and Italy at loggerheads and draw Mussolini toward him....

¶ 6   It was these circumstances which gave birth to the Rome-Berlin Axis. On October 24, after conferences with Neurath in Berlin, Count Galeazzo Ciano, Mussolini's son-in-law and Foreign Minister, made the first of his many pilgrimages to Berchtesgaden. He found the German dictator in a friendly and expansive mood. Mussolini, Hitler declared, was "the leading statesman in the world, to whom none may even remotely compare himself." Together, Italy and Germany could conquer not only "Bolshevism" but the West. Including England! The British, Hitler thought, might eventually seek an accommodation with a united Italy and Germany. If not, the two powers, acting together, could easily dispose of her. "German and Italian rearmament," Hitler reminded Ciano, "is proceeding much more rapidly than rearmament can in England.... In three years Germany will be ready...."

¶ 7   The date is interesting. Three years hence would be the fall of 1939.

¶ 8   In Berlin on October 21, Ciano and Neurath had signed a secret protocol which outlined a common policy for Germany and Italy in foreign affairs. In a speech at Milan a few days later (November 1) Mussolini publicly referred to it without divulging the contents, as an agreement which constituted an "Axis"—around which the other European powers "may work together." It would become a famous—and, for the Duce, a fatal—word.

¶ 9   With Mussolini in the bag, Hitler turned his attentions elsewhere. In August 1936 he had appointed Ribbentrop as German ambassador in London in an effort to explore the possibility of a settlement with England—on his own terms. Incompetent and lazy, vain as a peacock, arrogant and without humor, Ribbentrop was the worst possible choice for such a post, as Goering realized. "When I criticized Ribbentrop's qualifications to handle British problems," he later declared, "the Fuehrer pointed out to me that Ribbentrop knew 'Lord So and So' and 'Minister So and So.' To which I replied: 'Yes, but the difficulty is that they know Ribbentrop.'"...

¶ 10   On January 30, 1937, Hitler addressed the Reichstag, proclaiming "the withdrawal of the German signature" from the Versailles Treaty—an empty but typical gesture, since the treaty was by now dead as a doornail—and reviewing with pride the record of his four years in office. He could be pardoned for his pride, for it was an impressive record in both domestic and foreign affairs. He had, as we have seen, abolished unemployment, created a boom in business, built up a powerful Army, Navy and Air Force, provided them with considerable armaments and the promise of more on a massive scale. He had singlehandedly broken the fetters of Versailles and bluffed his way into occupying the Rhineland. Completely isolated at first, he had found a loyal ally in Mussolini and another in Franco, and he had detached Poland from France. Most important of all, perhaps, he had released the dynamic energy of the German people, reawakening their confidence in the nation and their sense of its mission as a great and expanding world power.

**SET B
Exercise 1
(Optional)**

The following statements use "history" in one or the other of its two crucial meanings, referring either to the *reality* that is the past or to an *account* of the past (someone's version of the reality). Your task here is to decide which meaning of history the author of each statement intended. Use "R" to refer to its usage as "reality" and "A" to refer to its usage as "account."

_____ **1.** "History consists, for the greater part, of the miseries brought upon the world by pride, ambition, avarice, revenge, lust, sedition, hypocrisy, ungoverned zeal, and all the train of disorderly appetite." (Edmund Burke)

_____ **2.** "I know histhry isn't thrue, Hinnessey, because it ain't like what I see ivery day in Halstead Street." (Mr. Dooley [Peter Finley Dunne])

_____ **3.** "History is the witness of the times, the torch of truth, the life of memory, the teacher of life, the messenger of antiquity." (Cicero)

_____ **4.** "History does not usually make real sense until long afterward." (Bruce Catton)

_____ **5.** "The deepest, the only theme of human history, compared to which all others are of subordinate importance, is the conflict of skepticism with faith." (Goethe)

_____ **6.** "Every work of history constructs contexts and designs, forms in which past reality can be comprehended. History creates comprehensibility primarily by arranging facts meaningfully and only in a very limited sense by establishing strict causal connections." (Johann Huizinga)

_____ **7.** "Fellow citizens, we cannot escape history." (Abraham Lincoln)

_____ **8.** "What we call history is the mess we call life reduced to some order, pattern and possibly purpose." (Anonymous)

_____ **9.** "But history is neither watchmaking nor cabinet construction. It is an endeavor toward better understanding." (Marc Bloch)

_____ **10.** "History is, in its essence, exciting; to present it as dull is, to my mind, stark and unforgivable misrepresentation." (Catherine Drinker Bowen)

**SET B
Exercise 2
(Optional)**

The second exercise is intended to deepen your understanding of the essentially *re-creative* character of history. As we have seen, historians use various conventions in trying to make the past comprehensible. We would like you to identify several such conventions in the passage that follows. More specifically, we want you to find specific usage of the following conventions, citing the point in the passage or the sentence in which you see the convention exemplified.

1. Characterization of an individual: _____

_____

2. Description of perceptions, motivations, etc.: _____

_____

_____

3. Shift of scene: _____

_____

4. Value judgment of author: _____

_____

5. Analysis of significance of a development: _____

_____

_____

6. Manipulation of time (two examples of this, please—check the description of this convention given in our discussion earlier)

a. _____

_____

b. _____

_____

The passage is taken from Crane Brinton, et al., *A History of Civilization*.[6] It is concerned with Peter the Great, the Russian Tsar from 1682–1725.

The Early Years of Peter the Great

¶ 1 The young Peter was almost seven feet tall, and extremely lively. Highly intelligent, he had learned to read and write (but never to spell) from a drunken tutor who was the only academic instructor the troubled times afforded. Even in his early years, Peter was fascinated by war and military games. He set up a play-regiment, staffed it with full-grown men, enlisted as a common soldier in its ranks (promoting himself from time to time), ordered equipment for it from the Moscow arsenals, and drilled it in war games with unflagging vigor, himself firing off cannon or pounding on a drum with equal enjoyment. He discovered a broken-down boat in a barn, and unraveled the mysteries of rigging and sail with the help of Dutch sailors settled in the foreigners' suburb of Moscow. Sailing remained one of his keenest passions. Though he married at the age of sixteen, Peter neglected his wife, and preferred working on his military maneuvers, sailing his boats, and relaxing with his peculiar circle of cronies.

_____

[6]Crane Brinton, J. B. Christopher, R. L. Wolff, *A History of Civilization*, Vol. II, 3rd ed. (Englewood Cliffs, N.J.: Prentice-Hall, 1967, pp. 222-4. Reprinted by permission of Prentice-Hall, Inc.

¶ 2   This rowdy lot smoked huge quantities of tobacco (which horrified the conservative Muscovites, who believed that smoking was specifically forbidden by the Biblical text which says that what cometh out of the mouth defileth a man), and regularly got completely drunk. Then they would engage in obscene parodies of church services, or play elaborate and highly dangerous practical jokes on the unoffending citizenry, roaring about Moscow in winter late at night on sleighs and treating the sleeping populace to shrieking serenades. Masquerades and parties lasted for days; staid Moscow ladies, accustomed to almost harem-like seclusion, were commanded to put on low-necked evening dresses in the western style, and dance and engage in social chit-chat. They were literally forced to drink with the Tsar and his friends: if a lady refused, Peter simply held her nose, and poured the wine down her throat. Peter spent enormous sums of state revenue on this sort of party, and richly endowed his boon companion Lefort, a young Swiss soldier of fortune who became Field Marshal, Grand Admiral and "chief diplomat."

¶ 3   The almost frantic energy that Peter devoted to pleasure reflected only part of his appetite for new experience. Just as he served in the ranks of his own play-regiment and sailed his boats himself, so he eagerly learned any new technique that came to his attention. At various times he took up carpentry, shoe-making, cooking, clock-making, ivory-carving, etching, and—worst of all—dentistry. Once he had acquired a set of dentist's tools, nobody was safe, since Peter did not care whether the intended victim had a toothache or not; whenever he felt the need to practice, he practiced—and those were the days before anesthetics. Preferring to wear shabby work clothes, driving his own horses, neglecting formal obligations and paying little attention to court and church ceremony, Peter in his own person was a shock to the Muscovites, and not in the least in keeping with their idea of a proper tsar....

¶ 4   In 1695, anxious to try his hand at war, Peter led a campaign against the Turks at Azov in the area of the Black Sea. He failed, but in the next year, with the help of Dutch experts, he assembled a fleet of riverboats on the Don, sailed them downriver, and defeated the Turks at Azov. Since the Habsburgs at the time were waging a long war against the Turks, this rather surprising Russian contribution aroused much interest and curiosity. The project of forming a league against the Turks with the states of western Europe now gave Peter the pretext for a trip outside Russia, the first undertaken by a Russian sovereign since the Kievan period.

¶ 5   Though ostensibly traveling incognito as a Russian noncommissioned officer, Peter naturally failed in his efforts to conceal his identity: after all, there were no other authoritarian seven-footers in the party. What fascinated him was western "know-how," especially naval. He planned to go to Holland, England, and Venice, where the best ships (in his opinion) were made, find out how they were made, and bring the knowledge back to Russia for the advancement of Russian aims. He hired several hundred technicians to work in Russia, raised money when he needed it by selling to an English peer the monopoly of tobacco sales in Russia, and visited every sort of factory or museum or printing press he could find. The huge Russian Tsar in all his vigor and crudity, emerging into the air of western

Europe from his antiquated and stagnant country, made an unforgettable impression.

¶ 6   From the celebrated western trip many well-known pictures emerge: Peter laboring as a common hand on the docks in Holland; Peter and his suite, drunk and dirty, wrecking the handsome house and garden of the English diarist, John Evelyn, near London: "There is a house full of people," wrote Evelyn's harassed servant, "and that right nasty." Less well known perhaps are the spectacles of Peter dancing with a German princess, mistaking her whalebone corsets for her ribs, and commenting loudly that German girls have devilish hard bones; of Peter receiving an honorary degree at Oxford; of Peter deep in conversation (Dutch) with William Penn about the Quaker faith; of Peter gobbling his food without benefit of knife or fork, or asleep with a dozen or so of his followers on the floor of a tiny room in a London inn with no windows open.

¶ 7   Before Peter could get to Venice, the western trip was interrupted by news that the *streltsy* had revolted again (1698). Peter rushed home, and personally participated in the punishment of the alleged plotters; he and Menshikov rather enjoyed chopping off the heads of the victims. Though many innocent men suffered torture and death, Peter had broken the *streltsy* as a power in Russian domestic life.

¶ 8   From the West, Peter had returned more determined than ever to modernize his country and his countrymen. The very day of his return he summoned the court jester, and with his assistance went about with a great pair of shears, stopping his courtiers and clipping off their beards. Though this may seem a trivial joke, in fact it was an action full of symbolism. The tradition of the Orthodox Church held that God was bearded; if man was made in the image of God, man must also have a beard. Deprived of his beard, man was no longer made in God's image, and was a natural candidate for damnation. This was the way the Muscovite nobles and churchmen felt. Peter now decreed that Russian nobles must shave, or else pay a substantial tax for the privilege of wearing their beards. Bronze beard-tokens worn around the neck certified that the tax had been properly paid; without such a token a bearded man ran the risk of being clipped on sight.

¶ 9   Presently, Peter issued an edict commanding that all boyars, members of the gentry class, and the city population generally must abandon traditional Russian dress, which included long robes with flowing sleeves and tall bonnets, and adopt western-style costume. The manufacture of the old-fashioned clothes was made illegal, and Peter added point to his decree by taking up his shears again, and cutting off the sleeves of all the people he met wearing the forbidden robes. The enactments on the beards and on dress were regarded by the victims as an assault on precious customs and a forcible introduction of hated foreign ways.

History
and the
Disciplines

We have seen in Chapter One that the central aim of the historian is to "light up" a segment of the human past, a past that has vanished, yet a past that can still be studied through the records that have been left behind. This is the essential paradox of history: The actual events of the past are gone forever, but they are as "real" as all the human activities you see around you every day. As the British historian G. M. Trevelyan wrote:

> History starts out from this astonishing proposition that there is no differ-
> ence in degree of reality between past and present. Lady Jane Grey was
> once as actual as anyone in this room. And we had best be careful before
> we think of her as a phantom lady with her head under her arm, for we
> are of her succession, and shall soon be no more and no less ghostly than
> she. We, too, are only queens and kings for a day. We are all food for
> history. No one century, not even the twentieth, is more real than any
> other.[1]

The historian's task is as challenging as any on earth. Unlike the scientist who can experiment directly with the objects of his research, the historian is many times removed from the events that are the object of *his* study. Much that happened in the past (indeed *most* of what happened in the past) was never recorded; much that was recorded has been lost; and the records that remain are often contradictory, imprecise, and misleading. Furthermore, the historian himself is a factor in the equation. Not only is he fallible and capable of error, but his own biases, political beliefs, economic status, religious persuasion, and personal idiosyncracies can subtly and unconsciously influence the way in which he interprets the sources that do exist. For instance, a conservative Republican might "read" the evidence of the Watergate Affair in a much different light than, say, a liberal Democrat. (See Chapter Six for a further discussion of this problem.)

Given the maddeningly tentative nature of historical knowledge that results from the inherent limitations of the evidence and the human fallibility of

---

[1] "History and Fiction," *Clio, A Muse and Other Essays*, new ed. (London: Longmans, Green, 1930), p. 100.

historians, let us consider further the nature of historical study. More specifically, how does the work of the historian compare and contrast with the work of the scientist, social scientist, and artist? This is not the place for an in-depth consideration of this problem. But a few words should be said about history's relationship to the sciences, social sciences, and humanities, for history is at once all of them and none of them.[2]

To even the most casual observer it is apparent that the discipline of history is an intellectual chameleon. In its attempt to establish solid "truths" (or at least viable hypotheses) about man and his world, history shares a good deal with science; as a discipline concerned primarily with women and men as *social beings*, it shares much with the social sciences; and as a discipline that so often emphasizes telling a story about the past in a literate and engaging fashion, it aspires to the status of an art. Yet the differences between history and her sister disciplines are as striking as the similarities.

HISTORY AND SCIENCE

In the nineteenth century some of the pioneers of modern historical studies were convinced that history could attain the status of a pure science like chemistry or physics. N. D. Fustel de Coulanges, a nineteenth-century French historian, was typical when he claimed: "History is and should be a science." A moment's reflection will show that such optimism was misplaced.

The aim of science is to discover regularities in nature—"laws"—which can be used to generalize (i.e., predict) about future occurrences. Precise measurement and laboratory experiments are the basic methods used for establishing such scientific "laws." For instance, if one experiments by heating water (at sea level) to 212° Fahrenheit, it will boil and turn to steam. If, time after time, the same transformation occurs at 212°F., the researcher can conclude that the boiling point of water at sea level is 212°F. The researcher can generalize further that such always was the case and always will be the case in the foreseeable future.

It should be obvious that history, in this sense, can never be a science as physics and chemistry can. Past events are unique and unrepeatable. The historian cannot "experiment" on the past. He cannot run the French Revolution over and over again to discover which variables were the critical ones. Nor can he interview the participants or have them submit to lie-detector tests. The historian can never establish the boiling point of a human community with anything like the precision with which the scientist can establish the boiling point of a liquid. The historian, then, does not aim, as the scientist does, to establish general universal laws. Given the nature of his subject matter (unique, concrete events), the historian is more interested in reconstructing *specific episodes* in all their diversity and particularity. He aims at truth, but not universal, timeless truth.

In spite of the above, history shares more with science than first meets the eye. First of all, originally "science" simply meant "knowledge." And if we think of a science as any search for knowledge based on a rigorous and objective examination of the evidence (whether the evidence is a beaker of boiling water

---

[2]An excellent introduction to the debates on these issues can be found in Hans Meyerhoff (ed.), *The Philosophy of History in Our Time* (New York: Doubleday, 1959).

or a diplomatic dispatch), then clearly history has some claim to being a "science." Second, not even all the so-called sciences are totally experimental in approach. Such disciplines as astronomy, geology, medicine, and even biology are much akin to history in their methodology. All, like history, rely heavily on systematic observation and classification of data. Moreover, sciences like astronomy and geology are (like history) primarily concerned with studying the "records" of *past* events. The geologist studies rock formations and mountain ranges that betoken upheavals thousands of years ago. The astronomer examines light and radio waves that originated eons in the past. Even the physician needs to be somewhat of a historian in that a patient's unique personal medical history must be taken into account before diagnosis and treatment.

To sum up, even though history can never hope to achieve the level of certainty that is possible in the pure experimental sciences, it can still, through the application of rigorous canons of research, strive to attain closer and closer approximations of the "real" past it seeks to recover. Remember, as difficult as it is to reconstruct the events of the past, those events *did* happen. The heroes, villains, and nameless masses actually lived and breathed. They loved and hated, built and destroyed, worked, played, and died. Just as the scientist is concerned with the concrete realities of the natural world, so too is the historian concerned with real people and real events. To the extent that past reality can be recaptured, however faintly, history can stand with the sciences as one more technique for better understanding the world in which we live.

HISTORY AND THE SOCIAL SCIENCES

History is related even more closely to the so-called social and behavioral sciences (e.g., anthropology, sociology, political science, economics, psychology). Indeed, many would include history among the social sciences. Whether history is a bedfellow or simply a close relative of the social sciences need not, for the moment, concern us. What is clear is that historians and social scientists share much in common. On the simplest level it is fair to claim that history provides much raw material for the social sciences. It would even be arguable (rightly we think) that history is in many ways the father of the social sciences. Historians Jacques Barzun and Henry Graff have noted that the social sciences "are in fact *daughter* disciplines [to history], for they arose, each of them, out of historical investigation, having long formed part of avowed historical writing."[3]

Both history and the social sciences are bodies of knowledge that deal with *women and men in society.* Indeed, it is often difficult to tell where one discipline leaves off and another begins. It is best to think of history and the social sciences not as distinct categories, but as colors in an intellectual spectrum where one hue shades imperceptibly into another. But as much overlap as there is, each discipline approaches the study of the individual and society in a slightly different way.

Anthropology literally means the "study of man." Physical anthropologists study the centuries-long physical evolution of human beings, whereas cultural anthropologists attempt to describe similarities and differences among ethnic

---

[3]*The Modern Researcher*, rev. ed. (New York: Harcourt, Brace and World, 1970), p. 218.

and cultural groups and to explain the evolution of human social patterns. The work of the cultural anthropologist is not so different from the work of the historian. Anthropologists *are* historians of a sort, and some have defined history as "retrospective cultural anthropology." In general, though, the anthropologists have traditionally concentrated on primitive or preliterate peoples, whereas the historians have emphasized the study of civilizations for which there are *written records.*

Sociology, a close relative of anthropology, studies the characteristics and behavior of social aggregates and groups, especially their institutions and modes of social organization. Whereas anthropology has typically emphasized the study of primitive societies, sociologists have focused their attention on the more advanced, technologically sophisticated societies. To the extent that anthropology and sociology might study the *same* cultural groups and institutions, they are almost indistinguishable as disciplines. Again, the overlaps with history are many. Much sociology is based on historical evidence, and many historians have adopted a sociological approach in their historical studies of social classes, occupational groups, institutions, and the like.

Political science, like sociology, attempts to unlock the secrets of institutional and group behavior, but, as the name implies, concentrates especially on political behavior and governmental institutions. The evolution of political and legal ideas (political theory) has also been a longtime interest of the political scientist. The shared interests of the political scientist and historian are many, since law, politics, war, and diplomacy are among the most traditional objects of historical study. Many scholarly works on government, international relations, and politics are impossible to categorize as history or political science with any degree of certainty. Theodore White's well-known *Making of the President* volumes, for example, might equally be used as texts in both political science and history courses.

Economics is the science that attempts to lay bare the mechanisms through which a society produces, trades, and distributes material goods. That the historian too is vitally interested in the economic side of human affairs goes without saying. Ever since Karl Marx (1818–1883) proposed an entire theory of historical change based on the operation of economic forces, historians have been able to ignore the material (economic) side of life only at their own peril.

Finally, *psychology* is the "science of mental, emotional, and behavioral processes." The psychologist is interested in the unseen forces within the individual and within the environment that make people behave the way they do. More than the other social and behavioral sciences, *psychology emphasizes the mental processes and behavior patterns of the individual*, although some branches of psychology (e.g., social psychology) do deal with group behavior. Recently, historians have shown a growing interest in the psychological dimension of human behavior. Indeed, a hybrid field, psychohistory, has lately grown into respectability. Both historians and psychologists have attempted to apply the insights of psychology and psychoanalysis to historical individuals and groups—with uneven success.

Clearly, there are many parallels between history and the various social sciences. But how do they differ? First, and this verges on massive oversimplification, a major preoccupation of the social sciences is to explain how societies, economies, groups, governments, institutions, and individuals behave *today*.

History, on the other hand, is more interested in explaining how societies functioned and *evolved* in the past—that is, *how they changed through time.* Of course, the political scientist or economist does not ignore history (i.e., the past); nor does the historian ignore the lessons of the present. But generally the social sciences are much more "present oriented" than is history. The social scientist (often using historical evidence) tries to account for present behavior; the historian (often using contemporary insights) tries to account for past behavior.

History and the social sciences diverge in yet another way. The social sciences, like the physical sciences, emphasize the precise quantification (i.e., measurement) of data, experiments (when appropriate), and the development of "laws" that allow prediction (and even control) of future behavior. *Whereas the historian attempts to reconstruct individual events in all their uniqueness, social scientists attempt to discover general principles of behavior that can be used to understand many events.* To oversimplify, the historian examines the uniqueness of past events; the social scientist searches for the commonalities. For instance, a historian may desire to know all there is to know about the Kennedy-Nixon election of 1960 in order to write a definitive history of that election. A political scientist, however, might want to compare the voter behavior in 1960 with that in 1964, 1968, 1972, and 1976 in order to discover voting patterns that might help him predict the outcomes of future elections. Now, the historian will be more than happy to utilize whatever information the political scientist discovers (intellectual parasitism has a long and noble history), *but* it is not the historian's *primary* purpose to establish such regularities. Nor is the historian especially interested in prediction. He feels it is difficult enough to find out what has already happened. "It is the historian's aim," claims one writer, "to portray the bewildering, unsystematic variety of historical forms—people, nations, cultures, customs, institutions, songs, myths, and thoughts—in their unique, living expressions and in the process of continuous growth and transformation."[4] To this abundant description one might only add that it is the historian's further aim to portray all that variety in a systematic and readable manner.

Whether history is a bona fide social science or just a close relative is a matter best left open for debate. What is not open for debate is the fact that many historians (and the number is growing) are self-consciously trying to move history away from the time-honored narrative (storytelling) tradition in favor of the analytical and comparative format of the social sciences. (Recall the discussion of these forms in Chapter One.) Many historians (sometimes successfully, sometimes not) have applied the models, theories, and methodologies of the social sciences to historical problems. This trend is especially visible among social and economic historians who have taken to computers, statistical formulas, economic models, and sociological jargon with immense gusto. A good example is the controversial *Time on the Cross* by Robert W. Fogel and Stanley Engerman. Engerman and Fogel attempt an elaborate cost-benefit analysis of the slave economy of the American South before the Civil War. To do so they utilize elaborate mathematical formulas and economic models. It is in studies like this that history comes closest to being a full-fledged member of the social-science fraternity.

In spite of the boom in quantitative sociological history, however, most history

---

[4]Meyerhoff, *op. cit.*, p. 10.

is still "traditional" in that it is based on the careful reading and interpretation of literary evidence—chronicles, memoirs, letters, debates, diplomatic dispatches, and the like—and it is presented in a more-or-less narrative format. For many areas of historical inquiry, quantitative and statistical techniques will forever remain irrelevant either because the proper raw data is unobtainable or is not susceptible to quantification. It would be counterproductive, for instance, to attempt to understand the ideas of Plato or Thomas Jefferson with a computer and a set of statistical tables.

HISTORY AND ART

If, in studies like *Time on the Cross*, history seems to "belong" to the social sciences, in many other instances it seems to belong more to the literary arts. After all, in its most basic form, history is, as the name suggests, a "story." To tell a story well, the good historian is called upon to utilize the literary skills of the novelist or poet. Arnold Toynbee, the famous British historian, has claimed that "no historian can be 'great' if he is not also a great artist." In fact, some of the very greatest historians have been superb literary stylists and their works are worth reading on literary merit alone. The war histories of Winston Churchill, Lord Macaulay's *History of England*, Edward Gibbon's *Decline and Fall of the Roman Empire*, and Carl Sandburg's volumes on Lincoln are just a few examples of works that will live as literature no matter how one judges them as history. And, as history, we might add, they are quite respectable.

The historian must be an "artist" in another sense. To make the past come alive for the current era, a historian must be able to *re-create* in his own mind, and on paper, the passions, beliefs, and feelings of people long dead. This requires more than literary grace. The *historian must empathize and sympathize* with individuals, institutions, customs, and ideas that may seem foreign or strange (see Chapter Five). Like the poet or novelist, the historian must be able to make an imaginative leap in order to "feel" himself into the period he is studying. Dispassionate objectivity is, of course, essential to good history; but so too is the imaginative insight of the creative artist. The basic difference between a great historian and a great novelist is that the historian must confine the workings of his imagination to the known facts. The plausibility of the historian's narrative is determined by its adherence to the evidence. Good fiction, on the other hand, must be internally consistent and it must correspond to commonsense notions of how human beings behave, but it need not conform to any external body of source materials.

A SUMMARY: THE MAIN FEATURES OF HISTORY

If you are still somewhat confused about exactly where history fits into the jigsaw puzzle of intellectual life, do not despair. The lines that separate one branch of knowledge from another have never been precise. In simplest terms, the basic characteristics of history are three:

1. *History is concerned with man in society.* The historian is not concerned with the origins of the earth—that is the task of the geologist; he is not concerned with organic life processes—that is the task of the biologist; he is not concerned with when and how mankind came on the scene—that is the task of the

anthropologist. The historian's work only begins in the presence of reliable records—especially *written* records—which indicate that a specific human group shared a specific set of experiences in a specific time and place.

2. *History is concerned with change through time.* Quite obviously, "man in society" as described above is the central concern of disciplines other than history. Cultural anthropology examines similarities and differences among human ethnic groups; sociology studies a society's institutions and modes of social organization; political science concentrates on the political forms in a society; and economics on the mechanisms by which a human society provides material goods and services for itself. As distinct from these disciplines, however, history explains a society's *movement through time*—the events that marked its course, the problems that altered its direction, the individuals that affected its momentum, the ideas that shaped its destiny—in other words the changes (and the stabilities) that characterized that society's life from one point in time to another. Finally, it is important to note that true history does not just *list* events like a chronicle or diary does; history attempts *to explain* how and why events occurred as they did.

3. *History is concerned with the concrete and the particular.* This is not always true, of course, because even in history generalizations can and *must* be made. But in the final analysis a basic defining characteristic of the discipline in history's continuing preoccupation with the unique circumstance, and with the particulars that give substance to generalizations and distinctiveness to a given point in time. In other words, generalization, however important, is secondary to a knowledge of a *particular* past.[5]

---

[5]For a fuller discussion of history's three basic concerns, see Arthur Marwick, *What History Is and Why It Is Important* (Bletchley, England: The Open University Press, 1970, pp. 22–4.

EXERCISES

SET A
Exercise 1[6]
The preceding chapter has been devoted to outlining some of the major similarities and differences between the study of history and the other disciplines. In the selections below, see if you can distinguish the examples of historical writing from those drawn from a variety of other disciplines. Before doing so, however, recall the central characteristics of history: (1) a concern with man in society, (2) a preoccupation with change through time, and (3) a preference for explaining the interrelationship of concrete, particular events rather than elaborating comprehensive generalizations or hypotheses. Also, historians generally limit themselves to the study of societies for which there are written records.

Mark the passages drawn from history with an "H." Mark the passages drawn from other disciplines with an "O." You need not identify the other disciplines specifically. But do indicate your reasons for choosing as you do, specifically using the criteria (1, 2, 3) above.

Example:

_____ **A.** We have now got so close to our present that we have to count in tens of thousands of years rather than in millions. Beginning at some undefined point in time, perhaps 70,000 years ago, Neanderthal Man appeared on the scene. As we shall see in Chapter IX, he represents the beginning of civilized man in the sense that he went in for religious observances, which suggests an intellectual capacity for abstract concepts. It also suggests that he must have had the kind of spoken language we have, if less refined and subtle. Indeed, his brain was as large as ours, although presumably rather different, for his skull was low-browed and bun-shaped rather than domed.... They inhabited Europe, the Middle East, and central Asia until roughly 35,000 b.p. [before the present], when they disappeared, perhaps because they were unable to compete with or defend themselves against men of our own kind, who were replacing them.

> **Commentary:**
> This passage is challenging to categorize. If you labeled it history, we would not object too strenuously. The passage does deal with men in society (note the reference to religious observances), and it attempts to describe and explain change through time. Yet we would label this passage with an "O" because the author is describing a period long before the invention of writing and hence written records—a period often referred to as "prehistoric." The subject matter belongs more properly in the domain of the anthropologist.

_____ **B.** Naturally, the larger and more massive a star, the more tremendous a red giant it will balloon into. The red giant into which our Sun will someday bloat will not be a particularly impressive specimen of the class. Red

---

[6]The inspiration for this exercise came from Marwick, *ibid.*, pp. 25–30.

giants such as Betelgeuse and Antares developed out of main sequence stars considerably more massive than the Sun.

> **Reasons:**
>
>
>
>
>
>
>
>
>

_____ **C.** Leadership of Europe moved north to France, England, and Holland in the seventeenth century. In France, Henry IV (1589–1610) restored the monarchy to authority after a long bout of civil and religious wars. The state remained officially Catholic; but French national interests were kept carefully distinct from the cause of the papacy or of international Catholicism. Effective royal control of the Church in France dated back to the fourteenth century and was vigorously and successfully maintained against the revivified papacy in the sixteenth and seventeenth centuries.

> **Reasons:**
>
>
>
>
>
>
>
>

_____ **D.** What role do the opinions of the general public play in democracy? The average citizen clearly plays little part in initiating or directing day-to-day policies. Recent research has amply borne out arguments Walter Lippmann offered thirty years ago. The average citizen has little interest in public affairs, and he expends his energy on the daily round of life— eating, working, family talk, looking at the comics (today, TV), sex, sleeping. Not knowing what the government is doing about public problems, he has no basis for opinions on most policies of his government. Even if he had an interest in politics, he would have great difficulty getting accurate information; since the events of politics take place at a great distance, he cannot observe them directly, and the press offers a partial and distorted picture.

> **Reasons:**

____   **E.**   The Administration that came to power in January 1961 under President John F. Kennedy presented an attitude towards American responsibilities for "leadership" of the free world that one could call either "vigorous" or "frenzied," depending on how one felt about it. Our NATO allies were quickly apprised of the fact that the Americans had many new ideas for the defense of Europe, and that the Europeans would have to make some endeavor to understand and implement them. These ideas were themselves significant for what was to happen in the Far East, because they involved a complete dismantling of the "massive retaliation" concept in favor of a whole new complex of ideas stressing the use of conventional forces in limited wars. The man who as a true believer presided intimately over this change was the new Secretary of Defense, Robert S. McNamara.

> **Reasons:**

____   **F.**   Seventeenth-century America had none of the speculative vigor of English Puritanism. For Massachusetts Bay possessed an orthodoxy. During the classic age of the first generation, at least, it was a community of self-selected conformists. In 1637 the General Court passed an order prohibiting anyone from settling within the colony without first having his orthodoxy approved by the magistrates....Here was a community formed by free consent of its members. Why should they not exclude dangerous men, or men with dangerous thoughts? What right had supporters of a subversive Mr. Wheelwright to claim entrance to the colony?

> **Reasons:**
>
>
>
>
>
>
>
>
>
>

_____ **G.** 410   In this year Rome was destroyed by the Goths, eleven hundred and ten years after it was built. Then after that the kings of the Romans no longer reigned in Britain. Altogether they had reigned there 470 years since Gaius Julius first came to the land.

596   In this year Pope Gregory sent Augustine to Britain with a good number of monks, who preached God's word to the English people.

671   In this year there was the great mortality of birds.

715   In this year Ine and Ceolred fought at "Woden's barrow."

733   In this year Aethelbald occupied Somerton, and there was an eclipse of the sun.

> **Reasons:**
>
>
>
>
>
>
>
>
>

_____ **H.** There are obviously two kinds of pressure at work in the market. On one side is the willingness of consumers to buy larger or smaller quantities of the product, depending on its price. On the other side is the willingness of manufacturers to produce and bring to market various amounts of the product, depending on the price which they expect to receive. Demand-supply analysis is a way of separating these forces, analyzing each in turn, and then bringing them together to explain price and output.

Reasons:

Sources

A. Louis J. Halle, *Out of Chaos* (Boston: Houghton Mifflin, 1977), p. 241.

B. Isaac Asimov, *The Universe* (New York: Avon, 1966), pp. 162–63.

C. William H. McNeill, *The Rise of the West* (New York: Mentor, 1965), p. 635.

D. M. D. Irish and J. W. Prothro, *The Politics of American Democracy*, 2nd ed. (Englewood Cliffs, N.J.: Prentice-Hall, 1962), p. 262.

E. Bernard Brodie, *War and Politics* (New York: Macmillan, 1963), pp. 124–25.

F. Daniel Boorstin, *The Americans: The Colonial Experience* (New York: Random House, 1958), p. 7.

G. *The Anglo-Saxon Chronicle* from B. L. Blakeley and J. Collins (eds.), *Documents in English History* (New York: John Wiley & Sons, 1975), p. 18.

H. Lloyd G. Reynolds, *Economics* (Homewood, Ill.: Richard D. Irwin, 1963), pp. 93–94.

**SET A
Exercise 2** We have noted that recently many historians have applied some of the categories, insights, and methods of the various social sciences to historical problems. In the *history* passages below see if you can determine which of the social-science approaches (i.e., anthropology, sociology, political science, economics, psychology) the historians have tried to utilize. If more than one answer seems appropriate, please so indicate. Also, identify those passages that simply narrate "what happened" in a more traditional manner. Use the word "traditional" for such passages. You might want to review the brief definitions of the various social sciences on pages 19–20.

A. Among the Navaho, witches are active primarily at night. This is also so among the Tale, the Azande and the Amba, but there is little trace of night meetings in Essex, [England]. Navaho witches are believed to meet most frequently in a cave, and there is general agreement that all types of witch activity must be carried on away from home. Likewise, witches among the Kaguru meet in unfrequented places....

B. On Saturday, March 19, two days before the examination of Martha Corey, the Reverend Deodat Lawson arrived in Salem Village. He had been its minister from 1684 to 1688 and had now returned as a visiting preacher and for personal reasons as well; the afflicted girls were saying that his wife and daughter, whom he had buried there, had been killed by

_____

witchcraft. He tells us that there were at that time ten afflicted persons—three girls from nine to twelve years old...three adolescent girls...and four married women....He conducted both the morning and the afternoon services on Sunday, but not without incident.

C. Early in the year 1692 several girls of Salem Village (now Danvers), Massachusetts, began to sicken and display alarming symptoms [interpreted later as manifestations of witchcraft].... These symptoms are readily recognizable. The most cursory examination of the classic studies of hysteria—of Charcot, of Janet, of Breuer, and Freud—will demonstrate that the afflicted girls in Salem were hysterical in the scientific sense of that term.

_____

D. Almost every indicator by which the two Village factions may be distinguished, in fact, also neatly separates the supporters and opponents of the witchcraft trials.... The connection is clear: that part of Salem Village which was an anti-Parris stronghold in 1695 (the nearest part of Salem Town) had also been a center of resistance to the witchcraft trials, while the more distant western part of the Village, where pro-Parris sentiment was dominant, contained an extremely high concentration of accusers in 1692.... Similarly with wealth:...the average 1695–96 tax of the Villagers who publicly opposed the trials was 67 percent higher than that of those who pushed the trials forward....

_____

E. Our discussion will focus on a set of complex relationships between the alleged witches and their victims....Who were these witches, accusers, and witnesses? How did their lives intersect? Most important, what traits were generally characteristic and what traits were alleged to have been characteristic of each group?

_____

F. The fifteenth century witnessed a vast expansion of witch literature and witch trials. In part this geometric progression of the witch phenomenon can be attributed to the decay of those ideas and institutions that had held medieval society together. Deprived of the old securities, people responded in panic that at that particular time found vent in terror of witchcraft.

_____

Discussion:
For which passage(s) would more than one answer be appropriate?

Sources

A. A. D. J. MacFarlane, *Witchcraft in Tudor and Stuart England* (New York: Harper & Row, 1970), p. 211.

B. Chadwick Hansen, *Witchcraft at Salem* (New York: Mentor, 1970), p. 72.

C. *Ibid.*, pp. 21–22.

D. Paul Boyer and Stephen Nissenbaum, *Salem Possessed* (Cambridge, Mass.: Harvard University Press, 1974), p. 185.

E. John Demos, "Witchcraft in Seventeenth-Century New England," *AHR*, 75, (June 1970), 1312–13.

F. J. B. Russell, *Witchcraft in the Middle Ages* (Ithaca, N.Y.: Cornell University Press, 1972), p. 227.

SET A
Exercise 3

Among historians there is disagreement whether history is more a social science (like political science or sociology) or a humanity (like literature). As we have seen, history shares characteristics with both camps. Usually historians do not state explicitly where they stand on this issue, but often their attitudes are implicit in the books and articles they write. In the passages below indicate whether you think the historian in question seems to view history more as a social science or a humanity.

One clue to look for is the emphasis given to *literary evidence* (written records) versus *statistical and quantifiable evidence*. A preference for the latter would indicate a social scientific frame of reference. Another clue would be the relative weight given to description and narration versus analysis and generalization. Again, the latter emphasis *may* indicate a more "scientific" approach to the study of the past.

On a scale of 1 to 3, mark the most social-science-oriented passages with a "1" and the most traditional or "literary" passages with a "3." Those that you feel are in the middle, or for which you are unsure, mark with a "2."

_____ **A.** [In the Middle Ages] one sound rose ceaselessly above the noises of busy life and lifted all things unto a sphere of order and serenity: the sound of bells. The bells were in daily life like good spirits, which by their familiar voices, now called upon the citizens to mourn and now to rejoice, now warned them of danger, now exhorted them to piety. They were known by their names: big Jacqueline, or the bell Roland. Every one knew the difference in meaning of the various ways of ringing. However continuous the ringing of the bells, people would seem not to have become blunted to the effect of their sound.

_____ **B.** At whatever level one conducts research, roll-call votes offer versatile data that can be used to explore a variety of questions. Along with collections of session-laws and statutes, they comprise the most systematic body of data extant on the legislative process in the states. Roll calls offer data with which to discriminate systematically between contested and consensus issues and to compare the levels of voting conflict evoked by particular policy areas among various states.

_____ **C.** The extravagant conversations recorded by Hermann Rauschning for the period 1932–34, and by Dr. Henry Picker at the Fuehrer's H.Q. for the period 1941–42, reveal Hitler in another favourite role, that of visionary and prophet.... The fabulous dreams of a vast empire embracing all Europe and half Asia; the geopolitical fantasies of inter-continental wars and alliances; the plans for breeding an _élite_, biologically pre-selected, and founding a new Order to guard the Holy Grail of pure blood; the designs for reducing whole nations to slavery—all these are fruits of a crude, disordered, but fertile imagination soaked in the German romanticism of the late nineteenth century....

_____ **D.** To be more precise, only one of the manifestations of sexual change will occupy us here: a rapid increase in the incidence of illegitimate births between the mid-eighteenth and mid-nineteenth centuries.... We may bring to bear other kinds of evidence as well upon sexual history, such as the observations of contemporaries, various 'medical' surveys of the population conducted by the cameralist governments of western and central Europe, court records on sexual crimes and aberrancies, or the study of pornography.... Yet in this paper, I wish to present the evidence of illegitimacy alone.

First we examine potential objections to illegitimacy data as a measure of real sexual attitudes and practices; second, we briefly discuss the dimensions of the increase in illegitimacy between mid-eighteenth and mid-nineteenth centuries; third, a review of some current theories about sexual behavior and illegitimacy is in order; fourth, a general model linking modernizing forces to sexual change and illegitimacy will be proposed; finally I shall present empirical data confirming some of the linkages in this model from a region of central Europe which participated in the illegitimacy explosion—the Kingdom of Bavaria.

_____ **E.** In 1941 Frederick Williams introduced Frederick Mosteller to the problem which we shall consider in detail in this paper, namely the problem of the authorship of the disputed _Federalist_ papers. Williams and Mosteller, influenced by the work of Yule and of C. B. Williams (1939), studied the undisputed _Federalist_ works of Hamilton and Madison but found that sentence length did not discriminate between the two authors. They then computed for each known paper the percentages of nouns, of adjectives, of one- and two-letter words, and of _the_'s. On the basis of these data they constructed a statistic that was intended to separate Hamilton's writings from Madison's. This statistic, however, was not sensitive enough to assign the disputed papers with any degree of confidence, although it pointed to Madison for most of them.

_____ **F.** Joan [of Arc (1412–31)] was born in that atmosphere of legend, of folklike dreamings. But the countryside offered another and very different kind of poetry, fierce, atrocious, and, alas! all too real: the poetry of war... War! That single word sums up all the emotions; not every day was marked by assault and pillage; but rather by the anguished expectancy, the tolling of the alarm bell, the sudden awakening, and, far in the plain, the sullen glare of fire.... A horrible condition: yet with an aura of poetry: even the most down-to-earth of men, the Lowland Scots, turned into poets amid the perils of the *Border*; from that blasted heath, which still seems under a curse, the ballads blossomed forth like wild and vigorous flowers.

G. John Stuart Mill [1806–73] is thought of today as the archetype of the liberal, the author of that classic of liberalism, *On Liberty*. But there was another John Stuart Mill, who was anything but the perfect liberal and whose writings were of a quite different character.... Mill's responsibility for the creation of his own stereotype is only now becoming apparent. The publication of his correspondence with Harriet Taylor, for twenty years his intimate companion and later his wife, and the more recent publication of the original draft of his *Autobiography*, are enormously revealing. It remains for scholars to collate these materials, as well as to re-examine his early writings in their original versions.

H. It all seems clear and consistent enough. The women in Shakespeare's plays, and so presumably the Englishwomen of Shakespeare's day, might marry in their early teens, or even before, and very often did.

Yet this is not true. We have examined every record we can find to test it and they all declare that, in Elizabethan and Jacobean England, marriage was rare at these early ages and not as common in the late teens as it is now. At twelve marriage as we understand it was virtually unknown....

It is indeed hazardous to infer an institution or a habit characteristic of a whole society or a whole era from the central character of a literary work and its story.... The outcome may be to make people believe that what was the entirely exceptional, was in fact the perfectly normal.... This is a cogent argument in favour of statistical awareness, and of the sociological imagination, in studies of this sort.

I. For Churchill it [the Japanese attack on Pearl Harbor and U. S. entry into World War II] was a moment of pure joy. So he had won, after all, he exulted. Yes, after Dunkirk, the fall of France, the threat of invasion, the U-boat struggle—after seventeen months of lonely fighting and nineteen months of his own hard responsibility—the war was won. England would live; the Commonwealth and the Empire would live. The war would be long, but all the rest would be merely the proper application of overwhelming force. People had said the Americans were soft, divided, talkative, affluent, distant, averse to bloodshed. But he knew better; he had studied the Civil War, fought out to the last desperate inch; American blood flowed in his veins.... Churchill set his office to work calling Speaker and whips to summon Parliament to meet next day. Then saturated with emotion, he turned in and slept the sleep of the saved and thankful.

Discussion:

In what ways might the books/articles represented by the passages you labeled "1" (social-science approach) be superior *as history* to those books and articles represented by passages labeled "3"? Is one approach better than the other or do both approaches have potential benefits and liabilities?

Sources

A. J. Huizinga, *The Waning of the Middle Ages* (New York: Anchor, 1954), p. 10.

B. Ballard Campbell, "The State Legislature in American History: A Review Essay," *Historical Methods Newsletter*, September 1976, p. 193.

C. Alan Bullock, *Hitler*, rev. ed. (New York: Bantam, 1969), pp. 325–26.

D. Edward Shorter, "Sexual Change and Illegitimacy: The European Experience," *Modern European Social History*, ed. Robert Bezucha (Lexington, Mass.: D. C. Heath, 1972), pp. 231–32.

E. Ivor S. Francis, "An Exposition of a Statistical Approach to the Federalist Dispute," *Quantification in American History*, ed. Robert P. Swierenga (New York: Atheneum, 1970), p. 98.

F. Jules Michelet, *Joan of Arc* (Ann Arbor, Michigan: University of Michigan Press, 1967), p. 10.

G. Gertrude Himmelfarb, *Victorian Minds* (New York: Harper & Row, 1970), p. 113.

H. Peter Laslett, *The World We Have Lost*, 2nd ed. (New York: Scribner, 1971), pp. 84, 90–91.

I. James M. Burns, *Roosevelt: Soldier of Freedom* (New York: Harcourt Brace Jovanovich, 1970), p. 163.

**SET B
Exercise 1
(Optional)** Again, mark the passages drawn from history works with an "H." Mark the passages from other disciplines with an "O." You need not identify the other disciplines specifically. Simply note the reasons why you choose as you do.

_____ **A.** The Spanish-speaking countries of South America share common institutional features that inhere in cross-national configurations of law, administration, religion, and status assignment, all having historical roots in the ideals and orientations of post-medieval Spain. Spanish South America merits attention as a distinctive social order whose properties are illuminated by comparison with other regional cultures or complex civilizations.

Reasons:

_____ **B.** Our new knowledge of the history of the parts of the Universe close to us, that of the Earth and the solar system, has in the last decade given us the absolute time scale with which we can measure the stages leading to the origin of life as we know it now on Earth and, presumably, of life as it may occur in other places in the Universe.

Reasons:

_____ **C.** Because there is considerable variety in primate political organization, we can only summarize some of the most general characteristics, those common to a large variety of systems. However, it must always be remembered that man has had a peculiar evolutionary history during which he has evolved features peculiar to him as a species. Because he is a gregarious, terrestrial primate with a history of savanna living, it will help us to look at other terrestrial primates with a similar history and see what adaptions have ensured their success.

Reasons:

_____ **D.** The Commonwealth [of Massachusetts] escaped lightly from the cholera epidemic of 1832. Yet, without a major crisis, Boston appropriated a larger sum to clean the streets and alleys and care for the sick than any other American city, and it was similarly prepared to meet the next threatened cholera epidemic in 1849. In addition, the legislature in the spring of that year established a commission to prepare a sanitary survey of the state.... While the specific source of disease remained the subject of controversy, a new attitude toward health was revealed in the _Report of the Sanitary Commission._

Reasons:

_____ **E.** If science gave the world the hydrogen bomb, Edward Teller is the scientist who contributed the most to it. His dual role in both arguing the need for the bomb and making a vital contribution to its creation is unique. Newspapers, following Lewis Strauss's lead, dubbed him "the father of the H-bomb," and the phrase has more truth than most such newspaper epithets. Teller disclaims the title, but out of modesty rather than distaste.

Reasons:

_____ **F.** The combination of high birth rates and low or rapidly declining death rates now found in the less-developed countries implies two different characteristics of the population that have important implications for the pace of their economic development. One important characteristic is rapid growth...; the other is the heavy burden of child dependency which results from a high birth rate whether death rates are high or low.

> **Reasons:**
>
>
>

_____ **G.** In this chapter Ghana and Uganda represent emerging African societies which are economically underdeveloped and are members of a growing international sub-system. For the most part, all of the major directing decisions are made by a select elite.... Both Ghanian and Ugandan leaders were raised in the colonial era, both shared in the battle against British colonialism—though in Uganda it was a mild, almost indifferent rebellion against paternal power. However, there are also some significant differences....

> **Reasons:**
>
>
>

_____ **H.** The [Russian] revolution of 1917 broke out in the middle of the first world war, in which Russia, although belonging to an eventually victorious coalition of powers, suffered the heaviest defeats. The revolution may therefore appear to have been merely the consequence of military collapse. Yet the war only accelerated a process which had for decades been sapping the old order and which had more than once been intensified by military defeat.

> **Reasons:**
>
>
>

Sources

A. "South American Society," *International Encyclopedia of the Social Sciences*, ed. David L. Sills, vol. 15 (New York: Macmillan, 1968).

B. J. D. Bernal, *The Origin of Life* (London: Weidenfeld and Nicolson, 1967), pp. 3–4.

C. Lionel Tiger and Robin Fox, *The Imperial Animal* (New York: Holt, Rinehart and Winston, 1971), pp. 27–28.

D. Barbara G. Rosenkrantz, *Public Health and the State: Changing Views in Massachusetts, 1842–1936* (Cambridge, Mass.: Harvard University Press, 1972), p. 4.

E. Norman Moss, *Men Who Play God: The Story of the Hydrogen Bomb* (Harmondsworth, England: Penguin, 1972), p. 67.

F. National Academy of Sciences, "The Growth of World Population," in *Readings in Economics*, ed. Paul Samuelson (New York: McGraw-Hill, 1967), p. 18.

G. William G. Fleming, "Sub-Saharan Africa: Case Studies of International Attitudes and Transactions of Ghana and Uganda," in *Linkage Politics*, ed. James Rosenau (New York: Free Press, 1969), p. 96.

H. Isaac Deutscher, "The Russian Revolution," *The New Cambridge Modern History* (Cambridge: Cambridge University Press, 1960), XII, 386.

**SET B
Exercise 2
(Optional)**

As you have seen from Set A, often the line separating history from her sister disciplines is not always a clear one. Below are some more excerpts from works of history (or by historians). Again, identify the specific social-science approach(es) utilized in each passage. As before, sociology, anthropology, economics, political science, and psychology are possible answers. In addition, you might look for specific examples of two other specialties that figure large in much history writing:

1. *Demography.* Demography is a close ally of sociology and it refers to the statistical study of human populations. It is concerned with gathering statistical information about the growth and movements of population, about death-rates, birth-rates, marriage ages, family sizes, and the like. When applied to past populations, such an approach is called historical demography.

2. *Archeology.* Archeology is the study of the remains and monuments of the past (buildings, temples, fortresses, pottery, etc.). It is a close relative of history and a bulwark for the study of ancient civilizations.

For the passages below, if more than one answer seems appropriate, please so indicate. Identify those passages that simply narrate "what happened" by writing "traditional" in the space provided. Some answers may appear more than once; others not at all.

_____ **A.** Yet, while there was an increase in population, the manors belonging to [the monastery of] Saint Germain-des-Prés [in the ninth century a.d.] did not show a trend toward large families. The average number of children ranged from slightly more than one child per couple to slightly over three children per couple. Rarely did the households include other than those in the immediate family.

_____ **B.** Seventeenth-century children thus started life with a dangerous handicap. Almost invariably, they were going to encounter problems of a special magnitude in their attempts to "get" [food]. Erikson has indicated some of the possible consequences of maladaption in this stage. If the child's constant efforts to fill his stomach are to no avail, he may lapse into a state of "oral pessimism." Eventually, this pessimism can develop into a pervasive mistrust, a deeply rooted conviction that the world is a bad place and that individual initiative, because it is never adequately rewarded, is not worth the trouble.

Thinking along these lines, one might argue that the food deprivation experienced by seventeenth-century children created the foundation for that fatalism which is often associated with the peasant mentality of the period.

_____ **C.** Most of the Romano-British evidence is derived from dwelling-sites, whether military stations, towns or farms, where the medium used for building was generally stone. Many of these sites remain to this day undisturbed by the imposition of later buildings. By contrast, the Anglo-Saxons normally built of wood or similarly less durable material....

_____ **D.** The age-price profile is better explained by the pattern of earnings over the life cycle of slaves. Indeed, the age-price profile implies a corresponding earnings profile. Figure 17 presents the average net earnings, or profit, from male slaves in the Old South at each age about the year 1850.

_____ **E.** This study is an investigation of the use and purpose of military forces in civilized societies whose histories are largely histories of warfare....

Comparative studies of primitive societies lead to the general conclusion that the scope of warfare broadens as the level of civilization rises. Among most of the simplest hunting and gathering tribes, warfare functions chiefly as a mechanism to revenge homicide or to defend territory from incursions.

_____ **F.** These communities were, then, firmly a part of the urban-industrial order, oases in the midst of a predominantly rural nation.... By investigating their family and household structure we can perhaps get clues which will help us resolve the many paradoxes which appear when we compare pre-industrial England with the present day.

_____ **G.** The modern temperance movement began in the United States about 1770, when a member of a Quaker meeting at Philadelphia protested that he was "oppressed with the smell of rum from the breaths of those who sat around him." The first formal pledge to abstain from drink was taken by those attending a meeting at Moreau in New York State in 1808, though the signatories were still allowed to drink wine at public dinners, or beer and cider at any time, or to break the pledge on payment of a twenty-five cent fine, increased to fifty cents for getting drunk.

Sources

A. Emily Coleman, "Medieval Marriage Characteristics," in *The Family in History*, ed. Theodore K. Rabb and Robert I. Rotberg (New York: Harper & Row, 1973), p. 4.
B. David Hunt, *Parents and Children in History: The Psychology of Family Life in Early Modern France* (New York: Basic Books, 1970), 118–19.
C. P. H. Blair, *An Introduction to Anglo-Saxon England* (Cambridge: Cambridge University Press, 1966), p. 19.

D.   Robert W. Fogel and Stanley L. Engerman, *Time on the Cross: The Economics of American Slavery* (Boston: Little, Brown, 1974), p. 74.

E.   Raoul Naroll, et al., *Military Deterrence in History* (Albany, N.Y.: State University of New York Press, 1974), p. 1.

F.   Michael Anderson, "Family, Household and the Industrial Revolution," in *The American Family in Social-Historical Perspective*, ed. Michael Gordon (New York: St. Martin's Press, 1973), p. 60.

G.   Norman Longmate, *The Waterdrinkers: A History of Temperance* (London: Hamish Hamilton, 1968), p. 33.

Questions

In Chapter One, history was described as a "re-creation," a sort of intellectual contrivance by which a historian conveys a picture of some past reality. While picture making is a feature of both narrative and analytical history, it is most clearly observable in narrative history.

Narrative history is often written and taught with predominant concern for establishing and presenting (or determining) the "causes" of some particular event, as the "causes" of the Civil War or the "causes" of Hitler's rise to power in the 1930s. For various reasons this "cause mentality" has been deeply ingrained in historical literature. Perhaps it cannot (and, as some say, *should* not) be eradicated, but the fact remains that preoccupation with causality often obscures the nature of what it is that the historian does. Historians are concerned not with causes per se, but with establishing the *significant relations* between an event and the conditions, people, and ideas associated with it. They are often uncomfortable in applying the term *cause* to any of these conditions, people, and ideas, for to do so, given the complexity of the interrelationships involved, risks considerable oversimplification. Remember that the historian is painting a picture. To call excessive attention to any one facet as being the "cause" of the picture's validity does violence to the complex conception the historian seeks to present. Generally, then, the keynote of history is not the search for causes in and of themselves; it is, rather, the search for "significant relations," which only in a broad sense may be regarded as casual. The great Dutch historian Johann Huizinga summarized this point as follows: "History creates comprehensibility primarily by arranging facts meaningfully and only in a very limited sense by establishing strict causal connections."

Seen in this way, what the historian does in explaining any given event is offer a *cluster of relations*, with no single relation being sufficient to have caused the event, and with all of the relations being, in the particular historian's viewpoint, necessary for the event to have occurred. His account is not a "logic" of strict scientific explanation, but a "logic" of drama in which one force acts in the context of the presence of an opposing force. There is something of a dialectical framework in which one act brings a reciprocal response, and this process, along with necessary scene-setting by the historian, continues to the crisis or climax. In other words the historian tells a story—one that is solidly based on evidence—in which his judgment of "fundamental causality" is offered not in any ultimate sense but only as "a clue to the story being told." Historian Cushing Strout, writing about the U.S. Civil War, puts it this way:

> The pragmatic meaning of the assertion that slavery was "the fundamental cause" is only that the institution was so deeply entangled in the issues that divided the sections that it provides a valuable focus for examining the skein of events which culminated in war.[1]

If it be objected that when history is seen in this way one can scarcely read it for the purpose of deriving rules for application to the present or prediction of the future, one can only respond with Jacob Burckhardt's counsel that history's purpose is not to make us more clever for the next occurrence but rather "wise for every future occurrence."

ASKING QUESTIONS ABOUT THE PAST

A primary purpose of this chapter is to give you an understanding of the first stage of the historian's work as he explores some segment of the past. Typically, having singled out a given event as worthy of attention, the historian seeks to understand the ingredients that went into its making, in doing so "casting his net as widely as possible." What he wants, at this point, is information about individuals, groups, ideas, motivations, conditions, and developments that preceded and shaped the event. As we mentioned earlier (Chapter One), the historian has a general theory of how things typically happen, and on the basis of that theory he asks certain standard questions, which he "tries on for size" to see if they help him to get at pertinent factors that influenced the event.

We will examine these standard questions in a moment, but first there are several points to be made in connection with them. (1) The questions are really "starter questions." They are aimed at making sure the historian "touches all the bases," or follows a systematic "search pattern." Some of the questions will be found irrelevant when applied to a particular case. Others will yield results and, it is to be hoped, will lead to asking more exactly phrased and pointed questions through which a "cluster of relations" finally emerges. (2) While it is true that as a professional student the historian must ask and answer these "starter questions," it is also true that as a professional craftsman he usually, *as a matter of personal inclination*, winds up emphasizing only one or two of the questions when he presents his story. To be sure, a few historical series, such as the *Oxford History of England,* and an occasional textbook, such as *The Growth of the American Republic,* try to be exhaustive in their coverage. But most historians choose just one or two of the questions, leading to the several "varieties of history," such as intellectual history, economic history, social history, political history, constitutional history, and the like. (3) It is also worthwhile noting that a few scholars, notably certain philosophers, have recommended systems of inquiry that

[1]Lee Benson and Cushing Strout, "Causation and the American Civil War: Two Appraisals," *History and Theory,* Vol. I (1961), p. 182.

concentrate *exclusively* on one of the questions. Hegel is an example of a thinker who saw ideas as being the crucial factor in all reality; Marx saw economic systems in the same light. While perhaps profiting from the thought of such men, historians generally disagree with them, insisting on a wider perspective with which to view human affairs.

The "starter questions" that historians use may be grouped under six headings: (1) the influence of individuals; (2) the influence of organizations (groups, factions, nations, etc.); (3) the influence of institutions; (4) the influence of ideas; (5) the influence of economic and technological factors; and (6) the influence of the physical and biological environment. Each of these categories will be briefly discussed, with an effort being made to provide illustrations and/or further detailed questions.

1. *The influence of individuals.* This is not the place to engage in the debate over whether "the man makes the times" or "the times make the man"—the superman or "any man" argument. Suffice to say that since men do act, their personalities, their characters, and their motives are of inevitable importance in influencing events. Henry VIII, for example, was a spendthrift, and his extravagant ways made England a difficult place in which to live, thus preparing the way for "the great historic going forth of the English people" to America and elsewhere. Woodrow Wilson was a man of such lofty moral principle that he found it impossible to compromise with more mundane souls over the issue of his "morally right" League of Nations. Did he thus help set the stage for World War II? Lyndon Johnson was devious enough perhaps to have engaged in questionable election practices in his native Texas, but also was compassionate enough to have made an extensive civil-rights program a reality in the mid-1960s. The point of these examples is to show that individuals—in their quirks, in their principles, in their virtues and vices—do affect the course of events. Concerning the man or woman who was at or near the center of the event, some of the questions pertinent to this category are:

> What features dominated the personality?
> To what and to whom was that individual loyal?
> Did temperamental factors enter into his or her choice of action?
> How is the individual reflected in his or her policies?
> What qualities of leadership did he/she conspicuously display (or conspicuously lack)?
> What were his/her relations with other major figures, and how much did their support (or nonsupport) influence matters?

The foregoing does not pretend to be an exhaustive list. It is merely indicative of the kinds of questions one might ask concerning individual actors in the historical drama.

2. *The influence of organizations.* Concerning the role of groups or organizations in history, historian David Potter put it this way:

> It is one of the basic characteristics of history that the historian is concerned with human beings but that he does not deal with them primarily as individuals, as does the psychologist or the biographer or the novelist.

Instead he deals with them in groups—in religious groups, in cultural groups, in ideological groups, in interest groups, in occupational groups, or in social groups.[2]

Without denying the validity of what was said in the previous paragraph about the potential importance of individuals, it seems reasonable to say that individuals very often act in the interests of some organization, and that this puts them in opposition with some other organization or faction. Actually, the matter can get fairly complex. Take, as an illustration, the case of President Jimmy Carter. At times in his acts he has represented the Democratic Party, at other times the Administration, and at still others he has represented the American nation as an organized social group; but there is more: he is a Baptist, a Navy man, a businessman, a populist, and a southerner, each of these reflecting, possibly, a group that seeks expression. He has been opposed, upon occasion, by a liberal group of Democrats, by conservative Republicans, by steel interests, by coal miners, the oil lobby, the legislative branch, and many others. The point of this is to reemphasize the validity of Potter's statement above—that historians naturally gravitate to questions about groups (parties, factions, interests, nations, etc.). The major ones are political groups, nationality groups, geographical groups, and perhaps interest groups voluntarily joined. Raising the questions of organizations and their activities is especially fruitful in discovering the "significant" relations that surround a given event.

3. *The influence of institutions.* To a sociologist, institutions are organized ways of dealing with various recurrent human problems, including the problem of maintaining civil order (leading to an institution called "government"), the problem of regularizing male and female relationships (the institution of marriage and family), the problem of culturally training the young (the institution of education), the problem of squaring oneself with God (the institution of religion), the problem of national defense (the institution of the military), the problem of making a living (the institution of business), the problem of leisure (the institution of formal entertainment). These are the major institutions of American society at least.

In addition to this broad, generalized definition of "institution," there is a more concrete and conventional meaning. It can refer to specific organizations (as described under 2 above) that play an important and *continuing* part in a society: the Supreme Court, General Motors, Harvard University, the NAACP, the American Legion, the United States Navy, the American Medical Association—and hundreds of other organizations that have become more or less a permanent part of the culture. They are the "establishment" so to speak. Finally, "institution" can be used to describe certain established customs or practices in a culture, such as presidential inauguration ceremonies, the celebration of Thanksgiving, Sunday afternoon pro football, the morning coffee break, and the practice of dating.

Very generally, historians are interested in institutions because they represent cultural continuities that are a part of every historical situation. Social institutions such as the Navy or the Internal Revenue Service have flesh-and-blood spokesmen (often part of a bureaucracy) who are completely convinced of the value and

---

[2]David M. Potter, "The Historian's Use of Nationalism and Vice Versa," *American Historical Review*, Vol. 67, (July 1962), p. 924.

importance of their institution and who actively seek not only its perpetuation but an enhancement of its power, often at the expense of some other institution. This is simply institutional "scrimmaging" that goes on all the time, and sometimes becomes historically important. In the United States the Army and Navy have often been "at war" with each other as each has sought a larger slice of the budgetary pie. This continuing war affected American military capabilities in the months preceding the Pearl Harbor attack in 1941. It is also true that certain institutions become "power centers," such as Congress, political parties, and regulatory commissions, and various groups and interests compete for control of them.

When historians speak of the "institutional factor," they are generally referring to some fixed component of a historical situation, often some organizational component that reflects a set of interests and values of its own and is quite resistant to change. One of the most obvious examples of the influence of the institutional factor in history is that of the French military bureaucracy of the 1920s and 1930s which remained impervious to the appeals of young Charles de Gaulle that the next war would be one of quick strikes and rapid movement.

Among the questions to be asked in assessing the role of institutions are: What kind of position allowed an institution to exert its influence politically and economically? How did the fixed processes of the institution affect the situation? How did one gain access to power within the institution? What kinds of specific powers were available to clever operators within the institution? What institutional oppositions to the ruling party could be observed?

4. *The influence of ideas.* The aphorism that "men do not possess ideas, rather they are possessed by them" has much truth, especially if "ideas" are taken to include ideals, attitudes, and values. No one can dispute, for example, the influence of the idea of mercantilism as a guiding concept for the colonization of America, or the influence of the principle of reason as the throne upon which the French Revolution sat. Other examples: the impact of *Uncle Tom's Cabin* upon American attitudes toward slavery in the pre-Civil War period; the influence of the ideas on seapower of Alfred T. Mahan upon Kaiser Wilhelm in the late nineteenth century; the influence of John Maynard Keynes upon American economic practice; and, in longer perspective, the influence of the Christian ideal upon Western civilization. Various questions that one might ask in exploring the role of ideas in shaping a given event are: Had any particular idea become newly fashionable? Had certain familiar and almost axiomatic truths begun to be questioned? What prestigious old ideas continued to hold the loyalty of major individuals and groups that were involved in the event? Is there any evidence of manipulation of opinion by appeals to traditional ideas? Does it appear that some individuals and groups were in a sense "imprisoned" by certain ideas? Did any individual's *conception* of the situation or of his role in it have importance? Was there a distinctive "public mood" that appears to have aided any groups or individuals? Did the "intellectuals" have marked influence at any particular point? Again, these questions are but suggestive of the angles of inquiry that may be pursued.

5. *The influence of economic and technological factors.* For an individual and for business organizations the "economic problem" is simply one of "getting ahead" or of getting a larger piece of the pie in a situation where others hanker for a larger piece of the pie too. This competitive situation is but rarely a contest between the "haves" and the "have nots"; rather it is a contest between various groups of "want more ofs," with each group trying to shape the situation to its maximum benefit, especially by gaining a major voice in some facet of government. Looked at in a larger framework the "economic problem" is a national problem as a society, using its resources, (1) struggles to support itself under circumstances of reasonable domestic tranquility (the government having the problem of maintaining this reasonable level of tranquility) and (2) attempts to maintain sufficient economic strength to deal effectively with its national enemies. Questions one asks in assessing the weight of economic factors include such considerations as: What economic groups regarded the situation as affecting their interests? How strongly organized were the groups involved and upon what basis did their power rest? What actions, either threatening or coercive, did they take? What political levers did the economic groups have? Was the economic problem reflected in the event symptomatic of a larger problem of resources in the society as a whole?

Related to the economic factors are the technological developments that influence a society's productive process, its potential, and its life-style. One needs to look no further than the invention of the cheap internal-combustion engine powered by gasoline to confirm the great importance of technological developments. Questions that may be asked about any given event might be: Does any interest group feel threatened by advancing technological change? What resources appear to be more necessary because of technological advances? What institutional changes must be made to accommodate the innovations that have occurred? What changes in public policy were necessitated by technological changes?

6. *The influence of physical and biological environment.* Though perhaps the physical environment often has no more than a remote influence upon an event, still the geographical question must be asked, and sometimes it is a fruitful vein of inquiry. Did any major natural phenomena (such as storms, drought, extended cold periods) influence the general situation? Are new resources being developed in the area, or is a critical resource such as coal or oil, "running out"? How does the area fare in relation to other areas? Is its potential growing or declining? Do the transportation capabilities favor the area or handicap it? With respect to the biological environment, one can ask to what extent diseases or other ecological disturbances altered the situation. After all, it was an epidemic of plague (1348–49) that still constitutes one of the greatest disasters in European history; and it was the Irish potato blight that had a lot to do with supplying the cheap labor to build the American railroad system in the mid-nineteenth century.

Remember that the six foregoing categories offer "starter questions," which give a historian an assurance that he will have touched upon all the major types of influence. As a total list they may seem a bit forbidding, but please remember they are intended to widen one's perspective. You do not have to answer each and every question. Rather use them as appropriate, until that moment occurs when you grasp the most essential relations by which an event "makes sense."[3]

---

[3]For a fuller discussion of the major types of questions that historians ask, see Carl G. Gustavson's admirable *A Preface to History* (New York: McGraw-Hill, 1955).

EXERCISES

The study of history can and should be a mind-widening experience, not only because it takes us out of the often narrow perspective of the here and now, but also because it can lead us to be more systematic in the way we look at experience. In this chapter we have discussed the several "starter questions" that historians use. The exercises that follow are intended to promote a questioning pattern that has proven quite fruitful in historical studies and is also usable in other circumstances. The selections that follow were written by experienced, highly regarded historians. You may be sure that in doing their research they asked all the questions we have discussed in this chapter. Keep those questions in mind as you read their accounts, and then see what you can do with the items in the exercises that follow each account. You may want to check the exercise questions on pages 51–52 before you read the selections.

SET A The following passage, dealing with the early years of Theodore Roosevelt's presidency, was drawn from George E. Mowry, *The Era of Theodore Roosevelt*.[4] For our purposes here, the rather extensive footnotes have been omitted.

¶ 1 Some months after Roosevelt's spectacular action against the Northern Securities Company, the administration was confronted with a labor crisis of major proportions which, had it been handled badly, might have endangered its political future. In May, 1902, over fifty thousand anthracite coal miners enrolled in the United Mine Workers walked off their jobs in northeastern Pennsylvania, demanding a 10 to 20 per cent increase in pay, recognition of the union, an eight-hour day, and other fringe benefits. A similar strike in the preceding election year of 1900 had won a settlement granting a 10 per cent increase, due largely to the mediating influence of Mark Hanna. Hanna had been disturbed by the possible effect of the strike on McKinley's election prospects, and had persuaded the reluctant operators that four more years of McKinley Republicanism was worth a 10 per cent wage raise.

¶ 2 From 70 to 80 per cent of the anthracite fields were owned by six railroads crisscrossing the region. The rail presidents, headed by George F. Baer of the Reading and W. H. Truesdale of the Lackawanna, insisted that this time there should be no political compromise. Relying upon the fuel needs of the seaboard cities from Boston to Washington, they closed down the mines, rejected all offers of negotiation, and waited for the union to crack. Led by the able John F. Mitchell and financed by contributions from the soft-coal miners, the United Mine Workers held their ranks through July, September, and into October. As winter approached even schools and hospitals had empty coalbins, and the public temper became increasingly ugly. Senator Lodge reported that civil commotion was imminent in Boston, and the President felt that there was real danger of riots in New York City.

¶ 3 By September it was obvious that the bulk of press opinion was opposed

---

[4]New York: Harper & Brothers, 1958, pp. 137–40. Reprinted by permission of Harper & Row, Publisher, Inc.

to the stand of the mine operators. Some of the more conservative journals, it was true, labeled the strike as an "insurrection" and demanded that force be used against the unions. Occasionally an eminent individual like the newly elected president of Princeton University defended capital's side of the argument. Woodrow Wilson interpreted the strike not as one over wages and hours but as a union attempt "to win more power...." But the weight of opinion was with the unions. Labor's orderly conduct of the strike during its first three months, and its repeated willingness to arbitrate the issues, were in favorable contrast with the intransigent stand and the incredibly foolish statements of the operators. To a proposal that the dispute be referred to Archbishop Ireland for arbitration, George F. Baer replied, "Anthracite mining is business and not a religious, sentimental or academic proposition." A month later he claimed that the Deity had conferred the large property rights of the country exclusively upon the Christian men who now directed the nation's corporations, a divine-right property doctrine which President W. H. Truesdale of the Lackawanna Railroad promptly supported.

¶ 4 Such paleolithic statements elicited public protests even from conservative sources, and as the viewpoint of the operators remained unchanged, public opinion rapidly hardened against the coal roads. By early September not a few of the country's leading newspapers were tentatively suggesting government ownership of the mines, while others demanded compulsory arbitration. "The economic harmonies of free contract," one paper commented, "were no longer working in the coal fields." Others vigorously asserted the "paramount rights of the public welfare" to any and all considerations of private property. In October an action of the New York Democratic State Convention recalled the days of the Populists and the bad times of the early nineties. "We advocate," the platform stated, "the national ownership and operation of the anthracite coal mines."

¶ 5 As early as the middle of June, Roosevelt had sent the Commissioner of Labor into the coal fields to investigate and propose a solution in the event the strike was not soon settled. But despite the almost unanimous approval of the press for government intervention, Roosevelt refused to act during July and August. Since Knox, Root, and Lodge all advised that the government was without constitutional power to intervene, the President found himself at his "wit's end." The whole affair proved to him again that it was necessary to have government supervision over big corporations. As September rounded into October, as temperatures fell and the public pressure mounted, Roosevelt determined to intervene, advice or no advice. On October 1, telegrams went out from the White House inviting the chief coal operators and the union leaders to a conference on October 3. Exactly what took place at the day-long conference has in the past been guessed at. Apparently, Loeb, the presidential secretary, took notes, but the notes have never been unearthed. Among the papers of Philander C. Knox, however, a long unannotated memorandum, hitherto undetected, gives a purported blow-by-blow account of the day's events. According to the Knox memorandum, Roosevelt opened the short morning session at eleven with the disclaimer that he "had any right or duty to intervene in this way on legal grounds." The urgency of the situation and the national interest, however, made his intervention necessary. Mitchell spoke first for the miners. They were prepared to meet the operators at any time to adjust their differences. If such a meeting was not agreeable, the union was willing to accept the findings of an arbitral commission appointed by the President, provided that the operators also agreed to accept its awards. Roosevelt then asked both parties to think over the offer and adjourned the meeting until three o'clock.

¶ 6 At the afternoon session Baer and his colleagues ignored the labor leaders completely and adamantly refused to talk with the unions either directly or indirectly. What the President was asking them to do, John B. Markle said, was "to deal with outlaws" who were responsible for the "existing anarchy." Baer then started a long diatribe against the unions, accusing them of daily violence against the fifteen to twenty thousand peaceful miners who wanted to work. If the power of the state of Pennsylvania was not sufficient to meet the challenge to peace, it became the duty of the President to restore order. "Free government," he concluded, was "a contemptible failure if it can only protect the lives and property and secure comfort of the people by compromise with the violaters of law and instigators of violence and crime." After much the same line had been taken by E. B. Thomas, chairman of the board of the Erie Railroad, and by Markle, representing the independent coal operators, David Wilcox, vice-president of the Delaware and Hudson, charged specifically that the miners had committed twenty murders. Mitchell immediately objected that the charge was false and offered to resign his position if the operators would name the men responsible for the alleged murders and show that they were guilty as charged. Ignoring Mitchell's interruption, the operators demanded that a permanent injunction be granted against the strikers and that the President "put an end to the anarchy in the coal fields" by using the Army, if necessary, as in the Pullman strike, and by starting an immediate suit against the unions under the Sherman Law. When the President finally asked the operators whether they would agree to Mitchell's proposal for arbitration, he was met with a blunt refusal. Upon his further inquiry whether the owners had anything else to suggest, they replied they had no other proposal except that the miners should return to their jobs and leave the determination of their grievances to the decision of the judge of the courts of common pleas in the districts where the mines were located. After twice "insulting" the President and the Attorney General, the operators left the conference without once addressing a word directly to the union representatives. Three days later the Attorney General received a formal petition from the general attorney of the Delaware, Lackawanna and Western Railroad, asking that an injunction be issued against the strikers for interference with interstate commerce and that federal troops be sent to Pennsylvania to restore order. The miners, Knox was told on the same day by the vice-president of the Delaware and Hudson Railroad, should be proceeded against as Eugene Debs was proceeded against in Chicago some ten years before.

¶ 7 During and after the conference Roosevelt was beside himself at the operators' "arrogant stupidity." But the meeting had given him one constructive idea. Suggesting to Root and Knox that they could write letters of protest if they desired to disclaim responsibility, he indicated that he was prepared to send ten thousand federal troops to dispossess the operators and produce coal. By previous constitutional interpretation the President had the authority to send federal troops into a state to assure the exercise of duly authorized federal powers or when they were requested by a governor or a state legislature to preserve peace and order. Nowhere was the right to seize and operate private property even hinted at, much less specified. Nevertheless, the President talked with General J. M. Schofield and through Senator Mathew Quay arranged for the governor of Pennsylvania to request the intervention of federal troops. Spurred by this terrible specter of state socialism, the friends of capital began to move fast. On October 8, Senators Quay and Penrose held a conference with John Mitchell. Two days later, together with Senators Odell and Platt, they met with Baer. On October 11, with Roosevelt's blessing, Root journeyed to New York for a secret conference with J. P. Morgan. The "Great Mogul of Wall Street" was induced to put pressure on the railroad presidents, and at a White House conference on October 13 the groundwork for a compromise was worked out between the President and agents of the acknowledged autocrat of American finance and industry, Morgan. The miners were to go back to work, and a five-man commission appointed by the President, consisting of one Army engineer, a mining engineer, a "businessman familiar with the coal industry," a federal judge, and an "eminent sociologist," was to arbitrate the points at issue. Subsequently the commission was raised to seven members, and the President, in order to meet labor's objections to the òne-sided nature of its personnel, agreed to appoint E. E. Clarke, president of the Brotherhood of Railroad Conductors, as the "eminent sociologist." In March, 1903, the commission made public its awards: the miners were given a 10 per cent raise on the average, working hours were reduced in some cases to eight and in most to nine, recognition of the union was not conceded, and the traditional manner of weighing coal was to be continued. The commission also recommended a 10 per cent increase in the price of coal, a proposal of which the operators quickly availed themselves.

¶ 8 During the presidential campaign of 1904 Roosevelt described his actions in the coal strike as simply giving both labor and capital a "square deal." The phrase was to stick in public memory as so many of Roosevelt's did, and perhaps it started the twentieth-century fashion of likening national political programs to phrases in an ethically operated game of chance. The President's actions during the strike set many important precedents. For the first time in a labor dispute representatives of both capital and labor were called to the White House, where the influence of the government was used to obtain a negotiated settlement. For the first time the President had appointed an arbitral board whose decision both sides promised to accept. In order to obtain capital's consent to arbitration, Roosevelt, for the first time in American history, had threatened to use troops to take over and operate a major industry. Whether he would have gone that far or not is problematical. As Root said later, the President was "a bit of a bluffer" at times. But both by his actions and threats Roosevelt had moved the government away from its traditional position of isolation from such economic struggles. The government, by precedent if not by law, had become a third force and partner in major labor disputes.

Save pages 47-51 for use with Exercises in Chapter Nine.

QUESTIONS This section is based upon the "starter questions." In the episode you have just read is there any basis for saying that

1. Certain individuals seemed to have played an important role?

   a. Specify three of them and briefly explain their importance: _____

   _____

   _____

   _____

   _____

   _____

   _____

   b. Which of them seemed to have been of decisive importance and why?

   _____

   _____

2. Certain groups (organizations, interests) were active in the situation? Specify:

   _____

   _____

3. Certain institutions seemed to have shown enhanced strength or weakness? Briefly explain: _____

   _____

   _____

4. Certain ideas (attitudes, moods, conceptions) made the situation what it was, or influenced it, or changed it in some way? Specify and briefly explain:

   a. _____

   _____

   _____

   b. _____

   _____

   _____

   c. _____

   _____

5. Certain economic interests were involved, and pursued their objectives in various ways? Specify, and briefly explain:

a. _____

_____

_____

b. _____

_____

_____

6. Certain technological factors had any importance? Please specify: _____

_____

_____

7. Certain physical environments had any importance? Please specify: _____

_____

_____

SET B
(Optional)

This excerpt, which deals with Franklin D. Roosevelt's "court-packing" effort of 1937, was taken from William E. Leuchtenburg, *Franklin D. Roosevelt and the New Deal.*[5] Once again the extensive footnotes have been omitted here.

¶ 1 Roosevelt's Second Inaugural Address on January 20, 1937, indicated he was ready for a more radical turn. "I see one-third of a nation ill-housed, ill-clad, ill-nourished," the President declared. For the next two weeks, the country waited to see what specific legislation the President would demand to improve the lot of this "one-third of a nation." When Roosevelt did act, he caught the country by surprise. In a message which electrified the nation, he asked not for new social legislation but for reform of the Supreme Court.

¶ 2 In the spring of 1936, the Court, which had already wiped out the NRA and the AAA, had gone out of its way to find the Guffey Coal Conservation Act unconstitutional. A month later, in the Morehead Case, the Court shocked even conservatives by ruling, once more by a 5–4 vote, that a New York state minimum wage law was invalid. In the field of labor relations, the Court seemed to have created, as President Roosevelt protested, a "'no-man's-land,' where no Government—State or Federal"—could function. The decisions in these two cases suggested that the Wagner Act would not survive a test in the courts, and that a wages and hours law was

[5]New York: Harper & Row, 1963, pp. 231–39. Reprinted by permission of Harper & Row, Publishers, Inc.

out of the question. Roosevelt, it seemed, not only faced the prospect of seeing past accomplishments like the Social Security Act destroyed but had been forbidden to attempt anything new.

¶ 3 For at least two years, Roosevelt and his aides had explored proposals to make the Court more amenable to New Deal legislation. The President originally favored amending the Constitution, but he came to feel that this strategy bristled with difficulties, for a modest expenditure could forestall ratification in thirteen legislatures. Moreover, any law passed under such an amendment would still be subject to Court review. The real problem, Roosevelt came to feel, lay not with the Constitution but with the Court. Since so many decisions had been handed down by a divided bench, any reform should be aimed at swelling the Court majority.... The President decided that the only feasible solution was Court packing, a proposition he had earlier viewed with distaste. Yet he moved warily, because he knew Court packing violated taboos, and he sought a formula that both had historical precedent and would divert attention from his desire for a more liberal Court by raising a new issue of judicial reform. The President took puckish delight in the fact that the plan Attorney General Homer Cummings finally hit upon was based upon a recommendation made in 1913, albeit in a different form, by none other than Justice McReynolds.

¶ 4 On February 5, 1937, the President sent Congress his design for reorganizing the judiciary. Roosevelt declared that a deficiency of personnel had resulted in overcrowded federal court dockets; in a single year, he asserted, the Supreme Court had denied 87 per cent of petitions for hearings on appeal, without citing its reasons. In part, this could be attributed to "the capacity of the judges themselves," a problem which raised "the question of aged or infirm judges—a subject of delicacy and yet one which requires frank discussion...." To "vitalize the courts," Roosevelt recommended that when a federal judge who had served at least ten years waited more than six months after his seventieth birthday to resign or retire, the President might add a new judge to the bench. He could appoint as many but no more than six new justices to the Supreme Court and forty-four new judges to the lower federal tribunals. The President's proposal presented Court packing not as a political ruse but as devotion to a principle: the retirement of aged justices in the interest of efficiency.

¶ 5 In this oblique approach to a fundamental issue of government, Roosevelt was too clever by half. Opponents of his plan had no difficulty in proving that Court inefficiency was a bogus issue and showing that what the President really wanted was a more responsive Court. The over-age argument made little sense since one of the President's most consistent supporters had been the eighty-year-old Louis Brandeis, and the President's message offended many of the Justice's admirers. Septuagenarian senators put little stock in the argument that the faculties of septuagenarian judges might be impaired....

¶ 6 Roosevelt could scarcely have bungled the presentation of the Court plan more. The proposition had never been mentioned during the recent campaign, and he had handed it to Congress without a word of warning to congressional leaders. Speaker Bankhead protested to Representative Lindsay Warren, who had served with him as one of Roosevelt's assistant floor managers at the 1932 convention: "Lindsay, wouldn't you have thought that the President would have told his own party leaders what he was going to do[?] He didn't because he knew that hell would break loose." Save for Cummings, not even Roosevelt's cabinet officers knew of the proposal, nor had the President taken into his confidence most of his political intimates. The Supreme Court bill reflected less the thinking of New Deal intellectuals than the narrow shrewdness of an Attorney General who had been a Democratic national chairman. Yet too much can be made of Roosevelt's tactical failings. He had little choice save to hand the opposition the one issue around which it could rally.

¶ 7 Men who had feared to oppose his economic policies, because they anticipated popular disapproval, now had the perfect justification for breaking with the President and going to the people. Representative Hatton Sumners, chairman of the House Judiciary Committee, announced: "Boys, here's where I cash in my chips." The administration turned to the Senate only to meet the opposition not just of conservatives like Glass but of usually reliable Roosevelt men like Joseph O'Mahoney of Wyoming, Tom Connally of Texas, and Burton Wheeler of Montana. O'Mahoney protested that nothing in the bill limited the Court's powers of judicial review, nor remedied either the defects of old age or of divided decisions. New judges, he wrote, "would be just as likely to disappoint him as, in similar circumstances, Oliver Wendell Holmes disappointed Theodore Roosevelt when shortly after his appointment, he dissented in the Northern Securities Case." . . .

¶ 8 In attempting to alter the Court, Roosevelt had attacked one of the symbols which many believed the nation needed for its sense of unity as a body politic. The Court fight evoked a strong feeling of nostalgia for the days of the Founding Fathers, when, it seemed, life was simpler and principles fixed. One constituent urged Senator McCarran to take a stand "against what Cornwallis and Howe fought for in 1776." The greater the insecurity of the times, the more people clung to the few institutions which seemed changeless. Congressmen were deluged with letters expressing intense anxiety over the fate of the Court. When Senator Bailey announced his opposition to the plan, a South Carolina lady wrote: "Bully for you! Oh Bully for you! *Don't*, don't let that wild man in the White House do this dreadful thing to our country."

¶ 9 Roosevelt had counted on conservative opposition, and had probably anticipated some of the liberal defections, but he failed to reckon with the power of the Court itself. On March 29, in a 5–4 decision in which Roberts joined the majority, the Court upheld a Washington minimum-wage law similar to the New York statute it had erased in the Morehead Case. Two weeks later, Roberts joined once more in a series of 5–4 rulings which found the Wagner Act constitutional. These decisions marked a turning point in the history of the Supreme Court. They upset the historic verdict in the Adkins Case and appeared quite contrary to the Court's rulings in the Carter and the Schechter cases. . . .

¶ 10 On May 18, prodded by Senator Borah, Justice Van Devanter announced his retirement from the bench. Since Roberts' "conversion" had given Roosevelt a 5–4 Court willing to approve New Deal legislation, Van

Devanter's departure made possible a 6–3 division. The need for drastic reform no longer seemed pressing. Chief Justice Hughes struck another effective blow at the Court bill. In response to a letter from Senator Wheeler, Hughes composed a devastating reply to Roosevelt's charge of inefficiency. He pointed out that the Court had heard argument on cases it had accepted for review only four weeks earlier, and claimed that an increase in justices would only produce delays: "more judges to hear, more judges to confer, more judges to discuss, more judges to be convinced and to decide." On May 24, the Court gave fresh evidence that the crisis had ended, when in two 5–4 decisions it validated the unemployment insurance provisions of the Social Security Act, and in a third opinion it ruled 7–2 that old-age Pensions were constitutional.

¶ 11 The cluster of decisions, Van Devanter's resignation, and Hughes's letter killed the Court reform bill. Before these events, the Senate was probably evenly divided. After them, wavering members joined the opposition, and the proponents lost heart. Senate leaders pressed for a compromise. Senator Byrnes queried: "Why run for a train after you've caught it?" The Senate majority leader, Joe Robinson, thought he could get the President "a couple of extra justices tomorrow," even though men like Borah regarded "two as bad in principle as six." But the President refused to yield. The margin represented by Roberts' switch seemed too thin, especially since Roosevelt had had to promise the next vacancy on the Court to Robinson, who was a conservative. Besides, he had his Dutch up.

¶ 12 Begun in winter, the court fight was consuming all of spring, and now threatened to run its weary way through summer. By mid-June, when Vice-President John Garner, who loathed the Court plan, packed his bags and went home to Texas, the Democratic party was tearing itself apart. Still Roosevelt pushed on with the hopeless struggle. In mid-July, in his apartment in the Methodist Building across from the Capitol, the loyal Senator Robinson collapsed and died. His death destroyed what little hope remained for a favorable compromise. Five days later, Roosevelt's close political ally, Governor Herbert Lehman of New York, gratuitously announced his opposition to the proposal. The President had no choice but surrender; on July 22, Senator Logan moved that the bill be recommitted. "Glory be to God!" Hiram Johnson shouted. After 168 days the historic Court battle was over. Vice-President Garner designed a substitute measure in order "not to bloody Mr. Roosevelt's nose"; enacted in August, it embodied procedural reforms, but abandoned altogether the President's proposal to appoint new judges.

¶ 13 In later years, Roosevelt claimed he had lost the battle but won the war. In one sense, this is true. The very month of the defeat of the Court bill, August, 1937, he named to the Van Devanter vacancy Alabama's Senator Hugo Black, the *bête noire* of southern conservatives. Black's appointment, Herbert Hoover protested, meant that the Court was "one ninth packed." Black survived an ugly episode when an enterprising reporter revealed that he had once been a member of the Ku Klux Klan and in his service on the bench more than vindicated those who believed him neither a racist nor a bigot but a champion of minority rights. Within two and a half years after the rejection of the Court measure, Roosevelt had named five of his own appointees to the nine-man bench; Black, Stanley Reed, Felix Frankfurter, William O. Douglas, and Frank Murphy. The new Court—the "Roosevelt court" as it was called—greatly extended the area of permissible national regulation of the economy while at the same time safeguarding the civil liberties of even the most bothersome minority groups. Yet, in another sense, Roosevelt lost the war. The Court fracas destroyed the unity of the Democratic party and greatly strengthened the bipartisan anti-New Deal coalition. The new Court might be willing to uphold new laws, but an angry and divided Congress would pass few of them for the justices to consider.

Save pages 52-56 for use with Exercises in Chapter Nine.

QUESTIONS This section is based upon the "starter questions." In the episode you have just read is there any basis for saying that

1. Certain individuals seemed to have played an important role?
   a. Specify three of them and briefly explain their importance:

   1. _____

   _____

   2. _____

   _____

   3. _____

   _____

   b. Which of them seemed to have been of decisive importance and why:

   _____

   _____

2. Certain groups (organizations, interests) were active in the situation? Specify:

   _____

   _____

3. Certain institutions seemed to have shown enhanced strength or weakness? Briefly explain: _____

   _____

   _____

4. Certain ideas (attitudes, moods, conceptions) made the situation what it was, or influenced it, or changed it in some way? Specify, and briefly explain:

   a. _____

   _____

   _____

b. _____

_____

_____

c. _____

_____

5. Certain economic interests were involved, and pursued their objectives in various ways? Specify, and briefly explain:

a. _____

_____

_____

b. _____

_____

_____

6. Certain technological factors had any importance? Please specify: _____

_____

_____

7. Certain physical environments had any importance? Please specify: _____

_____

_____

Evidence

The famous soldier-scholar Lawrence of Arabia once wrote a friend: "The documents are liars. No man ever yet tried to write down the entire truth of any action in which he has been engaged."[1] Lawrence exaggerated, but he certainly had a point. Not all documents are "liars," but they do not always contain the unalloyed truth either. Whatever the imperfections, documents and similar historical records and artifacts are the basic raw materials for even the simplest problem of historical reconstruction. In this chapter we will consider briefly the types of sources the historian uses to learn about the past and to write history. We will also examine some of the critical techniques used by the historian to evaluate and interpret the raw data of the past.

Before doing this it is necessary to reflect on the common problem every historian faces. As the historian seeks to discover the truth about some segment of the past, he finds himself dealing with what might be described as a filtration system. From an initially very large reservoir of human actions, interactions, and conditions that constituted a given historical situation, only a relatively small part was observed by those in a position to do so—the filter of *limited observation;* of all the richness of detail that was observed by any witness, only a relatively small part was remembered—the filter of *limited memory;* of all that was remembered by a witness, only certain aspects of it could be committed to paper—the filter of *limited recording;* and, of all that was recorded, only some parts can be fully accepted—the filter of *limited credibility.* And so that large reservoir has been squeezed down to a few bucketsful—a figurative way of saying "evidence." Nonetheless, the historian must try to create a sense of the original reservoir (the past) even though the surviving evidence is lamentably sketchy and incomplete.

Not only is the evidence scattered and fragmentary; before it can be used constructively it must be thoroughly sorted and sifted by the historian. Evidence comes in mixed-up bundles, with relevant and irrelevant information intermixed like kernels of grain and their husks. Only a small part of the evidence will be relevant to the particular questions a historian may be investigating, and it is the historian who must separate the wheat from the chaff.

---

[1]Jacques Barzun and Henry Graff, *The Modern Researcher*, rev. ed. (New York: Harcourt, Brace and World, 1970), p. 50.

Moreover, the evidence only infrequently gives direct answers to important questions. For example, how much did President Franklin D. Roosevelt have to do with the unpreparedness of Pearl Harbor on the fateful day of the Japanese attack in December 1941? We'd all like to know the answer to that one, but the many bundles of evidence yield no direct answer. So one must examine, weigh, and finally *infer* an answer, and be ready to defend that answer against the criticisms of those who interpret the evidence differently. What all of this means in practice is that any historical account, given the limitations we have described, is inevitably a compound in which "the certain, the probable, and the speculative will co-exist." However maddening this state of affairs might be to a perfectionist, it is a typical characteristic of most professions, including law, medicine, economics—and history.

THE SOURCES: PRIMARY AND SECONDARY

The problem of weighing evidence is never an easy one, but its difficulty can be eased by an appreciation of the various types of sources the historian relies upon in his work. There are two basic categories of source materials used by the student of history, whether beginner or seasoned professional.

Primary sources are those that were written or created during the period that the historian is studying. Put another way, primary sources are those documents or artifacts produced by the eyewitnesses of, or participants in, the events the historian is attempting to reconstruct. Primary sources are the records that make the study of history possible: letters, reports, diaries, tax records, parish registers, newspapers, business accounts, works of art, buildings, and a host of others.

Secondary sources are the works of history *based* on the primary sources; they are works of reconstruction and interpretation written by the historian. Secondary sources attempt to transform the incoherent mass of primary (or original) sources into coherent accounts of past events. They also attempt to explain *how and why* events happened as they did. The books and articles through which we learn most of our history are secondary sources.[2]

The distinction between primary and secondary sources is not always as clear as the above definition implies. For instance, a newspaper story has many of the characteristics of a secondary source—that is, it is a narrative constructed by a journalist (a historian of sorts) based on documents or eyewitness testimony. Yet newspapers must still be considered primary sources for the period during which they were written. Also confusing is the fact that many sources can be categorized either as primary or secondary depending on the subject being studied. For instance, T.B. Macaulay's famous multivolume *History of England* (published between 1848 and 1861) is a *secondary source* for the study of English history between the 1680s and the early 1700s (the period covered by Macaulay's volumes). But Macaulay's *History* would be a *primary source* for a study of

---

[2]Textbooks and similar works represent a special category of *"tertiary"* source. Most general survey texts are not based on research into primary sources so much as they reflect the findings of a wide variety of secondary sources—that is, other history books. An author who attempts to cover the history of Western Civilization from 1500 to the present could not in a lifetime read all the primary sources necessary to discuss such a long and complex period. Such an author must, therefore, rely on the researches of other scholars (i.e., on secondary sources). Thus textbooks are a step or two further removed from the original sources than are most secondary works.

Macaulay himself or for a study of mid-nineteenth-century history writing. That is, it is a secondary source for the period it discusses (the late seventeenth century), but a primary source for the age in which it was written (the middle of the nineteenth century).

Finally, a note of caution: Many primary sources have been published in book form. In spite of the resemblance in form to secondary sources, these materials remain primary. Remember, the basic question to ask is when the materials originated, not when they were published or reprinted. For instance, a copy of the Declaration of Independence printed in a textbook is still a primary source even though the book itself is not.

USING PRIMARY SOURCES[3]

Primary sources are the historian's friends, for without them history as a discipline could not exist. Yet primary sources are notoriously fickle. Coaxing the truth from them can be a frustrating task. For some eras there are too few primary sources; for others, too many. They can be seductive or coldly aloof. They can mislead, lie, or lure one into a false sense of security. They can be written in the obscure languages of the ancients or the incomprehensible jargon of the modern bureaucrat. They can lead the intrepid researcher into blind alleys, false turns, and dead ends. Yet for all the frustrations, unlocking the secrets of the records of the past can also be an immensely satisfying task. The historian is a detective; the primary sources are the clues.

The variety of potential primary source materials is immense. Clearly, the largest category of primary sources is made up of many types of *written material*. In fact, even though human beings have been a recognizable species for tens of thousands of years, historians have typically limited themselves to the study of societies for which we have written records. Not all primary sources, however, are in written form. Remember our definition: A primary source is one that came into existence during the period that the historian is studying. From this perspective, just about anything that survives is fair game for the historical detective—buildings, tools, works of art, weapons, coins, and, more recently, films, tapes, records and the like.

For instance, peruse the list below and see if you can identify those items that could be used by the historian as a primary source.

Inscriptions	Works of art
Buildings	Baptismal and burial records
Pots/Artifacts	Pamphlets
Coins	Newspapers
Royal Charters	Magazines
Laws	Autobiographies/Memoirs
Government publications	Legislative debates
Diplomatic dispatches	Maps
Court records	Novels
Police reports	Films

---

[3]Techniques for reading and analyzing secondary sources are discussed in Chapter Ten.

Minutes of organizations	Photographs
Private letters	Folk songs
Diaries	Language
Business records	Furniture
Railroad schedules	Telephone books

Only a brief glance at the list should have convinced you that *all* of the above are potential primary sources. And the above list is far from complete, for *anything* that survives (including your aunt Matilda) is a primary source. At first it may seem dubious to categorize folk songs as primary sources. But songs, poems, and stories that pass from generation to generation (even if never written down) still originated sometime in the past, and, in spite of changes in form and content over the years, can still tell the historian something of that past time. Alex Haley, the author of the 1977 best-seller *Roots*, learned much of his early family background through such orally transmitted stories.

A more careful perusal of the above list should have convinced you that not all primary sources are equally "primary." That is, some would be more useful and/or credible than others. Newspaper accounts, for instance, are often not written by eyewitnesses or participants but by journalists (really contemporary historians) who piece together their stories from many sources. Thus newspaper stories are often further "removed" from the events they describe than other forms of written evidence. Also less "primary" are such things as autobiographies and memoirs. Often such accounts are written (much like a secondary source) years after the events they describe, and they are subject to distortions resulting from the failing memory and personal vanity of the authors.

Ideally it would be valuable for you to learn the relative merits and liabilities of each type of original source. In practice, it is enough at this point that you master the basic and important distinction between premeditated (intentional) and unpremeditated (unintentional) evidence. In the same way that an unposed candid snapshot can be more revealing than a posed photograph, unpremiditated evidence can be more revealing than material written or spoken with the intention of establishing a specific interpretation of a set of actions or events.

Premeditated (or intentional) evidence, then, is material that governments, businesses, individuals, and so on produce to "make a case," put forth their version of events, or even impress a constituency (stockholders, voters, future historians). Newspapers, autobiographies, contemporary histories, political speeches, pamphlets, and the like fall within this category.

Unpremeditated (unintentional) evidence is the body of material that is created when human beings are unself-consciously going about their business without thought of how a wider "audience" or posterity might judge them. The internal communications of organizations (armies, businesses, universities, etc.), diplomatic correspondence, private letters, personal diaries, statistical records, and a host of others belong in this category. Generally such unintentional evidence will tend to be more "honest," although such is not always the case. For instance, the private diary of a public official may be composed more with an eye on influencing the verdict of future historians than on recording the unvarnished truth. Unfortunately, so self-conscious have many public figures become about how "history will judge" them that it becomes more and more difficult to break through the public facade to the "real" individual beneath.

PRIMARY SOURCES AND CRITICAL METHOD

The most challenging job of the historian is to unravel the meaning of the records of the past. Here the historian has two aims, neither of them simple. The historian must first determine if the source is *authentic;* then he must establish the *meaning and credibility* of the contents. The first task is known as external criticism; the second, internal criticism.

External criticism, in the words of one historian, "authenticates evidence and establishes texts in the most accurate possible form."[4] This is clearly work for professionals and need not long concern us. Suffice it to say that many historical records lack precise dates or correct attribution (i.e., who wrote them). Many texts, after years of copying and recopying, are inaccurate. And forgeries are far from rare. Often highly specialized techniques are required to authenticate documents or artifacts: carbon dating, linguistic analysis, chemical analysis, and the like. Extensive knowledge of the period in question is also a prerequisite. Beginners rarely have either the background knowledge or the specialized skills for such criticism, so that we need not dwell on this aspect of analysis.

When the authenticity of a document has been established, the historian faces the far more important challenge of reading and interpreting the contents. This is *internal criticism.* Here the critical operations are less a mystery.

"Skepticism," argued the American novelist Edgar Saltus, "is history's bedfellow." So it is—or should be. Skepticism should be a habitual state of mind for the student of history. All too often we mere mortals have a tendency to believe anything if it is written down. If the material is very old it is often endowed with the attributes of absolute truth. But remember, our venerable ancestors could lie with as great facility as we.

Documents, like diplomats, do not reveal their secrets easily. Thus one must learn to question the evidence like an attorney in a courtroom—from different angles, from different perspectives, relentlessly, suspiciously. Even an account written by an individual of unimpeachable honesty can be marred by error and half-truth. It is the historian's job to separate the true from the false. What sort of questions should you ask? Space forbids a definitive list, but here are some of the most important.[5]

1. *What exactly does the document mean?* Often the *literal* meaning differs from the *real* meaning. For instance, diplomats are trained to phrase messages in such a restrained fashion that even the imminent end of the world can be made to sound totally innocuous. In other words, the historian must be familiar with the conventions of diplomatic correspondence in order to understand the *real* meaning of the dispatches. Likewise, words change meaning from one age to the next. A nineteenth-century reference to a "gay" person means something quite different from a similar reference in the 1970s.

2. *How well situated was the author to observe or record the events in question?* Here there are a number of subsidiary questions. What was the author's physical location? Was he/she a direct eyewitness or did he/she get the information from another? What was the author's *social ability* to observe? That is, might the person's social or economic position have influenced how he/she

---

[4] R. J. Shafer, ed., *A Guide to Historical Method* (Homewood, Ill.: Dorsey Press, 1969), p. 100.
[5] These questions are based on those printed in Shafer, *ibid.* pp. 137–38.

"saw" the event? A patrolman, for instance, might "see" a student-police confrontation differently than would a student radical. A person on welfare might be far more able to understand the impulse behind a hunger march than a member of the jet set. Finally, did the person have *specialized knowledge* that could affect the credibility of the testimony? A lawyer's report of a murder trial might be far more insightful than that of a sensation-seeker in the audience.

3. *When, how, and to whom was the report made?* Obviously, the longer the time between the event and the report, the greater the chance that memory will play tricks on the writer. This is one reason why personal memoirs can be treacherous sources for the historian. In addition, the intended purpose of the report should be discovered. An army officer reporting to a superior may tell his commander what he (the commander) wants to hear rather than the less-than-satisfying truth. Politicians are notorious for slanting their comments to please the audience of the moment. It is a very human impulse, after all, to tell others what we think they would like to hear.

4. *Is there bias, either in the report, or in yourself, that must be accounted for?* Personal bias can be the enemy of truth on two levels. The author of the document in question might have had personal beliefs or convictions that intruded themselves into his version of events. Here it is important to know as much about the author as possible. Likewise, *your own* values can often blind you to much that the sources reveal. A person who habitually regards all official government statements as lies or half-truths and the statements of social and political dissidents as gospel (or vice versa) is in a poor position to evaluate political documents dispassionately. (See Chapter Six for a more thorough discussion of bias in history.)

5. *What specialized information is needed to interpret the source?* Many times you will have to look up names, places, dates, and technical terms to get the full meaning of a given statement.

6. *Do the reported actions seem probable according to the dictates of informed common sense?* Here the key words are *probable* and *informed common sense.* Absolute certitude is impossible for most questions in history, especially the most important questions. The test of the credibility of a given version of events, therefore, is the inherent *probability* of its being true. Note, the question is not whether the version is possible (just about anything is possible), but whether (given all the evidence) it is probable.

In determining this the historian's most useful methodological tool is simple common sense, seasoned with appropriate relevant information. When all is said and done the credibility of evidence must be judged in the light of our understanding of how people behave. But it should be pointed out that "common sense" may deceive us unless we also have all the special knowledge necessary to make it work. Reports that eighteenth-century armies performed spectacular feats of endurance on forced marches violates our "commonsense" notion of what an infantryman can accomplish. Yet such reports are too numerous to be fabricated. Thus as important as is basic common sense in dealing with the records of the past, the importance of getting all relevant information cannot be overstressed.

7. *Is there corroboration?* One of the most basic ways of establishing the credibility of a given piece of evidence is to find what lawyers would call corroborating testimony. That is, were there other witnesses who could substantiate the account. More will be said in another chapter on how to synthesize larger bodies of evidence. For now it is sufficient to note that just as corroborative evidence is essential in a courtroom, it is also basic to solid history.

This list of questions to ask of evidence (whether historical or contemporary) is meant to be no more than a rudimentary guide. In the end there is no critical or imaginative faculty that cannot be applied to the internal evaluation of evidence. Nor can you know too much. The more you know about the period in question, human behavior, and the workings of the natural world, the better off you will be.

EXERCISES

**SET A
Exercise 1:
Primary Sources**

As noted on pages 60–61, historians make a distinction between primary and secondary sources. Below are sources you might consult if you were preparing a paper on the origins of World War II (1939–1945). In the space provided indicate whether the source should be classified "primary" (P) or "secondary" (S) or both (PS). Remember, your hypothetical paper deals with the *origins* of the war in Europe, or the *period prior to 1939*.

_____ **1.** *Documents on German Foreign Policy 1918–1945*, Series D, Vols. I–VII (September, 1937–1939).

_____ **2.** Alan Bullock, *Hitler: A Study in Tyranny* (1953).

_____ **3.** Konrad Heiden, *Hitler* (1936).

_____ **4.** *The Goebbels Diaries*, edited by Louis P. Lochner (1949).

_____ **5.** A. J. P. Taylor, *The Origins of the Second World War* (1961).

_____ **6.** *The Speeches of Adolph Hitler, 1922–39*, edited by Norman H. Baynes, 2 vols. (1942).

_____ **7.** T. W. Mason, "Some Origins of the Second World War," *Past and Present* (December 1964).

_____ **8.** *The Times* (London), 1933–1939.

_____ **9.** *Triumph of the Will* (German-made documentary film—1935).

_____ **10.** Adolf Hitler, *Mein Kampf (My Struggle)* (1939).

**SET A
Exercise 2:
Premeditated and
Unpremeditated
Evidence**

On page 60 the distinction was made between "premeditated" and "unpremeditated" evidence. Reread the definitions of these two categories of evidence. For the potential sources listed below indicate whether each item should be categorized as "Unpremeditated" (U), "Premeditated" (P), or shares qualities of both (UP). For many items there is no absolutely right or wrong answer. The important thing is to categorize evidence according to the degree that it might contain conscious bias or propagandistic intent. Compare (if possible) your judgments with those of others in your class and discuss those items where you disagree. Put your answer to the left of each entry.

_____ Inscriptions

_____ Buildings

_____ Pots/Artifacts

_____ Coins

_____ Royal Charters

_____ Laws

_____ Government publications

_____ Diplomatic dispatches

_____ Court records

_____ Police reports

_____ Minutes of organizations

_____ Private letters

_____ Diaries

_____ Business records

_____ Railroad schedules

_____ Works of art

_____ Baptismal and burial records

_____ Pamphlets

_____ Newspapers

_____ Magazines

_____ Autobiographies/Memoirs

_____ Legislative debates

_____ Maps

_____ Novels

_____ Films

_____ Photographs

_____ Folk songs

_____ Language

_____ Furniture

_____ Telephone books

**SET A
Exercise 3:
Types of
Primary Sources**

There are both benefits and liabilities associated with every type of primary source. For instance, records of congressional debates provide invaluable insights into the deliberative processes of the House of Representatives and the Senate. Yet congressmen are allowed to insert into the *Congressional Record* speeches that were never delivered or edited copies of speeches that were delivered. Thus the *Congressional Record* is not an altogether accurate compendium of legislative debates. Also one can never be quite sure if the sentiments expressed in the recorded debates reflect the true beliefs of the speaker or statements intended to impress the constituents back home.

For the categories of primary sources listed below, list what you see to be the most serious *potential* problems in using that particular type of evidence. Remember that with any piece of evidence one is concerned with the accuracy and credibility of the document. (In this exercise, use your imagination. Many possible observations are not discussed in the text of the chapter. Rely on your wits and personal experiences.)

Example:

_____ **A.** Memoirs/Autobiographies

> **Sample comments:**
> The primary problems with this type of source are (1) potential bias on the part of the author (i.e., the author is writing about his/her own life); (2) potential memory lapses on the part of the author.

_____ **B.** Newspapers

> **Comments:**

_____ **C.** Diplomatic Documents

> **Comments:**

_____ **D.** Political Speeches

Comments:

_____ **E.** Novels

Comments:

(If you had trouble with this item refer to Chapter Two, Set A, Exercise 3, Item H.)

_____ **F.** Military Dispatches

Comments:

_____ **G.** Public Opinion Polls

Comments:

**SET A
Exercise 4:
Interpreting
Evidence**

The first task when dealing with primary sources is to make sure you understand the author's meaning. This is often not as simple as you might think, since styles of expression change from era to era and vary from individual to individual. Often (even today) you will confront material that is written in a style that seems foreign and confusing.[6] It is also important to be able to "translate" the material into your own words so that you are sure you understand it and can communicate it to a contemporary reader.

Below is an excerpt from *A Manual of Political Economy* written by the English political philosopher Jeremy Bentham (1748–1832). In this brief excerpt Bentham is discussing the proper role of government in dealing with the economic problems of English society in the late eighteenth century. In 3 to 5 sentences summarize *in your own words* Bentham's ideas concerning the nature of government and its proper role in society. Be sure to include the points you see as central to Bentham's argument.

> The practical questions, therefore, are how far the end in view is best promoted by individuals acting for themselves? and in what cases these ends may be promoted by the hands of government?
>
> With the view of causing an increase to take place in the mass of national wealth, or with a view to increase of the means either of subsistence or enjoyment, without some special reason, the general rule is, that nothing ought to be done or attempted by government. The motto, or watchword of government, on these occasions, ought to be—*Be quiet.*
>
> For this quietism there are two main reasons:
>
> **1.** Generally speaking any interference for this purpose on the part of government is needless. The wealth of the whole community is composed of the wealth of the several individuals belonging to it taken together. But to increase his particular portion is, generally speaking, among the constant objects of each individual's exertions and care. Generally speaking, there is no one who knows what is for your interest so well as yourself— no one who is disposed with so much ardour and constancy to pursue it.
>
> **2.** Generally speaking, it is moreover likely to be pernicious, viz., by being unconducive, or even obstructive, with reference to the attainment of the end in view. Each individual bestowing more time and attention upon the means of preserving and increasing his portion of wealth, than is or can be bestowed by government, is likely to take a more effectual course than what, in his instance and on his behalf, would be taken by government.

Your summary (3 to 5 sentences) of Bentham's arguments:

```



```
▶

---

[6]The United States and Britain, for example, have been described as two cultures separated by a common language. In a recent mystery novel one finds the very British sentence: "Pushing her pram onto the zebra, a nearsighted nanny stepped off the curb." Translation into American English: "Pushing her baby carriage onto the crosswalk, a nearsighted children's nurse stepped off the curb."

Summary, continued

**SET A
Exercise 5:
Analysis
of Evidence I**

The first shots of the American Revolution were fired at Lexington, Massachusetts, on April 19, 1775. British troops on their way to destroy colonial military stores in nearby Concord were confronted by colonial militiamen at Lexington Green. Shots rang out and military hostilities began.

Since neither party wished to appear the aggressor, both denied firing the first shot. Below are three brief accounts of the event in question. Your task is *not* to determine who fired the first shot, but to examine the reports with the critical eye of the historian. More specifically, what points about each item should be noted by the historian wishing to weigh the probable validity of each account? Use the seven questions on pages 63–65 to make pertinent observations concerning the authorship, circumstances of composition, content, and *potential* credibility of each piece of evidence.

1. The official deposition of the commander of the colonial militia, John Parker:[7]

Lexington, April 25, 1775

I, John Parker, of lawful age, and commander of the Militia in Lexington, do testify and declare, that on the nineteenth instant, in the morning, about one of the clock, being informed that there were a number of Regular Officers riding up and down the road, stopping and insulting people as they passed the road, and also was informed that a number of Regular Troops were on their march from Boston, in order to take the Province Stores at Concord, ordered our Militia to meet on the common in said Lexington, to consult what to do, and concluded not to be discovered, nor meddle or make with said Regular Troops (if they should approach) unless they should insult us; and upon their sudden approach, I immediately ordered our Militia to disperse and not to fire. Immediately said Troops made their appearance, and rushed furiously, fired upon and killed eight of our party, without receiving any provocation therefor from us.

John Parker.

---

[7]Excerpt 1 is taken from Peter S. Bennett, ed. *What Happened on Lexington Green* (Reading, Mass.: Addison-Wesley, 1970), pp. 13–14. Excerpts 2 and 3 are from Allen French, *General Gage's Informers* (Ann Arbor, Mich.: University of Michigan Press, 1932), pp. 53–4, p. 55.

2. British commander Major John Pitcairn's official report to General Gage:

I gave directions to the Troops to move forward, but on no account to Fire, or even attempt it without orders; when I arrived at the end of the Villiage, I observed drawn up upon a Green near 200 of the Rebels; when I came within about One Hundred Yards of them, they began to File off towards some stone Walls on our Right Flank—The Light Infantry observing this, ran after them—I instantly called to the Soldiers not to fire, but to surround and disarm them, and after several repetitions of those positive Orders to the men, not to Fire &c—some of the Rebels who had jumped over the Wall, Fired Four or Five Shott at the Soldiers, which wounded a man of the Tenth, and my Horse was Wounded in two places, from some quarter or other, and at the same time several Shott were fired from a Meeting House on our Left—upon this, without any order or Regularity, the Light Infantry began a scattered Fire, and continued in that situation for some little time, contrary to the repeated orders both of me and the officers that were present—It will be needless to mention what happened after, as I suppose Col. Smith hath given a particular account of it. I am sir

Boston Camp   Your most humble Servant,
26th April, 1775   John Pitcairn.

3. Personal account by British ensign Jeremy Lister written in 1832:

However to the best of my recollection about 4 oClock in the Morning being the 19th of April the 5 front [companies] was ordered to Load which we did, about half an hour after we found that precaution had been necessary, for we had then to [fire]...and then was the first Blood drawn in this American Rebellion. it was at Lexington when we saw one of their [Companies] drawn up in regular order Major Pitcairn of the Marines second in Command call'd to them to disperce, but their not seeming willing he desired us to mind our space which we did when they gave us a fire then run of[f] to get behind a wall. we had one man wounded of our [Company] in the Leg his Name was Johnson also Major Pitcairns Horse was shot in the Flank we return'd their Salute, and before we proceeded on our March from Lexington I believe we Kill'd and Wounded either 7 or 8 men.

Observations/Questions Pertinent to Evidence: In commenting on *each* piece of testimony ask the following questions (not all will be relevant to each item):
—What is the literal meaning of the document?
—How well-situated was the author to observe and record the event?
—When, how, and to whom was the report made?
—Is bias a factor? (ideological, class, personal?)
—Is specialized information necessary to understand the document? If so, for which parts?
—Does the report correspond to the dictates of informed common sense?
—Is there corroboration? (This is an important question but irrelevant here since you have access only to a small sample of documents.)

Comments

Excerpt 1:

Sample Comment:
"Parker was an American and would tend to blame the British for firing the first shot." (Note: This is only one of a number of possible comments. What other observations might be made for this item?)

Excerpt 2:

Excerpt 3:

**SET A
Exercise 6:
Using
Statistics**

In Chapter Two we noted the increasing number of historians who base their research on statistical and quantifiable evidence. It is not an aim of this book to provide a lesson in the use and misuse of statistical evidence. Yet it is an inescapable fact that statistical evidence continues to play a greater and greater role in historical writing. And students of history would do well to develop their ability to read and interpret graphs, tables, charts, opinion-poll data, and the like.

The exercise below does no more than scratch the surface in this area, but it will provide a taste of the sort of reasoning and analysis that the use of statistical evidence requires. Note, however, that the tables reproduced below do not represent primary sources in the purest sense. The historian who drew up the charts, John Demos, has culled the information from many original documents and has done the counting for you. Moreover, the organization of the information reflects the questions that Demos wished to investigate.[8] Nevertheless, the charts do represent raw data which does not "speak for itself." It must be interpreted by the historian.

---

[8]John Demos, "Witchcraft in Seventeenth-Century New England," *American Historical Review,* June 1970, pp. 1311–26. Statistical tables reprinted by permission of the author.

I. Persons accused of being witches:

Age	Male	Female	Total
Under 20	6	18	24
21–30	3	7	10
31–40	3	8	11
41–50	6	18	24
51–60	5	23	28
61–70	4	8	12
Over 70	3	6	9
Total	30	88	118

Marital Status	Male	Female	Total
Single	8	29	37
Married	15	61	76
Widowed	1	20	21
Total	24	110	134

II. Persons who accused others of witchcraft:

Age	Male	Female	Total
Under 11	0	1	1
11–15	1	7	8
16–20	1	13	14
21–25	0	1	1
26–30	0	1	1
Over 30	0	4	4
Total	2	27	29

Marital Status	Male	Female	Total
Single	5	23	28
Married	0	6	6
Widowed	0	0	0
Total	5	29	34

The tables categorize by sex, age, and marital status those people who, during the infamous Salem witchcraft trials in 1692, were either accused of being witches or who accused others of witchcraft. On the basis of the evidence presented, what general conclusions can be made concerning the "types" of people most likely to be accused of witchcraft (group I) compared with the "types" of people who accused others of witchcraft (group II)?

QUESTIONS: **1.** General characteristics of persons in group I: _____

_____

_____

_____

_____

2. General characteristics of persons in Group II: _____

_____

_____

_____

_____

3. Option: Write a brief paragraph summarizing the conclusions that can validly be drawn from the statistical data.

**SET B
Analysis of
Evidence II
(Optional)**

On August 16, 1819, a mass demonstration in St. Peter's Fields, Manchester, England, was held to dramatize grass-roots support for parliamentary reform and the democratization of voting rights. The local magistrates (town officials) saw the demonstration as a revolutionary threat to the stability of the state. Regular troops and the local cavalry (yeomanry) were sent to break up the "illegal" meeting and arrest the organizers. In their attempt to disperse the meeting hundreds were injured and about eleven people were killed. Radicals quickly dubbed the incident the Peterloo Massacre in mocking memory of Wellington's victory over Napoleon at Waterloo four years earlier.

There were many conflicting accounts of the events of that day, of which only a very few are printed below. Again, your job is not to determine what happened on that fateful August day, but to ask the "right questions" of the evidence. Use the seven questions on pages 63–65 to make pertinent observations concerning the authorship, circumstances of composition, content, and *potential* credibility of each piece of evidence. Put another way, what factors should the critical historian weigh when evaluating the items below?

1. Account of one of the reformers, Samuel Bamford, who attended the meeting. His account was published in his autobiography, *Passages in the Life of a Radical* (1844). "Hunt" refers to Henry "Orator" Hunt who was addressing the crowd when trouble began. The following excerpt is from Volume I, pages 207–08.

> On the cavalry drawing up they were received with a shout of good-will, as I understood it. They shouted again, waving their sabres over their heads; and then, slackening rein, and striking spur into their steeds, they dashed forward and began cutting the people.
> "Stand fast," I said, "they are riding upon us; stand fast." And there was a general cry in our quarter of "Stand fast." The cavalry were in confusion: they evidently could not, with all the weight of man and horse, penetrate that compact mass of human beings; and their sabres were plied to hew a way through naked held-up hands and defenceless heads; and then

chopped limbs and wound-gaping skulls were seen; and groans and cries were mingled with the din of that horrid confusion....

By this time Hunt and his companions had disappeared from the hustings, and some of the yeomanry, perhaps less sanguinarily disposed than others, were busied in cutting down the flag-staves and demolishing the flags at the hustings....

In ten minutes from the commencement of the havoc the field was an open and almost deserted space. The sun looked down through a sultry and motionless air. The curtains and blinds of the windows within view were all closed. A gentleman or two might occasionally be seen looking out from one of the new houses before mentioned, near the door of which a group of persons (special constables) were collected, and apparently in conversation; others were assisting the wounded or carrying off the dead. The hustings remained, with a few broken and hewed flag-staves erect, and a torn and gashed banner or two dropping; whilst over the whole field were strewed caps, bonnets, hats, shawls, and shoes, and other parts of male and female dress, trampled, torn, and bloody. The yeomanry had dismounted—some were easing their horses' girths, others adjusting their accoutrements, and some were wiping their sabres. Several mounds of human beings still remained where they had fallen, crushed down and smothered. Some of these still groaning, others with staring eyes, were gasping for breath, and others would never breathe more. All was silent save those low sounds, and the occasional snorting and pawing of steeds. Persons might sometimes be noticed peeping from attics and over the tall ridgings of houses, but they quickly withdrew, as if fearful of being observed, or unable to sustain the full gaze of a scene so hideous and abhorrent.

2. Account (c. December 1819) of Rev. Edward Stanley, later Bishop of Norwich. Stanley viewed the riot of August 16 from the window of a house that overlooked St. Peter's Fields.

As the cavalry approached the dense mass of people they used their utmost efforts to escape; but so closely were they pressed in opposite directions by the soldiers...and their own immense numbers, that immediate escape was impossible. The rapid course of the troop was of course impeded when it came in contact with the mob, but a passage was forced in less than a minute....On their arrival at the hustings a scene of dreadful confusion ensued. The orators fell or were forced off the scaffold in quick succession....During the whole of this confusion, heightened by the rattle of some artillery crossing the square, shrieks were heard in all directions, and as the crowd of people dispersed the effects of the conflict became visible. Some were bleeding on the ground and unable to rise; others, less seriously injured but faint with loss of blood, were retiring slowly or leaning upon others for support....The whole of this extraordinary scene was the work of a few minutes.

The rapid succession of so many important incidents in this short space of time, the peculiar character of each depending so much on the variation of a few instants in the detail, sufficiently accounts for the very contradictory statements that have been given; added to which it should be observed that no spectator on the ground could possibly form a just and correct idea of what was passing. When below, I could not have observed anything accurately beyond a few yards around me, and it was only by ascending to the upper rooms of Mr. Buxton's house that I could form a just and correct idea of almost every point which has since afforded so much discussion and contention.

3. Account of Francis Philips, an eyewitness, who published a book on Peterloo entitled *An Exposure of the Calumnies Circulated by the Enemies of Social Order.* . . . The book was published in November 1819.

I shall give a verbatim copy of a narrative I wrote at the request of a friend about six weeks ago. . . .

I mixed with the crowd, where pressure appeared the least, and was at one time within about twenty-five yards of the hustings, on the side nearest to the Magistrates. Although no direct affront was offered me, the observations, boldly and tauntingly made, convinced me of the revolutionary tendency of the meeting, and that they were confident of eventually overturning the Government. . . .

The Yeomanry . . . proceeded at a slow pace, it appeared to me, in file; but from the numbers before me I could not see distinctly. I was alarmed for their safety. . . . Whilst near me, I did not see a sword used, and I solemnly declare my firm belief that, if the crowd had given way to them, no cuts would have been given: a great dust arose when they [the yeomanry] quickened their speed, so that I could not distinguish all that passed, but certainly I did not see one person struck with the sabre. (pp. 22–24)

4. Account that appeared in the *Manchester Observer*, August 21, 1819.

The Boroughmongers [corrupt politicians], and their abettors, have at length filled up the measure of their iniquity to the brim!—The hand trembles, the heart shudders at the melancholy catalogue of cool-blooded murder which must this week occupy those columns hitherto devoted to the purposes of peace, and to the best interests of mankind. . . .

From Bolton, Oldham, Stockport, Middleton, and all the circumjacent country . . . came thousands of willing votaries to the shrine of sacred liberty; and at the period when the patriotic Mr. Hunt and his friends had taken their stations on the hustings, it is supposed that not less than one hundred and fifty thousand people were congregated in the areas near St. Peter's Church. . . .

[Cavalry arrived] and a scene of murder and carnage ensued which posterity will hesitate to believe, and which will hand down the authors and abettors of this foul and bloody tragedy to the execration of the astonished world.—Men, women, and children, without distinction of age or sex, became the victims of these sanguinary monsters; for "all are not men who bear the human form."

5. *The Manchester Mercury*, August 17, 1819.

The events of yesterday will bring down upon the name of Hunt, and his accomplices, the deep and lasting execrations of many a sorrowing family, and of the well-affected members of society at large. With a factious perverseness peculiarly their own, they have set at open defiance the timely warnings of the Magistracy; and having daringly invited the attendance of a mass of people, which ... may ... be computed at 100,000 individuals, they proceeded to address them with language and suggestions of the usual desperate and malevolent character.... Yesterday's proceedings showed, that the revolutionary attempts of this base junto, were no longer to be tolerated....

Now ensues a most painful and melancholy part of our recital; the necessary ardour of the troops in the discharge of their duty has led, we lament to say, to some fatal and many very serious accidents.

6. Statement of "Orator" Hunt, on occasion of a Parliamentary debate on the Peterloo incident, March 15, 1832. (Note: English Parliamentary debates are transcribed in the third person. Thus "I believe" is written "he believed.")

Proceedings had but commenced, when, without the least previous notice, the Manchester Yeomanry were let loose on the assembled multitude, ... with sabres newly sharpened for the occasion, they galloped over the people, cutting down all within reach. No resistance was offered or intended.... He [Hunt] believed he could prove, in opposition to the assertions of interested parties, that the Yeomanry had predetermined on slaughtering the people.

COMMENTS As before, "question" the evidence from the perspective of a critical historian. Note, for each item, which factors and considerations the historian should keep in mind when weighing the relative credibility of that piece of evidence. You might wish to review the discussion on pages 63–65 as well as the summary list on page 72.

Excerpt 1:

Sample observation:
"Account written long after the event."
Other observations:

Excerpt 2:

Excerpt 3:

Excerpt 4:

Excerpt 5:

Excerpt 6:

For discussion: Which accounts seem most "objective"? Least objective? Why?

Context

We have just examined many of the problems one confronts when reading and evaluating historical evidence. There still remains, however, a special problem that all historians must face—that of placing past events in the proper historical context and evaluating a past culture according to the standards and values of *that* culture and not those of the present day. It is no easy matter to understand the thoughts and actions of men and women who lived long ago and far away. Something of this difficulty can be understood by anyone who has traveled abroad and confronted a bewildering array of strange (from the visitor's point of view) customs, practices, laws, values, and the like. It is, for instance, worthy of no notice in Japan if a man takes off his trousers for a hot subway ride home. It would be scandalous (to say nothing of criminal) to do the same in the United States. A siesta during the searingly hot hours of midday is mere common sense to a resident of tropical climates. To an American, such a custom appears suspiciously close to laziness. The list of examples could be multiplied endlessly.

To the historian, the past is much like a foreign country. Things are done differently there. And just as the conscientious traveler today must learn the local customs, values, laws, and language to feel at ease in a foreign country, so too must the historian fully acquaint himself with the institutions, cultural habits, and beliefs of the society he is studying. Only then can the significance and complexity of the historical events under consideration be appreciated.

This brings us to the importance of *context* in the study of history—indeed in the study of any human actions whether past or present. Historical events can *never* be judged in isolation from the wider environment or situation in which they took place. To do so is to risk massive oversimplification or, worse, to misunderstand the events completely. For instance, as children we learned that at the Battle of Bunker Hill during the first year of the American Revolution (June 17, 1775) the commander of the American troops shouted something like: "Don't fire until you see the whites of their [the British troops] eyes!" Regardless of whether this romantic story is true or false, it illustrates perfectly the dangers of taking things out of their proper context. On the surface such an order seems to reinforce a rather idealized vision of the colonial rebels as supermen— determined, stalwart, and brave in the face of an attack by disciplined regular

British troops. However, a more intimate knowledge of the conventions and technology of eighteenth-century warfare reveals a more mundane explanation for the famous order. Actually, the muskets of the time were so inaccurate that a soldier had no hope of hitting an enemy infantryman unless he could see the "whites of his eyes." Military necessity, then, and not superior American valor, best explains the famous and stirring order.

This rather trivial example underscores the importance of knowing as much as one can about the historical period one is studying in order to put events in their proper context. The investigator's knowledge "must include an understanding of how men in other eras lived and behaved, what they believed, and how they managed their institutions."[1] Put another way, you should not judge or interpret past events and individuals on the basis of the standards of your own time, place, or social group, but by the standards of the society you are studying.

This is easier said than done. All too often the tendency to judge the distant past by one's own values and standards is inherent in the very nature of historical studies. One fact alone makes it impossible for the historian to see historical events exactly in the same way contemporaries saw them. The historian knows "how things come out," whereas the participants did not. In other words, historians evaluate and record the past with the enormous advantage of hindsight, and it is much easier to be a Monday-morning quarterback than to play the game itself. The "wisdom" of hindsight makes it very tempting for the historian to wax eloquent about the incompetence, naivete, and shortsighted-ness of those in the past whose vision was not so clear. Hindsight makes past problems seem much more simple (and more easily solvable) than they actually were, and "the leaders that dealt with them . . . smaller men."[2] Hindsight makes it very difficult for even the best-intentioned investigators to observe the rule of context.

Problems of context are especially thorny when moral values are involved. Many practices that, today, we would view as morally reprehensible, were viewed quite differently in other historical eras. Today the institution of slavery is universally condemned by all men and women of goodwill. Yet in many places, in many historical periods, men saw human slavery (or something very close to it) as part of the natural order of things. In the ancient world slavery was a prominent feature of Greek and Roman life; in the European Middle Ages serfs lived lives not far removed from formal slavery; and as late as the nineteenth century slavery was an integral part of the culture of the American South. In cases such as this, what position should the conscientious historian take? Should he condemn these peoples as "immoral" because they countenanced slavery? Should he become a moral "relativist" and judge those societies in terms of their own standards of right and wrong? Should he adopt some convenient middle-of-the-road position? There are no easy answers to these questions.

This is not the place to examine the question of moral judgments in history in detail. It is enough to say that the issue is still very controversial, with advocates on both sides: those who argue that certain moral precepts are timeless and

---

[1]Jacques Barzun and Henry Graff, *The Modern Researcher*, rev. ed. (New York: Harcourt, Brace and World, 1970), p. 116.

[2]Allan Nevins, *The Gateway to History* (Chicago: Quadrangle Books, 1963), p. 257.

universal and hence applicable to all historical eras; and those who argue that moral values are relative to time and place and therefore the moral standards of one era should not be applied to another.

Wherever your sympathies lie on this issue, it is necessary to keep in mind that there *is* a problem here for which there is no easy solution. It is the historian's job both to evaluate the past and understand it, and this is most difficult if basic moral values are in conflict. Perhaps the best advice is this: Be aware of the dilemma, so that in your own studies and researches you can act out of conscious choice rather than ignorance.

On Moral Judgments in History: A Dialogue[3]

Pro:
A sound historical morality will sanction strong measures in evil times; selfish ambition, treachery, murder, perjury, it will never sanction in the worst of times, for these are the things that make times evil—Justice has been justice, mercy has been mercy, honour has been honour, good faith has been good faith, truthfulness has been truthfulness from the beginning.

Goldwin Smith

Con:
Moral judgments on human beings are by their nature irrelevant to the enquiry and alien to the intellectual realm of scientific history.... These moral judgments must be recognised to be an actual hindrance to enquiry and reconstruction; they are in fact the principal reason why investigation is so often brought to a premature halt.

Herbert Butterfield

---

[3]Hans Meyerhoff (ed.), *The Philosophy of History in Our Time* (New York: Doubleday, 1959), p. 225; p. 230.

EXERCISES

The following excerpts are intended to help you appreciate the importance of trying to understand past events within the proper historical context. The passages (drawn from secondary sources) are all concerned with a notorious episode in the life of Oliver Cromwell (1599–1658), the English revolutionary leader who led the anti-royalist Parliamentary forces during the English Civil War (1642–49). By 1649 Parliament had won the civil war, had executed the king, Charles I, and Cromwell had become the effective ruler of England. In the same year Cromwell led an army to Ireland to snuff out an anti-English rebellion that had been raging since 1641. It is Cromwell's behavior in Ireland that is the primary concern of the passages that follow. When in Ireland, Cromwell's soldiers massacred the inhabitants of two towns, Wexford and Drogheda. The following passages attempt to examine the event by putting it in a broader historical context. The aim is not to justify a military atrocity, but to help you *understand* the event as thoroughly as possible.

After reading the initial passage, read the subsequent passages carefully in order to see what *new pieces of evidence* each presents. Note how a wider appreciation of the situation in 1649, the mind-set of Cromwell, the worldview of the seventeenth century, and the relevant historical background all help us to understand better the complex dynamics of a seemingly straightforward occurrence. Then answer the questions that follow.

The Event:

> Cromwell stayed in Ireland for a little over nine months—from August 1649 to May 1650. His siege of Drogheda lasted ten days (September 2–11), and its successful conclusion was followed by four days of general massacre directed by Cromwell himself, during which period some four thousand people were murdered. When on October 1, Wexford too was stormed, the same vengeance was exacted, and two thousand people more—men, women, and children, priests, nuns, and laymen—were put to death.... Having given this grim warning, Cromwell refrained from further atrocities in Ireland.... Nevertheless, on account of Drogheda and Wexford, Cromwell left behind him in Ireland a name for cruelty such as the passage of three hundred years has scarcely erased from memory.

Supplementary Information:

> **A.** What then is the explanation of Cromwell's cruel and compulsive behavior in Ireland? From childhood he had been raised in an atmosphere of paranoiac hatred for Catholicism. When he was only six, a group of desperate English Catholics had tried to blow kings, Lords, and Commons sky-high; after the Gunpowder Plot of 1605, a fear and loathing of Catholicism that was to last for many years swept England and formed the background of Cromwell's childhood education.... Finally, in Cromwell's adult years came the reports of the unspeakable atrocities committed by Irish Catholics in 1641—reports that, as we have seen, were grossly overstated but that seemed to establish irrefutably the unchanging nature of the evil that was Catholicism.

> **B.** The rules of war of the time, with regard to sieges, were clear. If a

commander refused to accede to a summons to surrender, and the town was subsequently won by storm, then he put at risk the lives not only of all his men, but of all those who could be held to be combatants. The significant moment was when the walls were breached by the opposing side: thereafter quarter could not be demanded.... Nor was the civilian population of the town necessarily protected from the rash consequences of the commander's refusal to surrender.... Grotius in *De Jure Belli ac Pacis*, a work first printed in 1625, that attempted to prescribe some limits to the vengefulness of war as a result of the appalling slaughters of the Thirty Years' War [1618–48], still postulated that it was lawful to kill prisoners of war, and furthermore, that "the slaughter of women and children is allowed to have impunity, as comprehended in the right of war and 137th Psalm."

C. Cromwell's Irish policy was not personal but national. When he crossed to Ireland in 1649 the Irish revolt against English rule...had dragged on for eight years. So long as it continued, Ireland offered a backdoor to foreign intervention against the regicide republic [Cromwell's Parliamentary party had beheaded King Charles I in January 1649], now isolated in monarchical Europe.... The government of the English republic decided that Ireland must be subdued quickly. Hence the massacres of Drogheda and Wexford, for which Cromwell is remembered in Ireland to this day.

D. In England [Cromwell] was prepared in fact to tolerate Catholics as well as Episcopalians: Roman Catholic historians agree that their coreligionists were better off during the Protectorate [the period of Cromwell's rule] than they had ever been under James or Charles I. But in Ireland it was different.... Again we must refer, by way of explanation though not justification, to the *political* associations of Irish Catholicism.... It was a *political* religion in a sense in which Catholicism in England had ceased to be political.

E. It is necessary to set this story in perspective because it has so often been used to picture Cromwell as a monster of cruelty, differing from other generals and statesmen in English history, and secondly because it is frequently assigned as a main reason for the poisoning of Anglo-Irish relations in modern times. In fact, Cromwell's Irish policy—wrongheaded as it may have been—was identical with that of Queen Elizabeth I, King James I, Strafford, and Pym. All of them sponsored the colonization of Ireland by Protestant settlers. To the Puritans Ireland was a nearer alternative to Massachusetts or Virginia and the natives as capable of absorption or extrusion as the Indians.

F. Cromwell resolved to put the garrison to the sword primarily for military reasons: "Truly I believe this bitterness will save much effusion of blood," he wrote.... To Sir Winston [Churchill] the atom bomb [in 1945] was a "miracle of deliverance"; to Cromwell the slaughter of the Drogheda garrison was "a marvelous great mercy."...

It was a grave and deliberate act of policy after full warning had been given (as at Hiroshima and Nagasaki); and Cromwell explained it and defended it as such.

Sources

A. Giovanni Costigan, *A History of Modern Ireland* (New York: Pegasus, 1970), pp. 76–77, 79.
B. Antonia Fraser, *Cromwell* (New York: Knopf, 1973), pp. 335–36.
C. Christopher Hill, "Political Animal," *New York Review of Books*, June 9, 1977, p. 40.
D. C. Hill, *God's Englishman* (New York: Harper & Row, 1972), pp. 121–22.
E. Maurice Ashley, *The Greatness of Oliver Cromwell* (New York: Collier Books, 1966), pp. 233–34.
F. *Ibid.,* pp. 232–33.

QUESTIONS **1.** For *each* passage (A through F) note the specific additional pieces of information that enable you to put the massacres of Wexford and Drogheda into a broader historical context:

Passage A: _____

_____

Passage B: _____

_____

Passage C: _____

_____

Passage D: _____

_____

Passage E: _____

_____

Passage F: _____

_____

2. The quoted passages help put Cromwell's expedition into historical perspective by supplying: (1) information on Cromwell the individual (*personal* values and beliefs); (2) commentary on the *immediate* political situation (i.e., 1649); (3) insights into the broad cultural, religious, and moral values of seventeenth-century society (the "worldview"); and (4) relevant historical background information (developments in England and Ireland *before 1649*) that had an impact on events.

Indicate by letter (A–F) the specific passage or passages that contain important information related to each of the general categories just listed.

    a. Cromwell the individual: _____

    b. Immediate political situation: _____

    c. Societal values/worldview: _____

    d. Historical background (pre-1649 in England): _____

DISCUSSION **1.** Generally, the quoted passages allow you to make a more balanced appraisal of Cromwell's Irish campaign because they suggest what a modern-day court of law would call "mitigating circumstances." The purpose is not to condemn or exonerate Cromwell's behavior, but to allow you to *view Cromwell's actions as his fellow countrymen in the seventeenth century might have viewed them.* In what ways do you think the seventeenth-century assessment would differ from a twentieth-century judgment? Why?

2. Passage F compares Cromwell's justification for the massacres in Ireland with the American and British justification for dropping the atomic bomb on Japan in 1945. In both cases it was argued that one act of violence would save lives in the long run by shortening the war. How valid or useful is this parallel? Why?

3. Which passage or passages added most to your understanding of the events in question? Least? Why?

SET A
Exercise 2:
Essay

Write a brief paragraph-length account of Cromwell's expedition. Be sure to include all the background information that you see as essential for a clear understanding of the events in question. You might find it profitable to compare your paragraph with those of your colleagues in class.

SET B
Exercise 1:
The Appeasement
Policy, 1933–1938
(Optional)

Few diplomatic policies have been as universally condemned as that called appeasement during the 1930s. So dramatic was the failure of appeasement that the policy became, in the words of one historian, "the most influential negative lesson for a whole generation of Western leaders" in the 1950s and '60s.

"Appeasement" refers to the attempts of the British and French, especially the British, to dampen the aggressive ambitions of Adolf Hitler's Nazi regime in Germany in the 1930s. Hitler (1889–1945) became Chancellor of Germany in 1933 and he immediately sought to overthrow the military and territorial restrictions imposed upon Germany by the Versailles Treaty after Germany's defeat in World War I (1914–18). Hitler embarked on a campaign of rearmament and territorial expansion, which, within a short time, made Germany the most powerful country in Europe. Eventually Hitler's aggressive actions (the remilitarization of the German Rhineland in violation of the Treaty of Versailles, the annexation of Austria, the dismemberment and ultimate invasion of Czechoslovakia, the invasion of Poland) led to the outbreak of World War II in 1939.

From 1933 until 1938 the British argued that the best way to satisfy Hitler and thus avoid war was to satisfy his territorial demands and ignore his violations of the Versailles Treaty. This was appeasement. The primary British proponent of appeasement was Neville Chamberlain, Prime Minister from 1937 to 1939. Chamberlain was the prime mover behind the September 1938 Munich Conference, which allowed Hitler to annex parts of Czechoslovakia without opposition. Munich was the most extreme example of the British determination to appease Hitler; and it was dubbed by one critic as "one of the most disastrous episodes" in British history. Most historians have echoed that sentiment. For rather than ensure peace, appeasement led to war. J. W. Wheeler-Bennett writes: "It is a tragic irony of history that this very will for peace was among the most important contributory factors to the Second World War, for it is clear that early and bloodless victories convinced Hitler that Britain and France would never oppose him by force. . . ."[4]

All of this is very obvious to us now. Appeasement was a failure. The appeasers were shortsighted and naïve. "The total upshot of their efforts was to aid Nazi-Germany to achieve a position of brutal ascendancy, a threat to everybody else's security or even existence, which only a war could end."[5] But is that enough of an explanation? No. Here, as elsewhere, the broader *context* is critical for an understanding of the attitudes and policies of the appeasers. Below are a series of passages that try to explore the historical context in which the appeasers worked. Read them carefully in order to discover as many factors as you can that might help you attain a better understanding of the appeasement policy. After you finish reading the excerpts, answer the questions that follow.

The Background of Appeasement

A. Appeasement rested on a number of assumptions. Perhaps its basic foundation was the conviction among the survivors of the First World War [1914–18] that Europe could not survive another such bloodletting. Every French town had its *monument aux morts* with its long list of the dead; no British village was without its war memorial. Even tiny villages displayed

---

[4]*Munich: A Prologue to Tragedy* (New York: Viking Press, 1965), p. 6.

[5]A. L. Rowse, *Appeasement* (New York: Norton, 1963), p. 118.

prodigious lists of casualties. Mutilated war veterans were conspicuous reminders, as was the arrival of the "hollow years" in the 1930's. Added to this were science fiction conceptions of the next war, with its aerial bombardments and poison gas. Millions of deaths were predicted....

B.   In one sense it [appeasement] was Chamberlain's own policy, and a very personal one; but it rested on illusions which were very widely shared. Chamberlain's hatred of war was passionate, his fear of its consequences shrewd. He believed...that much could be accomplished by personal diplomacy in conference; that there "must be something in common" between different peoples since "we are all members of the human race"; that there was a human side to the dictators, which could be appealed to, especially in tête-á-tête [face-to-face] discussions.

C.   One moral argument told strongly in Germany's favour: the argument which had been pressed, particularly by the Left, ever since the end of the first World War. The Treaty of Versailles had been presented as unjust, punitive, and unworkable. Germany was entitled to equality in armaments and everything else. The Germans of Austria, Czechoslovakia, and Poland were entitled, like other nationalities, to self-determination, even if this meant an increase in German power. More broadly, Germany was entitled to a place in Europe and in the world commensurate with her greatness in population, economic resources, and civilisation.

D.   Why then did Britain, the second beneficiary of the treaties [the Treaty of Versailles and others] look upon them as provisional or even objectionable, in part at least, while the French at the same time clung to them with an almost desperate devotion? The explanation lies partly in Britain's traditions and the happy experiences which she has had in her relations with the Dominions [e.g., Canada, Australia] and other parts of her Empire in applying a flexible policy. She has moved on from one temporary agreement to another, regarding each one only as a step in a continuous and inevitable historical evolution. It has also been suggested that a nation that has no written constitution and no codified law is more naturally skeptical about the permanency of any legal statutes and may at the same time have a more optimistic belief in the perfectibility of every settlement.

E.   Since the inauguration of the League of Nations in 1920 Britain had taken very seriously the obligations incurred under the Covenant, more particularly those involving the reduction of armaments, and this tendency had been further encouraged with the increase of economic burdens. In an honest but fatal endeavour to achieve universal disarmament, successive Governments had reduced the armaments of Britain to a point at which many believed them to be no longer compatible with the demands of national defence, in the vain hope that others would be moved to emulate such an example of unilateral rectitude....Under the insistent pressure of necessity occasioned by the economic crisis of 1931 [reflecting the onset of worldwide depression in 1929], the National Government of Mr. MacDonald and Mr. Baldwin reduced the armaments expenditure for the year 1932–3 to £102.7 millions, and the Labour Party, now in opposition, expressed the view that the reduction fell far short of what was expected.

At this moment it was believed by all parties that the risk of financial disaster was far greater than the menace from any rival Power.

F. J. M. Keynes said the Treaty [of Versailles] was filled with clauses "which might impoverish Germany now or obstruct her development in future." Many Englishmen read, and accepted, his criticisms. Ashamed of what they had done, they looked for scapegoats, and for amendment. The scapegoat was France; the amendment was appeasement. The harshness of the Treaty was ascribed to French folly.... France was blamed for having encouraged Britain in an excess of punishment. Justice could only be done by helping Germany to take her rightful place in Europe as a Great Power....

If Germany was to be won for friendship, France's friendship must be discarded. Dislike of France ran deep in English life.... While Germany gained a new master [Hitler] and a new discipline in 1933, France remained slovenly, excitable, under the influence of left-wing politicians.... German excesses there indeed were, but French weakness was as great a crime. It was a weakness the communists could exploit; a weakness which offered a chance of power to the agents of Moscow. A deal with France would be a deal with danger. But the Germans were wiser and stronger, and anti-communism was a leading point in Hitler's program.

G. [After World War I there was a] fashionable wave of pacifist thinking. In the decade after 1918 writers were little attracted by the theme of war; now, in the early thirties, there was an avalanche of war books...with a common theme, the senselessness of war.... Pacifism found other avenues of expression. David Low's popularity as a cartoonist began with his lampooning of war.... The Oxford Union in February 1933 voted 275–153 in support of the motion "that this House will in no circumstance fight for its King and Country."

H. Finally, and least explicitly of all, appeasement rested on domestic considerations of internal order. At the most elementary level, the appeasers assumed that a new war would lead to another round of revolutions like those of 1917 [the year of the Russian Revolution]. They had no stomach for another bout with the social tensions of total war. Regardless of how distasteful his manners or his regime were, Hitler was a barrier to Bolshevik [Russian Communist] expansion into central Europe. Two of Chamberlain's associates—Lord Halifax and Sir Horace Wilson—praised Hitler to his face in 1938 for his "great services" to the defense of European civilization from the Bolsheviks.

Sources

A. R. O. Paxton, *Europe in the Twentieth Century* (New York: Harcourt Brace Jovanovich, 1975), p. 417.

B. C. L. Mowat, *Britain Between the Wars, 1918–1940* (London: Methuen, 1968), pp. 590–91.

C. A. J. P. Taylor, *English History, 1914–1945* (Oxford: Clarendon Press, 1965), p. 417.

D. Arnold Wolfers, *Britain and France between Two Wars* (New York: W. W. Norton, 1966), pp. 214–15.

E. J. W. Wheeler-Bennett, *Munich: A Prologue to Tragedy* (New York: Viking Press, 1965), pp. 230–31.

F. Martin Gilbert and Richard Gott, *The Appeasers* (Boston: Houghton Mifflin, 1963), pp. 3, 8–9.

G. Alfred Havighurst, *Twentieth-Century Britain*, 2nd ed. (New York: Harper & Row, 1962), p. 233.

H. Paxton, *op. cit.*, p. 418.

QUESTIONS   **1.** For *each* passage (A through H) note the specific additional pieces of information that enable you to put the appeasement policy into a broader historical context:

Passage A: _____

_____

Passage B: _____

_____

Passage C: _____

_____

Passage D: _____

_____

Passage E: _____

_____

Passage F: _____

_____

Passage G: _____

_____

Passage H: _____

_____

2. Which passage or passages added most to your understanding of the events in question? Why?

3. Which passage or passages added least to your understanding of the events in question? Why?

**SET B
Exercise 2:
Essay
(Optional)**

Write a one or two paragraph account of the factors behind the appeasement policy. Be sure to include all the background information you see as essential for a full understanding of the appeasers and their policies. You might want to compare the factors you included in your essay with those chosen by your colleagues. (Note: An exercise in Chapter Seven also asks for an essay based on the appeasement passages. Ask your instructor whether you are to write an essay on the appeasement policy now, or later in Chapter Seven.)

CHAPTER SIX

The Conceptions and Theories of Historians

Nearly all of us have had the experience of riding through a strange city and getting glimpses of this and that—busy intersections, storefront displays, crowd movement, hamburger shops, residential streets, garish billboards—in all, a melange of assorted sights, and sounds, and smells. Later on when we are asked our impressions of that city, it takes us a while to sort it all out because there was such a variety of detail. The historian has just about the same problem. He has spent many hours viewing some foreign scene (some segment of the past), and there is a lot of sorting out to do before he can give his "impression." He must decide what things best characterized that scene, how much of this and of that to include, how much weight to give each item in his impression, and what to exclude. Actually, though, "impression" is not quite the right word. The more exact word is "interpretation," and it is the one that is commonly used. What it refers to, broadly anyway, is the distinctive color and emphasis the historian imparts to his picture, along with the frame he chooses as its setting. Put in another way, the historian's "interpretation" is his individual way of ordering, framing, and weighing the relations that have shaped the events of some segment of the past.

Any given historical interpretation is a mix of many elements, but certainly one of the most important is the historian's own conceptions and theories—his attitudes, interests, worldview. The historian's mind is not a "photographic plate, blank until exposed to the light cast by the evidence";[1] it is not a scale that can weigh past events with the precision of a finely calibrated chemical balance. Historians are as human as anyone else, and consequently share the prejudices, assumptions, and values of those around them. They are not "above the battle" in regard to such human tendencies, and their personal attitudes and values, while certainly not necessarily *determining* an interpretation of some given event, definitely do condition it. Their fixed ideas, even their temperaments, shape the way they look at things. Consider, for example, the old story about a little boy, a pessimist, who, after being put into a room filled to eye level with horse manure, complained and cried to be let out; another little boy, an optimist, exposed to the

---

[1]G. R. Elton, *The Practice of History* (New York: Thomas Y. Crowell, 1967), p. 96.

same conditions, searched feverishly through the manure saying, "I know there's got to be a new pony for me in here somewhere."

That historians' conceptions influence their works of history has its good side as well as its bad side. A fixed, decisive point of view is often the originating basis of a fresh and revealing insight into a past that has become excessively conventionalized by other historians. It can lead one to frame questions that, when honestly answered, provide an entirely different perspective on some segment of the past. The danger is, of course, that a fixed point of view may go further than merely framing questions. Too often the facts of history are bent or selected to fit that fixed point of view, and the "history" that emerges is a propaganda piece rather than "the best true story" about a past. What is called for is an intellectual honesty that forgoes serving some intense conviction and seeks instead the truth wherever it may lead.

Intellectual honesty is essential to the achievement of historical scholarship, but even when it is present, a reader of a historical work should remember that he is getting an angled view. The author of that work has certain conceptions and theories that have been etched into his mind over a lifetime, and inevitably those conceptions and theories affect the work in three ways: (1) they originate the questions that are asked; (2) they fix the point from which any given past is viewed; and (3) they shape the perception the historian has of that past. In all, that makes a historian's "conceptions and theories" a rather powerful filter, thus the validity of the advice that one should "study the historian" as well as the history he writes.

Though it is impossible to be comprehensive in naming the conceptions and theories that may color the historian's mind, certain broad and rather fluid categories may be named. These include what will be called here conventional "leanings," the climate of opinion, and grandiose historical theories. Each will be briefly discussed and illustrated.

CONVENTIONAL LEANINGS

At the outset let us recognize that the usual term for "leanings" is "bias." We have made a carefully considered decision not to use "bias" here because its meaning has become so heavily negative. Let the reader briefly reflect on the intent of the following fairly typical remarks:

—"The school board's bias was shown in its faculty hiring policies."
—"The bias of the judge made a fair trial impossible."
—"He made a biased decision against promoting a woman to the manager-ship."

In common usage "bias" has become a term of censure, often an epithet, and sometimes a code word for "I hate the S.O.B."

Under the circumstances, it is better to use a less negative term to describe the lurking, often muffled, yet ever-continuing presence of the historian in the story he tells. "Leanings" will do, for it suggest personal preferences or tendencies, emotional inclinations, warm interests, a partiality toward something. And that something, in many people's eyes, might be wholly admirable. Love of country, for example, does not disqualify one from writing effective history, nor does strong attachment to a church, nor does devotion to a principle of democracy, or aristocracy, or, indeed, to Marxist theory. All of these positions, or points of view, throw light on the past from different angles, thus illuminating different facets of it. Before dismissing as "poor history" a work written from any distinctive point of view, a reader should ask himself whether it might not be simply that he disagrees with that point of view.[2]

But, of course, it bears repeating that any historian's point of view can run away with him. He can "lean" so far that he falls flat. He can become so preoccupied with his point of view that he sees only those pieces of evidence that support it. His point of view can become so intrusive that *it* becomes the central focus rather than the past itself. It is certainly true, as historian Theodore Mommsen wrote, that history is neither made nor *written* "without love or hate." But the professional conscience of a historian must be strong enough to restrain love and hate when those passions begin to lead him away from truthful examination of evidence.

All of this does not mean that we should distrust works of history, only that they should be read with our eyes open. An author's leanings are usually unannounced. They often reveal themselves by what is left out, sometimes by excessive emphasis on one feature of a situation, occasionally by usage of emotionally charged language. Generally, in reading history one should follow the advice of historians Jacques Barzun and Henry Graff as they describe how to read the English historian Macaulay: "The reader proceeds by a sort of triangulation: here I stand; there, to left or right, stands Macaulay; and beyond are the events he reports. Knowing his position in relation to mine, I can work out a perspective upon events as I could not if I saw them exclusively through his eyes."[3] And so, one does not "dismiss" an author because he is found to be a nationalist, or a racist, or a Marxist, or something else. One reads him, perhaps understanding the reported events better, and certainly understanding the whole nature of history-as-a-personal-account better.

Besides the idiosyncratic likes and dislikes of individual historians, there are perhaps six conventional leanings that recurrently shape men's minds that one can find in history books. They are: (1) national feeling; (2) geographical feeling; (3) political feeling; (4) racial feeling; (5) religious or moral feeling; (6) class feeling. Each of these will be briefly described and/or illustrated.[4]

1. *National feeling.* To find nationalistic accounts one need not look across thousands of miles of ocean to Russia, where Soviet historians have labored so faithfully to doctor their stories to fit the party line. For better or for worse American historians have done the same, notably in high-school textbooks. For the most part the Americanism in textbooks is not so much an unequivocal "We're Number 1" kind of approach; rather it is contained in a warm endorsement of American ideals, often with ringing praise of democratic forms. Bragdon and McCuthchen's *History of a Free People* is representative:

BUT to say that American ideals have not been fully carried out is merely

---

[2]For a discussion of the possible merit of "passionate history," see G. M. Trevelyan, "Bias in History," in *An Autobiography and Other Essays* (London: Longmans, Green, 1949), pp. 77ff.

[3]Jacques Barzun and Henry F. Graff, *The Modern Researcher* (New York: Harcourt, Brace and World, 1970), p. 183.

[4]For the sake of illustration we will rely on examples from American history. Keep in mind, though, that all historians, wherever found, lean one way or another.

to say that Americans, being human, are not perfect. Taken as a whole, the history of the United States has been that of a bold and exciting experiment in founding a society on faith in human intelligence, human freedom, and human brotherhood. So far this experiment has been a success.[5]

It should be borne in mind that there are perhaps very good reasons for the nationalistic flavor of high-school textbooks. Certainly many people agree with the long-standing efforts of the American Legion, which in the 1920s set as one of its major goals the promotion of a favorable view of America in American-history textbooks.

2. *Geographical feeling.* At one time "geographical" (in American history writing) referred to works with an overwhelming regional consciousness, such as those characterized by a "northern" or "southern" point of view. Or, less often, it referred to the more chauvinistic of the state histories, which were written as texts for required state-history courses in high schools. In recent years, however, geographical bias has taken on something of the flavor of a preoccupation with the problems and distresses of the city, leading often to uneasy estimates of the American condition. One historian, for example, while acknowledging the warmth of small-town life, the continuation of neighborhood consciousness, and continuing ethnic identity, nonetheless finds little of a "binding sense of community at this late point in time." His assessment is a reasonable one, of course, provided one takes a strictly urban perspective. But some historians deny the overall validity of such a perspective (see *The Grass-Roots Mind in America*).[6]

3. *Political feeling.* By "political feeling" is meant not any expressed approval of one party or another, but a body of political beliefs that form the framework within which some segment of the past is viewed. Such beliefs range across the political spectrum, from a conservative distaste for governmental interference of any kind to a radical's rejection of the capitalist order. The following selection is taken from the works of a writer with impeccable liberal credentials, a man whose perspective is shaped by his unstated premise that social problems can be efficiently solved through governmental action.

> Eisenhower and his administration have lived off the accumulated wisdom, the accumulated prestige, and the accumulated military strength of his predecessors who conducted more daring and more creative regimes. If our margin for error is as great as it has traditionally been, these quiet Eisenhower years will have been only a pleasant idyl, an inexpensive interlude in a grim century. If our margin for error is much thinner than formerly, Eisenhower may join the ranks of history's fatal good men, the Stanley Baldwins and the James Buchanans. Their intentions were good and their example is pious, but they bequeathed to their successors a black heritage of time lost and opportunities wasted.[7]

The point here is not to profess disagreement or agreement with this writer's conclusion, but rather to point out that his interpretation is founded upon a premise that, while unspoken, is at least arguable.

---

[5]Henry W. Bragdon and Samuel P. McCutchen, *History of a Free People* (New York: Macmillan, 1954, 1956), p. xi.

[6]Conal Furay, *The Grass-Roots Mind in America* (New York: New Viewpoints, 1977), pp. 59ff.

William V. Shannon, "Eisenhower as President," in *Perspectives on 20th Century America*, Otis L. Graham, Jr., ed., (New York: Dodd, Mead, 1973), p. 323.

4. *Racial feeling.* However strong it might be in person-to-person living, racism in contemporary historical literature is for the most part passé. There are, though, observers who find a latent racism present in those works that fail to give what the observer regards as adequate coverage to the problems that have been faced by American blacks, Indians, and other ethnic minorities. In some cases such charges have been valid; in others, not. But it is beyond question that some past American historians had racial bias of a very active kind, as the following passage reflects:

> The first element in the negro problem is the presence in America of two alien races, both practically servants. The Indians were savages, and helped to keep alive savage traits in the souls of white settlers; but there was no considerable number of mixed bloods, and the Indians faded away as the white people advanced. The original slaves were also savages, just out of the jungle, who required to be watched and handled like savages, but they steadily increased in numbers, and from the beginning there was a serious race admixture. Their descendants in the second and third generation were milder in character, and were much affected by at least a surface Christianity; but their standards of character were much lower than those of the dominant white community, and tended to pull the superior race down. To the present day the low conditions of great numbers of negroes has a bad effect on the white race.[8]

5. *Religious or moral feeling.* Religious experience is or can be totally consuming, and so one can expect to find many works strongly dominated by religious points of view. Especially has this been the case in Reformation histories, in Irish histories, and in Puritan New England histories—all of them involving times and situations where religious differences occasioned violent conflict. Generally, though, in the United States, which for the most part has prided itself on tolerance, religious bias in historical literature (or its opposite, antireligious bias) is rarely pronounced, though one can find occasional exceptions. Note the following passage from *A New American History* by W. E. Woodward: "The *Book of Mormon* is a pack of nonsense, but it is not thereby deprived of historical significance. On the strength of his revelation and the book Joseph Smith founded a religion. Religious movements almost always have an improbable basis, and a fantastic mythology—the more fantastic the better. They are the rationalizing process in reverse."[9] Such outspoken statements are rare. More often antireligious bias, at least in the eyes of religionists, is reflected in certain historians' easy dismissal of the contemporary importance of religion, by their occasional tendency to treat fundamentalist religion as reflecting negative attitudes toward "progress," by associating religion with "bloc" mentality, and sometimes by associating religion with authoritarianism, thus suggesting negative attitudes toward democratic ideals. "Moral" feeling is often a derivative of religious feeling, or at least is tantamount to it, as would be illustrated by a historian taking as his fundamental principle that the freedom of speech is an *absolute* right.

6. *Class feeling.* Democracy does not mean the absence of economic and

---

[8]Albert B. Hart, "Negro Problem," *Cyclopedia of American Government*, (Chicago: Appleton, 1914), p. 513.

[9]W. E. Woodward, *A New American History* (New York: The Literary Guild, 1937), p. 422.

social classes, but it does imply a blurring of class lines, at least where rights and privileges are concerned. But, in the view of many American historians, this ideal of equality is more fiction than fact, and their histories reflect an intense class consciousness and a strong feeling in favor of less vocal elements of society. They frequently express a concern that privileged classes, whether of the economic or political establishment, are firmly in the saddle, and that the reforms that have been achieved are quite superficial. The following selection is representative:

> In acting to protect the institution of private property and in advancing the interests of corporate capitalism, the New Deal assisted the middle and upper sectors of society. It protected them, sometimes, even at the cost of injuring the lower sectors. Seldom did it bestow much of substance upon the lower classes. Never did the New Deal seek to organize these groups into independent political forces. Seldom did it risk antagonizing established interests. For some this would constitute a puzzling defect of liberalism; for some, the failure to achieve true liberalism. To others it would emphasize the inherent shortcomings of American liberal democracy. As the nation prepared for war, liberalism, by accepting private property and federal assistance to corporate capitalism, was not prepared effectively to reduce inequities, to redistribute political power, or to extend equality from promise to reality.[10]

Such are the leanings recurrently found in historical literature. Remember that their presence does not necessarily invalidate a historical interpretation. What they do is possibly frame the historian's perspective so that he picks and chooses his material to fit within its limits. And this is something of which his reader should be aware.

THE CLIMATE OF OPINION

In the preface to his play *Saint Joan,* George Bernard Shaw wrote: "It is difficult, if not impossible, for most people to think otherwise than in the fashion of their own period." There are always a few historians who will swim against the prevailing current, but most reflect the culturally fashionable ideas of their times. This tendency is well-illustrated by the varying views of the Civil War in American-history textbooks over the past one hundred years. At the turn of the century, during a time when American democratic institutions were being idealized, the war was seen fundamentally as a victory for democracy over a recalcitrant South. In the 1920s business had assumed institutional command over American life, and now the Civil War was portrayed as the victory of an industrial civilization over an agrarian one. In the 1930s Americans, viewing the resurgence of Germany, had generally become disillusioned with war as an instrument to achieve justice; the Civil War now began to be seen as an unnecessary war brought on by blundering politicians. Finally, as waves of civil-rights consciousness swept over the social landscape in the 1950s and 1960s, the Civil War came to be presented as a crusade over the moral issue of slavery.

---

[10]Barton J. Bernstein, "The New Deal: The Conservative Achievement of Liberal Reform," in *Past Imperfect,* Vol. II, Blanche Wiesen Cook, Alice Kessler Harris, and Ronald Radosh, eds., (New York: Knopf, 1973), p. 171.

Indeed, public opinion may not be something you can see, but all the same it is there—"sixteen pounds to the square inch," as one writer put it.

Of special importance to an understanding of historians' interpretations is familiarity with the "climate of opinion" that prevails during their careers. Climate of opinion refers to the "fundamental assumptions and attitudes shared by significant elements of a population at a given time." For historians, generally anyway, this means the assumptions and attitudes shared by the educated sector of the American people. The mechanics of how the historian is affected by the climate of opinion is well described by Robert A. Skotheim in this passage:

> From the mass of records left by the past, the historian selects and interprets data on the basis of what is meaningful and important to him. In this process, he is reflecting his climate of opinion, for he studies the past from the perspective of the present. His sense of what is meaningful and important significantly derives from the climate of opinion in which he lives.
> This is not to deny that he honestly tries to understand the past, or to suggest that he intentionally distorts the past because of his present interests. It is only to insist that the historian cannot jump out of his intellectual skin.[11]

Of the various "tempers" or fundamental belief patterns that have influenced American historians in the twentieth century, three are especially important in having shaped historians' interpretations. They are, in order, (1) the "progressive" temper; (2) the "liberal" tradition; and (3) the "new left" perspective.

The "progressive" temper. The body of beliefs characteristic of progressives flourished from the turn of the century up through World War II. Assumptions basic to progressives, at least so far as they affected history writing, were (1) a tendency to emphasize economic factors as the primary historical force; (2) a tendency to emphasize conflict between forces (liberalism vs. conservatism, capitalism vs. agrarianism, etc.) as the root process of national progress; (3) a brimming confidence in mankind's capability to create its future; and (4) a belief that a bad environment is the sole cause of human limitations.

The "liberal" tradition. Dominant in the 1940s and 1950s, the school of historians described as "liberal" grew out of a disillusionment with Europe occasioned by the trauma of two wars coupled with an enhanced sense that America's history is truly and wholly different from that of Europe. The American pattern was one of consensus, not conflict; of stability, not change; of individualism, not collectivism; of a homogeneous middle class, not a deeply fragmented class structure. Generally, America was celebrated as the home of a pristine liberalism that was moving to gradual perfection, even though at times privileged interests, notably business, somewhat slowed that movement.

The "new left" perspective. The turmoil of the 1960s produced a minority group of highly vocal young historians who rebelled against the "consensus" theme that had been dominant in the years preceding. (One should also keep in mind that this period found the United States deeply engaged in a Vietnam war that seemed to be fought predominantly by young men who were members of what some saw as "underprivileged minorities.") These historians reverted to

---

[11]*The Historian and the Climate of Opinion* (Reading, Mass.: Addison-Wesley, 1969), p. 2.

portions of the earlier progressive theme, including emphasis upon conflict in America and on the predominance of economic forces, but added to it a condemnation of almost all elements of the "establishment," along with a belief that history should actively further the cause of social and political reform.

GRANDIOSE HISTORICAL THEORIES
(SPECULATIVE PHILOSOPHIES OF HISTORY)

As we have seen, "doing" a piece of history inevitably involves a search for a cluster of relations, a *pattern*, by which an event "makes sense." The pattern gives meaning to what would otherwise be an assortment of disconnected facts. The next step in the progression is to find a pattern in several events taken together—some point of commonality according to which these events may be clustered together, given something of a common meaning, and called a "period." Moving to ever larger patterns, historians sometimes find a sufficient common ground for several periods to be called an "age." And so on. Carrying this pattern finding to its logical extreme means finding some common theme according to which all human history hangs together. To the extent to which such a pattern could be discerned, the historian becomes not only a perceptive reader of the human past, but also a prophet—with all of the acclamation and prestige that accompanies such charismatic power. The discovery of the larger pattern that lies at the bottom of—and gives meaning to—human history was a major enterprise of pre-twentieth-century scholars, and their speculations have continued to influence modern scholars.

The term "speculation" is used because none of the theories can be proven. The enormous variety of human cultures and the idiosyncracies of development in each of them, the huge confusion of historical fact along with the shortness of historical time, make it impossible to validate any common theme beyond the level of opinion. For this reason such speculations are usually referred to as "metahistory," as if to underline that they are essentially a form of metaphysical theorizing applied to history. Nonetheless, "metahistory," or "grandiose historical theories" as they are called here, remains influential. Each theory has the merit of simplicity, one gigantic engine powering all the movements, large and small, of the race.

Grandiose historical theories can be classified into two types: progressive and cyclical. Progressive theories all assume movement of the human race toward some usually distant goal. Mankind is on a ladder, so to speak, and while movement up the rungs may be occasionally hesitant, it nonetheless continues and the top rung *will* be reached. There are any number of major progressive theories, but only two of them have special contemporary importance: (1) *Marxism*, which promises that when the long-term conflict between economic classes has ended, the glorious day of the withering away of the state will inevitably come, and a perfected mankind will follow a rule of "from each according to his ability, to each according to his need." (2) *The Law of Progress*, originally an eighteenth-century conception but of continuing influence in modern historical literature. This theory assumes that human society is improving in all of its aspects—freedoms, rights, living circumstances, reason—albeit ever so slightly at times. One of the more interesting versions of man's upward progression is incorporated in the "Whig interpretation of history," a doctrine described by historian Bernard Norling as follows:

> The Whig's forte is studying the past not for its own sake but to discover how it shaped the present. Whig historians value chiefly those persons, practices, and institutions which seem to them forerunners of praiseworthy modern counterparts. They begin with certain assumptions: (1) history is the record of human progress, (2) the whole world wants democracy and is moving towards it, (3) Protestants have usually been the friends and promoters of progress and democracy, (4) Tories and Catholics have usually been against these laudable goals. Starting thus, they collect such information from the past as fits these assumptiosn and ignore what does not fit. Then they say their evidence proves their assumptions.[12]

Progress theories have held on especially well in America, as Americans' concept of themselves as "a people set apart" from lesser nations has remained a basic national assumption.

Cyclic theorists find the fundamental pattern of all history to be eternal recurrence of some basic process, as birth-childhood-adulthood-decline-death, or primitive, heroic and back to primitive. In other words, mankind is on a wheel, not a ladder, and the basic processes will go on into an indeterminate future. The most notable cyclic theorist of the twentieth century was the late Arnold Toynbee, who found a growth, breakdown, and dissolution pattern to have been characteristic of twenty-one civilizations of the past.

In summary, it is fair to say that the history you read is, in many ways, as much a product of the mind of the historian who wrote it as it is the product of the actions of the people who actually lived it. Written history reflects countless decisions on the part of the historian, and these decisions are shaped by personal leanings and the social and intellectual environment. Be alert to this as you read any work of history.

---

[12]*Timeless Problems in History* (Notre Dame, Ind.: University of Notre Dame Press, 1970), p. 57.

EXERCISES

While the intent of the following exercises is to provide you with a fairly wide exposure to examples of preconceptions and theories, still it is not possible to provide anything like full exposure. Some frames of mind, such as the progressive temper of the first part of this century, are discernible only in lengthy readings, which cannot be included here. It is also true that some leanings reveal themselves only after extended exposure to an author's occasional stereotyping and subtle innuendo.

Sometimes, however, an author's leanings can be detected in just a few sentences. The following quotations, which are taken from a wide range of written histories, reflect a number of the preconceptions just discussed. Specifically, you may find here evidence of the following:

National feeling   Class feeling
Geographical feeling   The "liberal" tradition
Political feeling   Cyclic theory
Racial feeling   Progressive theory
Religious or moral feeling

In the space provided indicate the feeling or theory you see as involved, and underline the words or phrases in the quotation on which you base your response. In some cases there is more than one correct answer.

SET A

1. Each white family [of the South] served very much the function of a modern social settlement, setting patterns of orderly, well-bred conduct which the negroes were encouraged to emulate; and the planters furthermore were vested with a coercive power, salutary in the premises, of which settlement workers are deprived. The very aristocratic nature of the system permitted a vigor of discipline which democracy cannot possess. On the whole the plantations were the best schools yet invented for the mass training of that sort of inert and backward people which the bulk of the American negroes represented.

2. An underlying weakness of his [Roosevelt's] leadership lay in his acceptance of the pragmatic approach to the solution of both domestic and foreign problems. In essence, it was a refusal to take the stand for a distinctively American approach to the basic problems of capitalism. No political program that emerged in the Roosevelt administration was distinctly the expression of the American tradition. In the course of twelve years, at home and abroad, the President stood with the radicals, using the political party parlance of the "middle way" in both instances.

3. In fighting the War for Independence in North America, the bourgeoisie led the popular masses of the colonies against the English landed aristocracy and against the colonial yoke of England. This war of the colonies for independence was a bourgeois revolution which overthrew the landed aristocracy and brought to power the American bourgeoisie in union with the slaveholders.

The American bourgeoisie used the struggle of the popular masses against the English as a means of achieving power; then, having come to power, like the English bourgeoisie of the seventeenth century, they oppressed the popular masses. In North America under the title "sovereignty of the people," (democracy), a so-called bourgeois democracy (in actual fact, the power of the bourgeoisie), was established.

4. The law of perfectibility is...absolute. Today everything leads to the conclusion that with the cessation of wars, with the establishment of a regime that will put an end to violent crises, no retrogression, not even a partial one, will ever again take place. There will be continuity and acceleration of the progressions among the whole of mankind, for peoples will teach one another and will sustain one another.

5. The Romanism of the present day is a harmless opinion, no more productive of evil than any other superstition, and without tendency, or shadow of tendency, to impair the allegiance of those who profess it. But we must not confound a phantom with a substance; or gather from modern experience the temper of a time when words implied realities, when Catholics really believed that they owed no allegiance to an heretical sovereign, and that the first duty of their lives was to a foreign potentate. This perilous doctrine was waning, indeed, but it was not dead. By many it was actively professed.

6. We love to indulge in thoughts of the future extent and power of this [American] Republic—because with its increase is the increase of human happiness and liberty....What has miserable, inefficient Mexico—with her superstition, her burlesque upon freedom, her actual tyranny by the few over the many—what has she to do with the great mission of...the New World....

7. The slaveholding regime...kept the main body of labor controlled, provisioned and mobile. Above all it maintained order and a notable degree of harmony in a community where confusion worse confounded would not have been far to seek. Plantation slavery had in strictly business aspects at least as many drawbacks as it had attractions. But in the large it was less a business than a life; it made fewer fortunes than it made men.

8. Roosevelt stood for the "common man"...but he was certainly not common himself. In fact he was a storybook Prince Charming, a fairytale hero to the millions; he ruled with a wand—even if it was an ivory cigarette holder. Out in the rain, men and women strove—literally—to touch the hem of his cape as he passed, this man who could not walk. The "common" people chose him, a prince, to lead them, and he did things for them, as a good prince should.

9. Human affairs form a circle, and...there is a circle in all other things that have a natural movement and coming into being and passing away. This is because all other things are discriminated by time, and end and begin as though conforming to a cycle; for even time itself is thought to be a circle.

Sources

1. U. B. Phillips, *American Negro Slavery* (Gloucester, Mass.: Peter Smith, 1959), p. 343.

2. Edgar E. Robinson, *The Roosevelt Leadership, 1933–45* (New York: Lippincott, 1955), p. 404.

3. *As Others See Us,* Donald Robinson, ed. (Boston: Houghton Mifflin, 1969), p. 43.

4. Henri de St. Simon, as quoted by Frank E. Manuel, *Shapes of Philosophical History* (Stanford, Calif.: Stanford University Press, 1965), p. 102.

5. James A. Froude, *History of England*, Vol. II (New York: Charles Scribner, 1872), p. 321.

6. Walt Whitman, editorial, *Brooklyn Daily Eagle* (July 7, 1846), quoted in *The Mexican War*, Ramon Ruiz, ed. (New York: Holt, Rinehart and Winston, 1963), p. 8.

7. Phillips, *op cit.,* p. 401.

8. John Gunther, *Roosevelt in Retrospect* (New York: Harper and Brothers, 1950), pp. 4–5.

9. Aristotle, *Physics.*

SET B
(Optional)

1. This is the story of the Roman Republic It is the story of the haves being challenged with protest and violence by the have-nots. It is a story remarkably like that of nineteenth- and twentieth-century Europe and America, where laboring men, farmers, immigrants, and women struggled for political and economic rights against those with business and property interests. In Rome and America an establishment class creates the myths, and makes the canons—or law—which become settled in the minds of many as the way of life.

2. God has not been preparing the English-speaking and Teutonic peoples for a thousand years for nothing but vain and idle self-contemplation and self-admiration. No, He has made us master organizers of the world to establish system where chaos reigns.

3. The slaveholders controlled the government of the United States during the first half of the nineteenth century. From the War for Independence until the Civil War of 1861–1865, almost all of the Presidents of the United States were slaveholders. The bourgeoisie submissively ceded the direction of governmental affairs to the slaveholders.... A democratic system, the sovereignty of the people, existed on paper in the United States. Meanwhile, not only the slaveholders but also the American bourgeoisie used this false mask as a cover. In a capitalist system where factories, mills, and land are the property of the bourgeoisie, there is no real democracy and the masses have to fight to utilize democratic institutions.... In a bourgeois democracy, the power of the capitalists is extremely burdensome to the masses.

4. We shall best show how marvellous and vast our subject is by comparing the most famous Empires which preceded,... measuring them with the superior greatness of Rome. There are but three that deserve even to be so compared and measured; and they are these. The Persians for a certain length of time were possessed of a great empire and dominion. But every time they ventured beyond the limits of Asia, they found not only their empire, but their own existence also in danger.... The Macedonians obtained domination in Europe from the lands bordering on the Adriatic to the Danube,... And yet... they still left the greater half of the world in the hands of others. They never so much as thought of attempting Sicily, Sardinia, or Libya.... The Roman conquest, on the other hand, was not partial. Nearly the whole inhabited world was reduced by them to obedience; and they left behind them an empire not to be paralleled in the past or rivalled in the future. Students will gain from my narrative a clearer view of the whole story, and of the numerous and important advantages which such [an] exact record of events offers.

5. During the last century the N.E. manufacturer imported the Irish and Fr. Canadians . . . thus the American sold his birthright in a continent to solve a labor problem. Instead of retaining political control and making citizenship an honorable and valued privilege, he intrusted the government of his country and the maintenance of his ideals to races who have never yet succeeded in governing themselves, much less anyone else.

Associated with this advance of democracy and the transfer of power from the higher to the lower races, from the intellectual to the plebian class, we find the spread of socialism and the recrudescence of obsolete religious forms.

6. It was a premeditated and predetermined affair, the war of the United States on Mexico; it was the result of a deliberately calculated scheme of robbery on the part of the superior power . . . there were enough . . . who were willing to lay aside all notions of right and wrong in the matter, and unblushingly to take whatever could be secured solely upon the principle of might. Mexico, poorer, weak, struggling to secure for herself a place among the nations, is now to be humiliated, kicked, cuffed, and beaten by the bully on her northern border, whose greatest pride is Christian liberty with puritan antecedents, whose greatest principle at this time finds exercise in hunting about for plausible pretexts to steal from a weaker neighbor a fine slice of land suitable for slave labor.

7. In broad outline we can designate the Asiatic, the ancient, the feudal, and the modern bourgeois modes of production as progressive epochs in the economic formation of society. The bourgeois relations of production are the last antagonistic form of the social process of production; not in the sense of individual antagonisms, but of conflict arising from conditions surrounding the life of individuals in society. At the same time the productive forces developing in bourgeois society create the material conditions for the solution of that antagonism.

8. Cuba, our land, emerged from the condition of being a Spanish colony at the close of the past century, only to become a protectorate and semicolony of the United States.

The efforts of the Cuban people to gain full independence and sovereignty—the heroic sacrifices of the Ten Years' War, the Little Way, the War of '95, the aspirations expressed . . . above all by Antonio Maceo and by Jose Marti—were frustrated and flouted by North American intervention in the Cuban-Spanish War at a time when the Cubans had practically defeated Spanish colonialism and were on the verge of gaining full independence.

In 1902 it was said that Cuba was a free and sovereign republic. It had an anthem and a flag. But above these symbols of sovereignty . . . we had the Platt Amendment, an instrument of oppression and of foreign domination over the country. . . .

The United States imperialists had militarily occupied the island. They maintained here their army of occupation; by trickery they had disarmed the Army of Liberation and had organized a rural militia and a police force under their command. . . .

9. In pride and vanity, he [Henry VIII] was perhaps without a parallel. He despised the judgment of others; acted as if he deemed himself infallible in matters of policy and religion; and seemed to look upon dissent from his opinion as equivalent to a breach of allegiance. He steeled his breast against remorse for the blood which he shed, and trampled without scruple on the liberties of the nation. When he ascended the throne, there still existed a spirit of freedom, which on more than one occasion defeated the arbitrary measures of the court; but in the lapse of a few years that spirit had fled, and before the death of Henry, the king of England had grown into a despot, the people had shrunk into a nation of slaves.

Sources

1. Frederick Gentles and Melvin Steinfield, *Hangups from Way Back*, Vol. I (San Francisco: Canfield Press, 1970), p. 136.

2. Albert J. Beveridge, *The Meaning of the Times and Other Speeches* (Indianapolis: Bobbs-Merrill, 1908), pp. 84–5.

3. Edgar E. Robinson, *The Roosevelt Leadership, 1933–45* (New York: Lippincott, 1955), pp. 100–01.

4. Polybius, *The Histories*, Evelyn S. Shuckburgh, trans., as quoted in Peter Guy and Gerald J. Cavanaugh, eds. *Historians at Work*, Vol. I (New York: Harper & Row, 1972), pp. 111–12.

5. Madison Grant, "The Passing of the Great Race," in *Antidemocratic Trends in Twentieth-Century America*, Roland L. DeLorme and Raymond G. McInnes eds. (Reading, Mass: Addison-Wesley, 1969), p. 45.

6. H. Bancroft, "The War as an American Plot," in *The Mexican War*, Ramon Ruiz, ed. (New York: Holt, Rinehart and Winston, 1963), p. 85.

7. Karl Marx, *The Critique of Political Economy*, quoted by Noah E. Fehl, *History and Society* (Hong Kong: Chung Chi College, 1964), p. 247.

8. Robinson, *op. cit.,* pp. 108–09.

9. John Lingard, *History of England*, Vol. IV (Paris: W. Galignani, 1840), p. 215.

Patterns, Interpretations, and Historical Synthesis

To this point we have done three things: (1) we have tried to get an idea of what history is, distinguishing history-as-written from history-as-actuality, and later distinguishing the discipline of history from the "other disciplines"; (2) we have considered questions to ask of the evidence, along with the problems of dealing with evidence (i.e., the *process of analysis*); and (3) we have examined the meaning of "interpretation," going on to explore some of the conceptions and theories the historian brings to his study of the past. All of these matters are necessary "prologue" to the discussion of the creative climax of the historian's work: his synthesis.

"Synthesize," as most readers know, means "to make by combining parts or elements into a complex whole." Applied to history, it refers to the culminating act of the historian. After he has accumulated, questioned, and assimilated the evidence, he joins several chosen "pieces" of a past together so that the events in question "make sense." Put in another way, it is the discovery by the historian of a pattern according to which a certain past "fits together." The matter of "pattern making" is so crucial to all written history that it must be discussed more thoroughly.

The search for a pattern is at the heart of all human mental activity. In educational psychology the literature is filled with such statements as "learning proceeds by recognition of meaningful wholes"; "structure or pattern is the basic feature of all experience"; "meaning is achieved by forming patterns"; "understanding is achieved when a pattern is recognized." Illustrative material like the following is common.[1]

1		2		3		4	
XAH	COJ	RIVER	HOUR	FOOT	ARM	HELP	MEN
YIX	YOF	DOOR	GIRL	MILK	EYE	BRING	SAFE
ZEQ	GYK	PEOPLE	EARTH	HAND	DRINK	THOSE	AGAIN
PYB	VEF	GENERAL	CALL	WATER	FOOD	WEARY	TO
QAJ	XUW	BLOW	BOOK	EAT	EAR	SAILOR	SHORE

[1]John M. Stephens, *The Psychology of Classroom Learning*, (New York: Holt, Rinehart & Winston, 1965), p. 146. Reproduced by special permission of Holt, Rinehart & Winston.

Nearly everyone passes over the first list quickly, seeing little or no pattern in the nonsense syllables; though the second list has better possibilities, it is still an assortment of words having little interrelationship; the third list soon leads many readers to cluster its items into the two patterns of "body parts" and "things related to body sustenance"; the fourth list is quickly perceived as a single pattern, a sentence with an unmistakable meaning. The tendency to search for a pattern is also illustrated by our way of reacting to partial figures such as the following:[2]

After a few seconds some individuals give up trying to "make sense" of the figure; those who stay at it for awhile, however, usually wind up seeing a child on a tricycle.

Pattern making is the root principle of all historical inquiry. Even such familiar concepts as the Age of the Renaissance, the Jacksonian Era, and the Roaring '20s are artificial constructs—patterns—used by historians to make the study of the past more manageable. But pattern making is more than a mere convenience. It is the basis of all historical synthesis. Usually, after studious consideration of the event, the historian sees, or begins to see, that event as part of a larger whole. The event is like a piece of a jigsaw puzzle, which suddenly makes sense when seen in the context of the other pieces. For example, Hitler's confidence that his invasion of Poland in 1939 would not be seriously challenged makes sense when seen in the context of his experience of the repeated British and French pacifism of the preceding years. Basically the historian comes to see an event as part and parcel of a whole composed of numerous individual actions, of certain prevailing conditions, and certain action-producing pressures. To put it another way, the historian comes to see an event as a part of an organic whole that includes specific

---

[2]R. F. Street, *A Gestalt Completion Test* (New York: Teachers College Press, 1931), p. 61. Reproduced by special permission.

people, special conditions, and certain antecedent events. In short he has found an appropriate frame of reference or pattern within which that event can be understood.

But it should not be supposed that the perceived pattern typically comes as a sudden sort of incandescent insight. On the contrary, its birth comes only after laborious questioning, and recurrent, often frustratingly inaccurate, speculations. Ordinarily at least, it springs not from some masterfully controlling metaphysical system or grandiose historical theory but from some modest "working hypothesis" that survives the trials of testing against the hard facts of reality. Nor is the perceived pattern anything whose truth can be regarded as certain. At best it is never anything more than probabilistic, because it is inevitably based on records that are incomplete. (Remember what was said in an earlier chapter about how little of what happens is ever recorded.) Further, it should be recognized that as a pattern it may not encompass *all* the facts; but it is important that it encompass the crucial ones.

The pattern that makes an event understandable is not one that, so to speak, "jumps out" of an assembled body of factual data. Rather it comes from an idea that rises into the historian's consciousness as he surveys the available facts. This subtle but important point is commented upon again and again by scholars of historical methodology. The remarks of G. J. Renier are representative: "It cannot be stated with sufficient emphasis that the historian's principles of serialization [fitting things into a pattern] are introduced into history by him, not deduced from it, that, in short, they are a *priori*."[3] What this means in practice is that the historian comes to his work with certain expectations about how human affairs work and tries out these expectations in each historical situation he attempts to analyze. His expectations originate in how his experience has taught him to read the world—what moves human beings, typical tendencies of motivation, relations between economic and political power, the relations between geography and economic development—generally all manner of regularities that his experience has taught him. (Recall the last chapter on "conceptions and theories.") What this means of course is that those with wide experience in human affairs have something of a head start in historical pattern making. But however wide one's experience, the rules of the game require that one's ideas should be applied in any given situation not as a formula but as a tool that may (or may not) prove useful in explaining the event under consideration.

A perceived pattern may be sophisticated or it may be simple; it may generate an overarching interpretation covering an entire period or it may only put a minor legislative committee's action in an appropriate context. It may tie together a large number of facts or only reflect a relationship between two or three facts. The scope of the synthesis very much depends on the sophistication of the historian. What is really important to note is that any given event may be patterned in a variety of ways. It may be plausibly seen as the end event of an economic sequence, or of a political sequence, or of an ideological sequence, or of a combination of various factors producing a sequence. For example, the election of Franklin D. Roosevelt in 1932 can be legitimately regarded as part of an expression of economic distress, as the product of a series of political failures by Republicans, as the end result of an ideological shift by the American people,

---

[3]G. J. Renier, *History: Its Purpose and Method* (New York: Harper & Row, 1965), p. 176.

or (in a more sophisticated way) as a combination of all these. What is involved in each of the syntheses is a certain *point of view*, and, starting from different points, historians inevitably must travel different roads to the same destination. Thus, interpretations vary, and each interpretation may have validity, just as different roads to a city may each have something to be said in its favor. Nowhere is this basic feature of history-as-written better expressed than in Patrick Gardiner's *The Nature of Historical Explanation*:

> ...there are no absolute Real Causes waiting to be discovered by historians with sufficiently powerful magnifying-glasses. What do exist are historians writing upon different levels and at different distances, historians writing with different aims and different interests, historians writing in different contexts and from different points of view.[4]

Because the pattern that a historian sees in events is much influenced by the theories and preconceptions he has come to accept, readers should expect to find wide variations in the ways several historians might interpret one single event. Such variation is well illustrated in the discussions of the Social Security Act of 1935 in the following passages, each of them written by a historian who is well regarded within the profession. Please note the marginal comments.

William E. Leuchtenburg, *Franklin D. Roosevelt and the New Deal* (New York: Harper & Row, 1963), pp. 129–30.

As seen by Leuchtenburg, the Social Security Act was part of the pattern of "doing something for everybody" that FDR had adopted early in his administration. This passage is preceded by descriptions of various relief agencies, such as the WPA and the NYA. But these agencies, and others like them, missed a good many Americans; hence, the Social Security Act.

By predepression standards, Roosevelt's works program marked a bold departure. By any standard, it was an impressive achievement. Yet it never came close to meeting Roosevelt's goal of giving jobs to all who could work. Of the some ten million jobless, the WPA cared for not much more than three million. Workers received not "jobs" but a disguised dole; their security wage amounted to as little as $19 a month in the rural South. The President split up the billions among so many different agencies—the Department of Agriculture got $800 million of it—that Hopkins had only $1.4 billion to spend for WPA. By turning the unemployables back to the states, he denied to the least fortunate—the aged, the crippled, the sick—a part in the federal program, and placed them at the mercy of state governments, badly equipped to handle them and often indifferent to their plight.

Roosevelt's social security program was intended to meet some of the objections to his relief operations.

---

[4]Patrick Gardiner, *The Nature of Historical Explanation* (London: Oxford University Press, 1963), p. 109.

Oscar Theodore Barck, Jr. and Nelson Manfred Blake, *Since 1900*, 4th ed. (New York: Macmillan, 1965), p. 479.

Emphasizing ideological factors, the authors of this passage see the depression experience as having eroded traditional American individualistic ideas. The change in national ideology was manifested early in the 1930s by the AFL resolutions and by a plank in the Democratc National Platform. Here the Social Security Act is seen as part of that same pattern of ideological change.

Another foundation stone of the Second New Deal was the Social Security Act of August, 1935. Behind its passage lay a reversal in prevailing American opinion. Old-age pensions, unemployment insurance, and provisions for sickness and accident benefits under government administration had been commonplace in Europe before World War I. But most Americans persisted in the belief that saving against old age and misfortune was an individual problem. The depression provided a cruel disillusionment. Thrifty citizens saw their life savings swept away by bank failures, while the average individual's inability to guarantee his own security in a complex economic system was demonstrated in many other ways as well. By 1932 there was a widespread demand for government action. The AFL passed resolutions asking unemployment insurance with compulsory payments by employers and the state—reversing its earlier hostility to the proposal— and the Democratic National Platform included a plank advocating both unemployment and old-age insurance under state laws.

But building a social security system exclusively on state legislation offered many difficulties.... Some Federal program to coordinate action on a national basis seemed to be required.... In January, 1935, the President transmitted to Congress... recommendations for joint Federal-state action.

Henry J. Carman, Harold C. Syrett, and Bernard W. Wishy, *A History of the American People*, Vol. II (Philadelphia Book Co., 1967), p. 634.

This is a most interesting passage that not only presents a pattern clearly different from the preceding two but also reflects an evident authors' bias. Note the editorial in line 5—"This move was long overdue." Note also the usage of such emotion-charged words as "quackery," "hating," "demagogues," and "Nazi Germany." The authors reflect a liberal, perhaps class-conscious point of view. As to the pattern they present, they see the Social Security Act as politically necessary because of the popularity of extremist proposals, including those of Huey Long, Francis Townsend, and Father Coughlin. The Social Security Act was part and parcel of the "turn to the left" of the Roosevelt administration in 1935.

For the first two years of its existence, the New Deal did little to provide long-range protection against the risks of a private economy for working people. But in 1935, it set up a social security program for the care of dependent children, the aged, the handicapped, and the temporarily unemployed. This move was long overdue....

Throughout the 1930's, but especially during the first years under the New Deal, the bitterness and frustration built up by the depression provided fertile grounds for demagogic movements and quackery of various sorts....

Some of the panaceas hawked for the illnesses of depression were harmless, but others were dangerous because of both their simplification of complex issues and their openly antidemocratic bias.... Senator Huey Long, dictator of Louisiana and self-styled "Kingfish," had promised to make "every man a king"; Dr. F. G. Townsend had assured his aged followers that his plan would give them $200 a month; and demagogues like Father Coughlin and Gerald L. K. Smith had outlined programs that were startlingly similar to those of Nazi Germany and Fascist Italy. The popularity of these and similar proposals among the poor, as well as humanitarian considerations, convinced Roosevelt that the national government could no longer put off the adoption of social-security legislation.

James MacGregor Burns, *Roosevelt: The Lion and the Fox* (New York: Harcourt, Brace, 1956, p. 226.

In this work Burns gives little systematic attention to the Social Security Act as such. He treats it as a continuation of Roosevelt's "middle way" pragmatism that had little to do with ideological position. Burns explicitly denies the validity of the pattern seen in the preceding selection—that the Social Security Act was part of a "turn to the left."

The theory that Roosevelt executed a swing left for ideological reasons as a result only of the NRA decision runs hard up against other strands of Roosevelt's development. His program had always embraced liberal measures as well as orthodox ones. Social security had long been in the works—Roosevelt in 1930 had been the first leading politician to advocate unemployment insurance—and it was put off to 1935 mainly because of administrative and drafting difficulties. The President urged the holding company bill throughout the session. He lined up for the Wagner Act before the NRA decision was announced. The speech he planned to give if the Supreme Court ruled against the abrogation of the Gold Clause would, except for the Court's 5–4 majority for the government, have precipitated a grave constitutional crisis in February 1935.

Roosevelt, in short, made no consciously planned, grandly executed deployment to the left. He was like the general of a guerrilla army whose columns, fighting blindly in the mountains through dense ravines and thickets, suddenly converge, half by plan and half by coincidence, and debouch into the plain below.

Norman A. Graebner, Gilbert C. Fite, and Philip L. White, *A History of the United States*, Vol II (New York: McGraw-Hill, 1970), p. 674.

The pattern presented here has strong similarities to that of the third passage (Carman et al.) in that it says Roosevelt was forced to the left by the "pie-in-the sky" proposals of Townsend, Long, Coughlin, and, additionally, Lundeen. But the pattern here is a bit more sophisticated as Roosevelt is seen as benefiting from an an already "strong movement" that had produced a congressional bill. Quite interestingly, in the first paragraph these authors describe the public mood as remaining individualistic. Contrast this view with the second passage (Barch and Blake). Thus, a vague part of Graebner's pattern is the image of Roosevelt as very much of an activist President who led, not followed, public opinion.

One of the most fundamental New Deal reforms was the Social Security Act approved by the President on August 5, 1935. Here the Roosevelt administration broke sharply with the past. Most citizens had accepted the idea that people should care for their own needs in old age and in periods of unemployment through individual savings.... Some states had passed old-age pension laws, but the payments were small and varied greatly from state to state.

By 1934 a strong movement already existed to make the federal government a participant in financing old-age pensions. The Dill-Connery bill provided for grants-in-aid to the states....

The increasing popularity of pie-in-the-sky panaceas undoubtedly prompted Roosevelt to become more concerned about suitable social security legislation. Dr. Francis E. Townsend of California had won millions of supporters for his old-age pension plan.... Meanwhile, Congressman Ernest Lundeen of Minnesota introduced a measure which would pay federal unemployment insurance to all of those over eighteen who were involuntarily unemployed. Huey P. Long of Louisiana advocated a Share-Our-Wealth program.... Father Coughlin, a Detroit priest, won millions of followers with his plan....

These growing demands for government action hastened passage of the Social Security Act of 1935.

Five different historians—five differing interpretations. It can be exasperating to a student—until the student learns the nature of this game called history. It is a game in which the facts do count, but what counts as much is the explanatory pattern that, according to his best lights, each historian presents. It is a game in which the "how" and the "why" count for more than the "what." And so when a student develops the habit of looking primarily for the patterns rather than simply for the facts, he will be well along the road toward mastery of the game.

EXERCISES

SET A
Exercise 1

There are two exercises in Set A. The first is intended to develop your skill in recognizing general features of the pattern present in each piece of historical writing. Each of the passages on the following pages tries to explain the government corruption during President Ulysses S. Grant's administrations of 1869–77. As you read them, keep on the lookout for three themes, each of which is found at least twice in the readings.

1. Emphasis upon Grant's character shortcomings

2. Emphasis upon the interrelationship between business interests and government

3. Emphasis upon the deterioration of value systems in American society as a whole.

1. Although Grant came into office on a wave of popular enthusiasm as "the Savior of the Union," he was to prove to be one of the most sorry failures as President that the country has ever known. The qualities that had made him a great leader of men during the war seemed to evaporate in the unfamiliar atmosphere of the White House. Completely out of his element, he was an easy prey to the scheming importunities of political sycophants. In the exacting role of President, this "dumb, inarticulate man of genius" was discovered to be indirect and irresolute, prejudiced and vindictive, incapable of making sound judgments about either men or affairs. It was not only that he lacked any real political aptitude and let himself be used by men whose sole concern was their own interests. He was seemingly unable to understand the responsibilities and obligations of the presidency. (Foster Rhea Dulles, *The United States Since 1865* [1969])

2. The most significant developments of Grant's second term were a series of revelations of widespread corruption in practically every branch of the government. As exposure followed exposure, the alliance between business and politics became increasingly clear. It soon became apparent that politicians of every rank had participated in the "great barbecue." Robert Schenck used his post as Ambassador at the Court of St. James to foist bogus mining stock on English investors; Senator James G. Blaine of Maine accepted a thinly disguised bribe in return for his efforts to secure a land grant for a western railroad; . . . and Secretary of the Treasury William A. Richardson had to resign when it was revealed that he had permitted one John A. Sanborn of Massachusetts to keep half of the $427,000 in back taxes that he had collected as a Federal agent. The internal revenue system was a center of corruption; taxes on tobacco, cigars, and, above all, on distilled liquors, were openly evaded. A "Whisky Ring," composed in part of high government officials, defrauded the treasury of enormous sums. Even General O. E. Babcock, President Grant's private secretary, was involved, and Grant himself was the recipient of many presents from members of the ring. (Harry J. Carman, et al., *A History of the American People* [1967])

3. Grant's presidency reflected the materialism of the day. Already during the immediate post-war years businessmen had showered this Union hero with lavish gifts. One group of millionaires headed by A. T. Stewart, the New York merchant, presented the general a mansion in Philadelphia. Another group contributed handsomely to the reduction of the $100,000 mortgage on his Washington house. Grant saw no need to curtail this flow of gifts after he entered the White House. Having spent years in poverty, he accepted with both hands the favors thrust upon him without ever suspecting the price that would be exacted of the nation for the presents he received. By entertaining Grant in Washington, Henry Cooke gathered information useful to his brother Jay, the financier. For a few boxes of choice Havanas, Jay Cooke laid his hands on a vast expanse of the public domain for the Northern Pacific Railroad. Grant accepted the use of private cars and yachts from such promoters as Commodore Vanderbilt, Jay Gould, and Jim Fisk. Perhaps Grant himself remained innocent of profiteering, but he could scarcely deny reasonable requests from his wealthy hosts whose cigars he smoked and whose riches he admired. (Norman A. Graebner, et al., *A History of the United States* [1970])

4.   During Grant's two terms as President, the word "politician" became synonymous with double-talking and self-serving. The corruption in Washington, and elsewhere in the country, was the result of a lowering in the moral tone of the nation during and after the Civil War. Immense fortunes in industry had been made during the war. Wealth was worshipped, and material display became a passion. Few politicians could resist the bribes for favors which businessmen dispensed freely. Grant was not responsible for this general moral laxity, but by his infatuation with business success and his negligence in office he allowed it to flourish. The early idealism of the Republican Party was smothered in this atmosphere of materialism. In fact, both major parties became agencies for obtaining and dispensing the spoils of office. (Rebecca Brooks Gruver, *An American History* [1976])

5.   The level of political morality sank to its lowest point during the eight-year administration of General Grant. With the possible exception of Warren G. Harding, nobody ever elected to the presidency has proved to have fewer qualifications. Totally ignorant of the problems of government, and an extremely poor judge of men, Grant surrounded himself with a shady group of adventurers, and was genuinely incapable of realizing that they were unworthy of holding office. A few men of ability and integrity served in his Cabinet at one time or another; but with the exception of Secretary of State Hamilton Fish, who provided the administration with its one substantial claim to respectability, all of them incurred Grant's disapproval and were dismissed. A man of unassuming manners and great simplicity of character, fond of horses, whisky, and cigars, Grant retained much of the personal popularity with the mass of the voters that he had earned during the Civil War, and this made him an invaluable asset to the Republican Party bosses. But as President he showed none of the energy, determination, and clearheadedness that had made him such a formidable military leader. (Henry Bamford Parkes, *The United States of America: A History* [1968])

6.   Profiteering, dishonesty, and political corruption neither began nor ended with Ulysses S. Grant; scandal had been disturbingly constant in

American political life. But during the Grant era no one seemed to mind. For a time Americans shrugged their shoulders at corruption, apparently figuring that the self-made politician compromised himself no more than the self-made industrialist, who made a fortune and became a folk hero. Even when the politician and the industrialist joined forces, the popular reaction seemed more often envy than disgust. (Henry F. Bedford, et al., *The Americans: A Brief History* [1976])

7. But even the most determined presidential effort could not have immediately tamed the spoils system. The sheer numbers, combined with the cost of maintaining party machinery, led to the development of a system which obliged party workers to pay fees for appointments, or incumbent officeholders were taxed an annual assessment on their salaries. Officeholders, well aware that their tenure was impermanent, unsurprisingly took it for granted that they were to milk the post for all it was worth. The result was inescapably a pervasive corruption. Efforts to control the system, as more than one president swiftly discovered, ran afoul of the congressional presumption that spoils were its peculiar prerogative—a presumption which if defied was promptly sustained by congressional refusals to support executive proposals. (J. P. Shenton, et al., *U.S. History Since 1865* [1975])

8. One of the many ironies in the reconstruction story is that some of the radical Republicans took the first steps toward destroying the political alliances on which the Republican political position in the South depended. During the first Grant administration a new set of leaders won a dominant position in the presidential circle. These were men who were most responsive to the economic pressures created by the cyclonic growth of American capitalism after the Civil War. They helped to make Congress, the state legislatures, and state political machines the willing collaborators of railroad, oil, textile, and steel interests that wanted government favors. The older crusading radicals found this new Republican leadership appalling, particularly as evidence of corruption began to come to light. "Like all parties that have an undisturbed power for a long time," wrote Senator James Grimes of Iowa, "(the Republican Party) has become corrupt, and I believe it is today the most corrupt and debauched political party that has ever existed." (Edwin C. Rozwenc, *The Making of American Society* [1973])

9. No President before 1869 had been so unqualified for office as was Ulysses S. Grant—a man who had no experience in politics, no capacity for absorbing such experience, no sensitivity for statescraft, and little judgment about men. Grant had impeccable personal integrity. He had as a soldier displayed the qualities of leadership and fortitude that won him deserved glory. He had, as his enemies in battle had learned, incomparable courage. But as a public servant Grant was a fool and a failure. He appointed an undistinguished Cabinet, of which several members were knaves who duped him shamelessly. He found most matters of public policy utterly bewildering. He did not himself generate the gross and greedy spirit of the time, but a stronger and wiser man would have yielded less readily than Grant to its rapacious temper. Truly pathetic in his inadequacies, he was also singularly obtuse about his choice of friends. He accepted expensive gifts from favor-hunters; he received personal loans from Jay Cooke, whose Northern Pacific Railroad was seeking federal subsidies; he welcomed the company of Jim Fisk, a conscienceless gambler in stocks. (John M. Blum, et al., *The National Experience* [1977])

10. Men like Blaine and Conkling remained the party's most influential national spokesmen throughout the period. They largely shaped national legislation during the era. Since they were Republicans, they believed in an effective and energetic national economic policy. In general, the purpose of this policy was to encourage industrial expansion. For this they were often criticized by Democratic politicians who retained their party's traditional faith. This Democratic faith rested on the belief that government should not meddle actively in the economic lives of Americans.

But the Republican Party, founded in an era when the national government had to expand its powers to preserve the Union, saw nothing wrong with continuing this trend at the war's end. To encourage economic development, party leaders aided business in every possible way. In accomplishing this purpose, they forged an informal alliance between the national government and the great majority of businessmen—bankers, industrialists, and merchants in foreign trade. While this alliance did further economic growth, it had other less fortunate consequences as well. It gave the era a reputation for corruption unparalleled in American history until then. (Allen Weinstein, et al, *Freedom and Crisis* [1974])

11. If the professional members of political machines frequently softened the animosities of political warfare by acting as "honest brokers" between contending economic forces, they also occasionally added to its acerbity by scandalous and corrupt practices which furnished targets for the enemy. Whenever any political party enjoyed a long tenure of power in federal, state, or municipal offices, ring-leaders were sure to accumulate large profits and hereditaments without regard for public decorum or at least without sufficient command over discretion. "What are we here for?" was the popular slogan of those who made politics itself a form of business enterprise. At Washington where the Republicans ruled the administration for more than two decades without interruption, the major delinquencies were assignable to members of their society; while in states and cities where the Democrats were in power, most of the letters of marque and reprisal were ascribed to them. Year after year, in spite of the best efforts of those who sincerely desired clean ceremonials, scandals in high places broke out with distressing regularity at the national capital. (Charles and Mary Beard, *The Rise of American Civilization* [1931])

Sources

1. Foster Rhea Dulles, *The United States Since 1865* (Ann Arbor, Mich.: University of Michigan Press, 1969), p. 129.

2. Henry J. Carman, Harold C. Syrett, and Bernard W. Wishy, *A History of the American People* (Philadelphia: Philadelphia Book, 1967), p. 45.

3. Norman A. Graebner, Gilbert C. Fite, and Philip L. White, *A History of the U.S.* (New York: McGraw-Hill, 1970), p. 31.

4. Rebecca Gruver, *An American History* (Reading, Mass.: Addison-Wesley, 1978), p. 600.

5. Henry Bamford Parkes, *The United States of America: A History* (New York: Knopf, 1968), p. 448.

6. Henry F. Bedford and Trevor Colbourn, *The Americans: A Brief History,* 2nd ed. (New York: Harcourt Brace Jovanovich, 1976), p. 288.

7. J. P. Shenton and Alan M. Meckler, *U.S. History Since 1865* (Homewood, Ill.: Learning Systems, 1975), p. 16.

8. Edwin C. Rozwenc, *The Making of American Society,* Vol. II (Boston: Allyn and Bacon, 1973), p. 596.

9. John M. Blum, Bruce Catton, et al., *The National Experience* (New York: Harcourt Brace Jovanovich, 1977), p. 369.

10. Allen Weinstein and R. Jackson Wilson, *Freedom and Crisis* (New York: Random House, 1974), p. 532.

11. Charles and Mary Beard, *The Rise of American Civilization* (New York: Macmillan, 1931), p. 305.

QUESTIONS In responding, use the author's name, referring to each passage no more than once.

1. Cite the authors whose interpretations strongly emphasize Grant's character shortcomings. Select a short phrase in each case that justifies your response.

_____

_____

_____

_____

_____

2. Cite the authors whose interpretations most strongly emphasize the interrelationship between business interests and government. Select a short phrase in each case that justifies your response.

_____

_____

_____

_____

_____

3. Cite the authors whose interpretations most strongly emphasize the deterioration of value systems in American society as a whole. Select a short phrase in each case that justifies your response.

_____

_____

_____

_____

_____

4. At this point you should have listed a total of nine passages as belonging in one or another of the above categories. Two passages remain. Briefly describe the theme of each.

_____

_____

_____

_____

_____

5. Now, read the following passage and see if you can identify any clear explanation of governmental corruption.

> While Grant was relieving southern whites of the wrath of Reconstruction, the wrath of reform was falling on his own head. Even while the campaign of 1872 was in progress, the first major Grant administration scandal, involving railroad bribery of congressmen, foreshadowed the history of his second term. After the Democrats won control of the House in the elections of 1874, the momentum of revelation and prosecution grew. Two affairs struck close to Grant personally. One concerned the "Whiskey Ring" in St. Louis, which, with the connivance of Orville Babcock, had defrauded the government of millions of dollars in internal revenue charges. Only Grant's incessant interference in Babcock's trial saved his old secretary from jail. The second affair led to the impeachment and resignation of Secretary of War W. W. Belknap, who, since assuming office in 1870, had been "kept" by traders in Indian Territory under his jurisdiction. (Richard Hofstadter, et al., _The Structure of American History_ [Englewood Cliffs, N.J.: Prentice-Hall, 1964], p. 227.)

Hofstadter's theme: _____

_____

(NOTE: If you had trouble identifying any theme, you're normal. This account simply presents the facts of government corruption and makes no effort to see it as part of a pattern.)

**SET A
Exercise 2**

In mid-February 1937, General Motors signed a collective bargaining agreement with the Congress of Industrial Organizations, a union of unskilled and semiskilled workers. A few weeks later in early March the United States Steel Corporation did likewise. The union victory over these industrial giants represented the greatest advance unions had made in all of American history.

Let us suppose that in relation to this event the following information, along with the above facts, is all that you have available. Your job is to synthesize these items, which is to say identify a pattern that makes understandable the decision of the two big companies. Please note that the items are chronologically mixed, as they would be in a research project, and so your first task might be to put them in some clear time order. Also, you are reminded that some of the items may not be particularly relevant according to your perspective.

After reading through and reflecting upon the information given, along with the facts above, write a four or five sentence paragraph that *explains* why the decision of the two big companies "makes sense." It may be helpful to use the "starter questions" discussed in Chapter Three, such as "What individuals played a crucial role?" "Were there any groups or organizations influencing the situation?" "Were certain ideas or points of view affecting what went on?" And so forth.

_____

_____

_____

_____

_____

_____

_____

_____

_____

_____

_____

_____

_____

1. Businessmen were much encouraged in the first four months of 1937 as sales rose steadily and industrial production surpassed its 1929 peak. The gross national product was a solid 5 percent over its mid-1929 level.

2. The Walsh-Healy Government Contracts Act of 1936 provided that "all persons employed by a contractor dealing with the U.S. government shall be paid not less than the prevailing minimum wages as determined by the Secretary of Labor and shall not be permitted to work in excess of 8 hours a day or 40 hours a week."

3. During the period 1934–36 General Motors alone spent nearly $1 million for private detectives whose job it was to keep down union organization. The major steel firms spent even more than that amount.

4. On December 28, 1936, the workers in the General Motors plant at Flint, Michigan, "sat down" at their work stations, refusing to leave, and lived at the plant for the next few weeks. Workers at General Motors plants elsewhere followed their example.

5. Section 7 of the National Labor Relations Act, signed into law by President

Roosevelt in 1935, reads as follows: "Employees shall have the right of self-organization, to form, join, or assist labor organizations, to bargain collectively through representatives of their own choosing, and to engage in concerted activities for the purpose of collective bargaining or other mutual aid or protection."

6. In November 1936, the American public resoundingly approved Franklin Roosevelt's New Deal by giving him a 523–8 electoral margin over Alf Landon of Kansas. It was an even greater landslide victory than that of 1932.

7. A majority of middle-class Americans strongly opposed the "sit-down strikes" as conducted at the General Motors plants. Nonetheless, Governor Frank Murphy of Michigan refused to send state troopers or the national guard to dislodge the strikers, despite the fact that they engaged in unlawful trespass.

8. On February 5, 1937, Franklin Roosevelt, angered by repeated Supreme Court rejection of major New Deal legislation, sent Congress a surprise message requesting legislation that would overhaul the judicial system and allow him to appoint up to six additional Supreme Court justices.

9. Upton Sinclair, an avowed socialist, favored the "sit-down strikes," commenting happily that "for seventy-five years big business has been sitting down on the American people, and now I am delighted to see the process reversed."

10. On February 3, 1936, William Knudsen, a high-ranking General Motors executive, broke off talks with the workers' committee of their plants. The next day he received a phone call from President Roosevelt: "Is that you, Bill? I know that you have been through a lot, Bill, and I want to tell you that I feel sorry for you, but Miss Perkins [Secretary of Labor] has told me about the situation and what you are discussing and I have called up to say I hope very much indeed that you will go through with this and that your people will meet a committee."

**SET B
Exercise 1
(Optional)**

In Set A each of the segments in Exercise 1 presented government corruption during the Grant Administration as flowing from some one particular influence of the times, such as Grant's shortcomings, the liaison between business and government, and so on. The occurrence of corruption was thus "single-framed," so to speak, by each of the historians. But historians' interpretations are often much more complex, with several influences being cited as having been important. Thus, one can speak of an occurrence as having a double, triple, or even quadruple frame. For example, the Japanese attack on Pearl Harbor in 1941 may be triply mounted as a failure of the Oahu Island defense system, as a masterpiece of Japanese military planning, and as a culmination of twenty years of aggravated relations.

Each of the passages on the following pages tries to explain American rejection in 1919 of the Treaty of Versailles (which included the League of Nations). By way of introduction to the passages, you should be aware that several influences are recurrently cited as contributing to the treaty's rejection. They are:

1. The shortcomings and limitations of *Woodrow Wilson*

2. Opposition of segments of *public opinion,* including isolationists, ethnic groups, and others

3. The role of *Henry Cabot Lodge*

Some authors see several of these influences as important; others place the rejection in a single frame. Read the passages and respond to the questions that follow.

1. At first, the Treaty's chances looked good. Wilson's prestige was still great, and the idea of a League of Nations had long attracted American support. Yet the Treaty aroused many kinds of opposition. Among its enemies were the disappointed minorities of German, Italian, and Irish descent, isolationists who feared that the League would involve America in European affairs, liberals who objected to the compromises of democratic principle, and, vaguer but crucially important, many Ameicans already reacting against wartime enthusiasm and sacrifice....

In the long struggle, opposition to the Treaty was marshalled by Henry Cabot Lodge, an enemy of Wilson and a master tactician. In order to attract the crucial Reservationists, Lodge proposed not the rejection of the Treaty but its passage with a number of changes. These were carefully calculated to sound plausible, but to be unacceptable to Wilson. Lodge knew his opponent. Wilson forbade Democrats to accept the reservations, thus making impossible a two-thirds majority. (Charles Sellers and Henry May, *A Synopsis of American History* [1969])

2. It [the League of Nations] was a useful proposal, but Wilson viewed it in terms of a mission so grand and all-encompassing, so noble in purpose, that no alteration was possible. Minor compromises would have secured ratification in the United States Senate of both the Peace Treaty and the League, and would not have weakened the League's chance to prove itself in the arena of world affairs. But Wilson was unable to compromise. In his mind the method had become totally identified with the goal; the League was world peace....

Wilson's tragedy was that faced with one of the great decisions of his life, he failed to recognize that there is more than one road to Rome. He became a prophet, not a leader. It is a dangerous matter to take on one's shoulders the burden of saving mankind, and to assume that you alone have the key to salvation....

[When] the Treaty came up for consideration in the Senate, he refused to give way, and without concessions from him the Treaty died. So did he, unrelenting, in 1924. (G. D. Lillibridge, *Images of American Society,* Vol. II [1976])

3. Wilson mistook his countrymen's flaming enthusiasm in World War I for an eagerness to accept international responsibility. He was not aware of the speed with which they were becoming indifferent to foreign affairs. The old American illusion about war—"The game's over, we've won, let's go home!"—had taken hold....so Senator Henry Cabot Lodge of Massachusetts, the suave and powerful "scholar in politics," had no difficulty in martialing opposition to the League, this "evil thing with a holy name."

Lodge hated Wilson with an implacable hatred. Even though he personally favored a world organization, he wanted none bearing the Wilsonian stamp. So Lodge moved to block the treaty by hobbling it with reservations and hamstringing it with debate....

When defeat of the League appeared imminent, he [Wilson] rejected advice to compromise with a fierce, "Let Lodge compromise! Better a thousand times to go down fighting than to dip your colors to dishonorable compromise."

This, from the same man who at the peace conference had made a religion of compromise. In the end the League did go down. On November 19, 1919, it was defeated in the Senate, and an attempt to rescue it the following year was also defeated. (Robert Leckie, *The Wars of America* [1968])

4. By 1919 Wilson's declining health...made him increasingly irrational, irritable, and temperamental. He handled the Senate particularly badly. Though he was aware that their two-thirds approval was vital for any treaty, he ignored them and did not consult with the powerful Foreign Relations Committee, perhaps because it was headed by a man he detested, Henry Cabot Lodge of Massachusetts....

The treaty was delayed by the Senate, which added reservations about America's Monroe Doctrine rights in the Western Hemisphere, tariffs, immigration policy, and armaments. The 14 "Lodge Reservations" were on the whole reasonable. They may have been unnecessary if Wilson had troubled to consult with the Senate beforehand. Lodge was not a blind isolationist who wished to wreck the League....

In fairness, President Wilson felt he had already compromised a great deal at Versailles. He ignored several political pointers, such as growing opposition to the League from particular American ethnic groups, not only German and Irish, but Italian-Americans, upset over the disposition of Fiume. The president was sick and out of touch with political realities....Self-deluded, he told Senate Democrats to vote *against* the treaty in two votes of November 1919 and March 1920. They obeyed....(Peter d'A. Jones, *The U.S.A.* [1976])

5. Lodge was well-aware that Wilson had the backing of a majority of the country, and he proposed to...delay and confuse the issue so thoroughly that the people would become tired of it and turn to other interests....If, as seemed likely, compromise reservations were proposed as the price of approving the Covenant, [Lodge] would quibble, hedge, perhaps accept them in the end—and then propose more and stronger ones....

The President's health had never been good, and now...six years of constant crisis had left him pale, trembling, and exhausted. Against the urgent advice of physicians and friends he embarked on a swing around the country....The climax of Wilson's tour came at Pueblo, where he spoke with tears in his eyes to an audience that gave him one ovation after another. The trip had weakened him cruelly....

Then on the train east of Pueblo Wilson's overworked nervous system collapsed....A few days later (early October) his left side was struck by paralysis....

Meanwhile the battle continued over the treaty....Wilson, unaware of or ignoring realities, and probably actuated by the pettishness of an invalid, directed Democratic Senators to oppose the amendments. Accordingly...it failed of the necessary two thirds....(Leland W. Baldwin, *The Stream of American History* [1952])

6. The failure of Wilson's larger aims was an American, as well as a personal, tragedy. The characteristically American ideal of a world order transcending the anarchy of power had no chance without the participation of the United States. But Wilson's stubborn righteousness of purpose prevented American support for his peace settlement at the moment when crusading idealism was evaporating in a feverish search for peacetime normality. The American people had been exposed too briefly and too superficially to the threat against their continental security to assume the continuing duties which their austere President had assigned to them. Instead they withdrew into isolation....

The man primarily responsible for scotching American membership of the League was Senator Henry Cabot Lodge. Lodge...represented those conservative nationalists who believed American interests best served, not by a moral crusade for a universal "collective security" but by the protection of American strategic interests, narrowly interpreted. In the mood of the 1920s conservative nationalism swung back from Roosevelt's interventionism to an isolationist phase from which it only reemerged after the attack on Pearl Harbor. (Frank Thistlethwaite, *The Great Experiment* [1955])

7. The leading opponent of the League of Nations in the Senate was Henry Cabot Lodge, a prominent Republican who was a lifelong friend of Theodore Roosevelt's. It has often been said that Lodge defeated the treaty. That is assuming a great deal. Mr. Lodge was not a big enough man to defeat anything that had a popular following....The anonymous authors of *The Mirrors of Washington* wrote of him that he "always creates the impression that it is a condescension on his part to God to have allowed Him to create a world which is not exclusively possessed by the Cabots and the Lodges and their connections."

No; the League Covenant was defeated by the American people. Wilson realized that public opinion was opposed to his cherished measure. He thought the people were not informed clearly as to its purport, and he went on a long speaking tour for the purpose of instructing them.

He was already a sick man, and the cold reception that he encountered broke his heart. At Pueblo, Colorado, on September 26, 1919, he had a paralytic stroke from which he never recovered.

On March 19, 1920, the treaty was voted down in the Senate [for the final time]. (W. E. Woodward, *A New American History* [1937])

8. Wilson returned to the United States confident that the Senate, despite the difficulties Lodge was stirring up, would ratify the treaty....

Through a combination of coercion and compromise he might have brought about ratification. But he was suffering from hardening of the arteries and, while in Paris, had been so ill that he may have been close to a stroke. His physical condition robbed him of political suppleness; instead of using patience and tact, he was more likely to shower his opponents with self-righteous anger....

Senator Lodge, applying all his brilliant intellect to his loathing for Wilson, was ready, as chairman of the Senate Foreign Relations Committee, to use every possible tactic to obstruct, delay, and defeat the treaty. Public sentiment seemed to favor ratification, and Lodge needed time to marshal forces against it. Consequently, he spent the first two weeks after it reached the committee reading aloud every word on its nearly three hundred pages....

Lodge managed to marshal the Republican senators so well that in November he obtained adoption of fourteen reservations....Although none of the Lodge reservations would have devitalized the League, Wilson preferred no ratification of the treaty to ratification with reservations....When the vote came...forty-two Democrats joined...to vote down the treaty....(Richard Current, et al., *American History: A Survey* [1971])

Sources

1. Charles Sellers and Henry May, *A Synopsis of American History* (Chicago: Rand McNally, 1969), p. 317.

2. G. D. Lillibridge, *Images of American Society*, Vol. II (Boston: Houghton Mifflin, 1976), p. 195.

3. Robert Leckie, *The Wars of America* (New York: Harper & Row, 1968), pp. 665–66.

4. Peter d'A. Jones, *The U.S.A.*, Vol. II (Homewood, Ill.: Dorsey Press, 1976), pp. 549–50.

5. Leland W. Baldwin, *The Stream of American History*, Vol. II (New York: Richard A. Smith, 1952), pp. 536–38.

6. Frank Thistlethwaite, *The Great Experiment* (Cambridge: Cambridge University Press, 1955), pp. 292–93.

7. W. E. Woodward, *A New American History* (New York: The Literary Guild, 1937), pp. 798–99.

8. Richard Current, T. Harry Williams, and Frank Freidel, *American History: A Survey* (New York: Knopf, 1971), pp. 601–02.

QUESTIONS

(Respond by using the name of the author)

1. Some of the passages give a three-framed explanation of the rejection of the treaty. Cite those that do, indicating in each case the several influences the author emphasizes.

	Wilson	Public Opinion	Lodge	Other
_____	_____	_____	_____	_____
_____	_____	_____	_____	_____
_____	_____	_____	_____	_____
_____	_____	_____	_____	_____

2. Some of the passages provide a two-framed explanation of the rejection. Cite those that do so, indicating the influences the author emphasizes.

	Wilson	Public Opinion	Lodge	Other
_____	_____	_____	_____	_____
_____	_____	_____	_____	_____
_____	_____	_____	_____	_____
_____	_____	_____	_____	_____

3. Some of the passages give a single-framed explanation. Cite them, indicating the influence the author emphasizes.

	Wilson	Public Opinion	Lodge	Other
_____	_____	_____	_____	_____
_____	_____	_____	_____	_____
_____	_____	_____	_____	_____
_____	_____	_____	_____	_____

4. In which passage is Wilson most favorably portrayed? Briefly explain your answer.

_____

_____

5. In which passage is Lodge most clearly blamed for the defeat of the treaty? Briefly explain.

_____

_____

6. Which two passages seem most compatible with each other? Briefly explain your answer.

_____

_____

_____

_____

7. Which two passages seem least compatible with each other? Briefly explain.

_____

_____

_____

_____

8. Which passage, in your opinion, most clearly reflects a decisive point of view of the author's? What evidence do you have for your opinion?

_____

_____

_____

_____

9. Which passage, in your opinion, is the best written piece of history? Why do you think so?

_____

_____

_____

_____

**SET B
Exercise 2
(Optional)**

In the Set B exercise in Chapter Five (pp. 89–92) you were given a number of passages relating to the English appeasement policy prior to World War II. *If you did not use those materials earlier,* go back and read them now. Your task is to synthesize the information presented in passages A through H, and, in a short essay paragraph, to *explain* the appeasement policy as an event in history. For this exercise assume that the information contained in those passages is all that is available.

Your paragraph should contain a clear topic sentence (introductory generalization) and a summary discussion of the factors which you feel best help us understand the events in question. Use the spaces below to write your paragraph.

Organizing for Writing

It has been legitimately said that writing is the highest of all the arts. It is therefore nonsense to suppose that any student can be taught "how to write" in the few paragraphs to follow. Better that one hear, ponder, and practice the counsel of the great and near-great literary masters, who, in their genius, say so much about writing in a few telling phrases: Winston Churchill, who said "Short words are best and the old words when short are best of all"; Nicolas Boileau, the seventeenth-century French writer, who counseled the writer to "twenty times upon the anvil place your work"; Mark Twain, who remarked that "as to the adjective: when in doubt, strike it out"; Alexander Pope, who pointed out that "whoever thinks a faultless piece to see, thinks what ne'er was, nor is, nor e'er shall be"; Robert Browning, who urged those who would write to "paint a picture"; L. M. Montgomery, who insisted that "the point of good writing is knowing when to stop"; H. L. Mencken, who approvingly described the man of "verbal delicacy...who searches painfully for the right word"; and, finally, the anonymous observer who saw as the crucial factor in writing "the length of time one could keep the seat of his pants in contact with the seat of his chair."

Skillful writing is perhaps "all of the above" and more. It presumes an empathy with the eventual reader's effort to understand, leading to patient presentation, to careful transitions, and to avoidance of convoluted sentences. This consciousness of the reader's situation brings careful attention to grammar, spelling, and punctuation, because with each mistake in one of these the thought flow is slowed or halted, and comprehension becomes that much more difficult. The following advice is given in a humorous vein, but the rule that each item violates is an important one:

1. Don't use no double negatives.
2. Make each pronoun agree with their antecedent.
3. Join clauses good, like a conjunction should.
4. About them sentence fragments.
5. When dangling, watch your participles.
6. Verbs has to agree with their subjects.
7. Just between you and I, case is important too.
8. Don't write run-on sentences they are hard to read.

9. Don't use commas, which aren't necessary.
10. Try to not ever split infinitives.
11. Its important to use your apostrophe's correctly.
12. Proofread your writing to see if you any words out.
13. Correct spelling is esential.[1]

Indeed, there are many necessary components of effective writing. But one stands out above all the rest: a clear, carefully developed *organization of ideas*. It is possible for a reader to overcome such deficiencies as excessive wordiness, faulty sentence structure, grammatical blunders, labored transitions, and other failures. It is even possible for him to look beyond a paper's logical fallacies and grasp its essence. But a reader cannot comprehend writing that flounders along without seeming purpose, without apparent connectedness, or without subordination of lesser ideas to larger ones. And what he inwardly says after a few exasperated efforts at comprehension is invariably along the lines of that great Truman Capote putdown: "That's not writing, that's typing!" A principle of order stands as the absolute first principle of all respectable writing. It is that principle, as applied to historical material, that will occupy our attention in the discussion to follow.

THE ORDERING OF HISTORICAL MATERIAL FOR PRESENTATION

It is important at this point to remember that "doing" a piece of history is a process. By the time a student comes to the stage of formally organizing historical material for writing he has already completed a good bit of the overall task, and so the work of writing is somewhat narrower than it might first appear. At the very start he framed the basic problem with which he would deal. He then asked a series of "starter questions," which gave him major leads and perhaps suggested certain analytical concepts with which to explore the problem. He next searched for evidence and evaluated it. After facing the evidence for a time and trying out his ideas on it, he got first a glimmer of basic relationships and from this emerged a synthesis according to which the occurrence of some event "makes sense." The initial historical problem was thus resolved as he came to see an explanatory pattern wherein the event is a logical culmination of certain things that went before it.

Many of the difficulties that students experience when writing history result from their failure to do full justice to one or more of these stages that precede writing. They short-circuit the process, with the result that either they have no synthesis at all or what they offer as a "synthesis" (interpretation) is a glittering generality that has little explanatory value. Such students literally have nothing to write, and usually compensate for it by providing a dreary recital of a string of facts or by forcing an interpretation that has little correspondence to the facts of the historical situation. The writing stage is difficult enough in itself without adding to it the burden and difficulties of the earlier stages.

When one comes to the writing stage fully prepared—having given each of the previous stages its due—there remain four organizational steps: (1) formal listing

---

[1]Harvey Jacobsen, *The Education Reporter*, October 19, 1966.

of the significant components of the historical situation; (2) formulation of a main thematic statement; (3) selection of a sequence of presentation of the components of the historical situation; and (4) selection of appropriate general headings.

1. *Formal listing of the significant components of the historical situation.* If the work of synthesis has been done this step should be relatively simple. It is nothing more than an analysis of the main factors that fed into the synthesis. Typically it involves putting down on paper a problem as perceived and experienced by certain historical figures, basic conditions that prevailed, crucial individuals and groups along with the ideas that influenced them, and pivotal actions taken. (Remember that Chapter Three required an analysis similar to this, so it should be nothing new to you.) The purpose of this step is to make explicit all that is implicit in the synthesis, thus assuring that nothing meaningful is left out.

2. *Formulation of a main thematic statement.* The task here is to put into exact language the crucial elements that explain how something happened as it did. This statement is often difficult to phrase, because it must *generalize*, but generalize with precision. It must not say anything that cannot be demonstrated in the discussion to follow. It involves a promise to the reader as to what will be done, and a commitment by the writer to go no further than the statement permits. This means, of course, that the writer agrees to bypass a lot of material that is interesting and even useful, but not vital, given the generalization the writer has made. A well-conceived thematic statement enables the writer to accomplish the final organizational steps with efficiency, because he will have thus named the pivotal components that make what happened basically logical. It is the centerpiece that will dominate all of the writing to follow and glue all the pieces together. (An example of how a real "pro" does this may be found in Chapter Ten, Edmund S. Morgan's "The Puritans and Sex," pages 183–93. Note the final two sentences of Morgan's first paragraph as he states his exact theme: that the Puritans were not the perpetrators of American squeamishness about sex.)

3. *Selection of a sequence for presenting the components of the historical situation.* Writing history is not simply a matter of "begin at the beginning" and then go on in chronological sequence to the end. The movement is usually chronological, but the overall framework typically combines chronology with much "stop-action" during which necessary description is given and/or explanatory comment is provided. Thus, there is an alternation between chronological movement and topical discussion.

In selecting a sequence of presentation, the material that has already been thought through mentally is now reviewed and explicitly organized for presentation so that the events being discussed make sense to a reader. The writer must at all times keep in mind the prospective reader's unfamiliarity with the subject matter, being careful to lead him slowly forward, pausing at times to describe crucial features of the historical scene and perhaps backtracking at other times to show the extended influence of ideas, institutions, and men. History-as-written is nearly always well laced with topical discussions that are crucial to the reader's "flow of comprehension." (As noted earlier, some histories are so heavily topical that the particular events of a period recede into relative unimportance. Such histories are referred to as predominantly analytical rather than narrative accounts.)

Though there are several basic approaches to organizing historical material, the most common one, at least in narrative political history, and the simplest one for most students to put into practice, is what may be called the problem-centered model. In it the writer typically uses the following format:

a. A problem develops for some group or nation, whether because of certain changed conditions, internal tensions, outside pressures, mismanagement of affairs, or some other influence. Whichever the case, the problem has certain significant dimensions that the historian must explore in a topical way.

b. A course of action in regard to the perceived problem is considered by someone or some group in a leadership position. The action is contemplated or taken because of the influence of certain ideas, certain groups, or certain practical realities. Whichever the case, the historian must examine the influences pertaining to the course of action that has been chosen. (Again, a certain amount of "stop-action" discussion is necessary.)

c. Opposition to the course of action develops, opposition that is animated by a certain point of view, that takes form under certain leadership, and that follows certain paths of resistance. The historian must detail all of this, along with the actions and reactions that led to a final resolution of the matter.

d. The matter comes to a conclusion, one way or another, and after a description of the now-changed situation, the historian often sets the narrative aside and editorializes on the meaning of the entire episode.

It is important for the student to recognize that at any point in the stages described above, the historian may engage in extended description or in structural analysis, depending on his point of view and interests. It is also important to remember that many trained historians, as well as many students, *prefer* analysis to narrative flow and focus their entire writing attention on some facet of a historical situation. But the "rule" remains the same: One must proceed in a logical order, moving *systematically* through "topics" rather than through events, as with narrative.

4. *Selection of appropriate general headings.* Once he has placed his material in some such format as that just described, the historian's one remaining organizational task is that of finding appropriate general headings under which to group the specific elements of his account. To help him in doing so, he has his "main thematic statement" (see Step 2), which contains the main points that must be made—usually two or perhaps three pivotal features of the historical situation. These points will unify his account as a whole. But these points must be fleshed out. Very useful in this respect is the problem-centered format, where the subpoints necessary for ensuring the prospective reader's flow of comprehension are singled out. Finally, the historian now selects the particular details that will give a fullness of meaning to each of the subpoints. Basically, this entire final operation is one of putting the general and the particular in proper relation to each other.

In writing the essay itself, two main considerations should be kept continually in mind. The first is that an academic essay is expected to have three identifiable parts: a clear-cut beginning (introduction), usually a full paragraph that familiarizes the reader with the subject matter and presents an unmistakable main thematic statement; a middle, consisting of a sequence of paragraphs, that develops and demonstrates the validity of the main thematic statement of the introductory paragraph; a concluding paragraph through which the writer ties up the loose ends of the historical situation he has described and summarizes the main features of the pattern according to which the events make sense. One writer has said all of this in a single breath: "Tell 'em what you're going to tell 'em, tell 'em, and tell 'em what you told 'em."

A second requirement of an effective essay is the necessity of writing in solid paragraph units. What this means in practice is that each paragraph must have a *topic sentence*, which gives it direction; all else in the paragraph supports, develops, or elaborates that dominant idea. Some writing authorities prefer the term *controlling sentence*, which states the theme and is the heart of the paragraph, contrasting it with *supporting sentences*, which explain, extend, or illustrate the meaning of the controlling sentence. Whichever expression one uses, "topic sentence" or "controlling sentence" or something else, the crux of the matter is that the eventual reader sorely needs "a nearby reminder of the objective of the details and ideas being presented."

Although carefully phrased topic sentences are vital, it is nonetheless important to note that strictly *narrative* paragraphs do not have topic sentences in the same way as those paragraphs that are primarily analytical in character. The purpose of a narrative paragraph is to move the reader ahead through a series of actions. What passes for the "topic sentence" is a sentence that gets the action started, such as, "The committee chairman called for a vote after the discussion had continued for an hour," or "The cavalry divided into two columns as they approached the base of the hill." What all this means in the task of writing is that the writer must be very clear at every point whether he is proceeding chronologically or topically.

All that has been said about organizing for writing in these few pages does no more than "set the stage" for the creative act of writing itself. Since effective writing is, after all, an *art*, it cannot be confined within a set formula or a recipe. Nonetheless, preparatory organization is an absolute precondition for effective writing, assuring not necessarily speedy writing (contrary to popular opinion most good writers do *not* write rapidly) but clarity of thought.

EXERCISES

**SET A
Exercise 1** Crucial to all effective organizing is the ability to subordinate lesser ideas to more general ones. In the spaces provided number the items from the most general to the most specific, using "1" for the most general and so on. In some cases the items are equal; in such cases use the same number. In the final exercise, note that a chronology is involved. Be careful with it.

a. legislative branch   _____
chairman   _____
government   _____
finance committee   _____
senate   _____

b. regional coal strike   _____
a family fight   _____
world war   _____
industrial turmoil   _____
local race riot   _____
national strife   _____

c. New York City   _____
United Nations   _____
State of New York   _____
United States Government   _____
State of Ohio   _____
France   _____

d. The automobile brought major social changes.   _____
Cars were used by children to get away from their parents.   _____
The total effect of the automobile has yet to be measured.   _____
The automobile ended the social isolation of the farmer.   _____
Industrial development was much advanced by the automobile.   _____

e. During the 1930s depression the WPA built 881 new parks and 1,500 new athletic fields.   _____
In the 1920s and 1930s organized recreation experienced a great surge in popularity.   _____
The head of the WPA was Roosevelt's closest advisor, Harry Hopkins.   _____
The twentieth century has seen enormous expansion of sports activity of all kinds.   _____
Local governments in the 1920s spent large amounts in building new city playgrounds and golf courses.   _____

**SET A
Exercise 2** Here we continue with another form of exercise aimed at enhancing the ability to subordinate specific ideas to more general ones. What follows is a scrambled paragraph; unscramble it, using numbers ("1" for the first sentence, "2" for the second, etc.) to indicate proper sentence order. It's a good idea to keep a couple

of points in mind, namely that identification of the topic sentence is half the battle and that in some cases chronology is a good clue to proper order.

_____ The administration quickly disposed of most of its war plants, usually by turning them over to private interests on very generous terms.

_____ Under such pressure, the politicians of both parties simply collapsed.

_____ Business was permitted to move ahead quickly into civilian production.

_____ The pressures for a return to civilian life were overwhelming by mid-1945.

_____ In November 1945, Congress approved a $6 billion tax cut, even though it would obviously contribute to inflation.

_____ Business interests demanded lower taxes, immediate demobilization, and the end of lend-lease and other measures assisting other foreign competitors in international markets.

_____ The armed forces, 12 million strong in 1945, had only 3 million by mid-1945, and but 1.6 million by mid-1947.

_____ Lend-lease shipments were cut.

_____ And—feeling secure with an atomic monopoly—it brought the boys home.

_____ Soldiers insisted on being allowed to come home, and officeholders were swamped with postcards from Asia labeled, "No boats, no votes."

Now read the sentences in order. Do they make sense?

**SET A
Exercise 3** Here are two paragraphs mixed together. Separate and order them, using 1a, 1b, 1c, and so on for one of the paragraphs and 2a, 2b, 2c, and so on for the other.

_____ Despite its sparse population, Nevada was admitted as a state in 1864, partly because the Republicans wanted its votes... and partly because Lincoln wanted another free state to support the constitutional amendment emancipating the slaves.

_____ The Dakota mining region produced its share of colorful characters, among them Wild Bill Hickok and Calamity Jane.

_____ In 1861 Congress created Nevada Territory out of western Utah.

_____ In *The Bonanza West* (1963), William S. Greever writes: "Certainly she gained experience as a prostitute, became expert at tying a diamond hitch, learned how to handle teams, and often wore men's attire."

_____ When she first came to Deadwood in 1876, she was thirty-five years old, with a dubious background that has since been gilded with myth.

_____ A reporter for the *Virginia City Enterprise*, Twain left an absorbing account of life on the mining frontier in *Roughing It* (1872).

_____ Secretary to the territorial governor was Orion Clemens, brother of Samuel Langhorne Clemens, better known as Mark Twain.

_____ It is said that while she was serving as a teamster with a military detachment, officers did not become aware of "her presence until they spied her form among those of troops taking a swim."

**SET A
Exercise 4**

One of the ways to secure good coherence within each paragraph is to remain conscious throughout its writing of the key word or words of the topic sentence. These words contain the controlling idea for the paragraph. In Exercises 2 and 3 you have worked up three paragraphs. Specify the key word or words of the topic sentence of each of them.

Exercise 2 paragraph: _____

Exercise 3 paragraph: _____

Exercise 3 paragraph: _____

**SET A
Exercise 5**

In the following exercise there are nine "pieces" that, when put together correctly, represent a simplified sentence outline for a short essay. Though much is missing, specifically included are a main thematic statement, three main points, four subpoints belonging somewhere under the main points, and a summary statement. Put all the pieces in their proper places (by number) in the form provided below.

1. There was another major division in the world of evangelical Protestantism [as]...Negroes [moved] in large numbers into their own denominations...

2. Traditional views of biblical authority, chronology, and interpretation were upset for many as the theory of evolution was popularized.

3. [During Reconstruction years (1865–77)]...many northern Christians regarded the South as open to ecclesiastical occupation, too, while southerners, resisting, saw northerners as having diluted the Gospel with political concerns.

4. From the conservative viewpoint the liberals, with their positive evaluation of...scientifically oriented culture, seemed to be wavering on first principles.

5. Though there were devoted missionaries from white denominations carrying out significant educational ministries among blacks, the two evangelical worlds...largely went their own ways.

6. In the thirty years following the Civil War, some uncomfortable realities [including sectional, racial, and theological differences] stood in the way of evangelical hopes for the early triumph of Christian civilization in America.

7. The Protestant world of the postwar period was shaken by another division...[as] the rise of liberal theology caused repercussions almost everywhere.

8. Handicapped by divisions and tensions, the evangelical Protestants faced some complex and formidable problems which became widely identified as seriously threatening the future of Protestantism.

9. The reunion of the nation did not lead to the reuniting of the sectional divisions of the denominational families.

    I. Main Thematic Statement
       A. Main point
          1. Subpoint (if any) _____
          2. Subpoint (if any) _____

    B. Main point
      1. Subpoint (if any) _____
      2. Subpoint (if any) _____
    C. Main point
      1. Subpoint (if any) _____
      2. Subpoint (if any) _____
    D. Summary statement

SET A
Exercise 6

The final exercise requires something comparable to laying out a total essay that has both narrative and topical elements. The sentences that follow, when unscrambled, will "tell the story" of the military aspect of the French and Indian War, which began in 1753. Your task is to put the following numbered items into essay form, recognizing that, for the most part, paragraphs will be incomplete. In the spaces provided on the next page present the story in full sentence form, using all the items. Note: In this war England was fighting France.

1. Within a year, the tide of the war had turned, as in 1759 the French lost Fort Niagara, Fort Ticonderoga, and Crown Point.

2. Personally arrogant and aggressive, he brought these qualities to British policy at a time when calamity seemed certain.

3. Though losing most of the early battles in the French and Indian War, the British rallied under the leadership of William Pitt and by 1760 had decisively defeated the French in America.

4. British General Edward Braddock's two regiments were defeated in 1755 by a French and Indian force that used the unconventional tactic of firing from behind trees.

5. Finally, he ordered a turn from the defensive to the offensive in North America.

6. The English needed the Ohio Valley as a settlement area for a growing colonial population.

7. The first in a series of British defeats began with the surrender of a small force led by Lt. Col. George Washington in 1753, as he sought to protect Virginia land claims in the Ohio Valley.

8. Pitt reformed the Army and Navy, replacing staid bureaucrats with talented young officers.

9. Later in that same year the French rollback continued with the defeat of General Montcalm at Quebec.

10. The geographical origin of the war was the Ohio Valley area south of the Great Lakes.

11. The complexion of the war began to change in 1758 with a major development in England.

12. The French needed the Ohio River as the vital link for their many small settlements west of the Appalachian Mountains.

13. The armies of Frederick the Great in Europe campaigning against the French were given financial aid, causing Pitt later to remark, "America has been conquered in Germany."

14. But for the genius and forcefulness of William Pitt, the French would likely have achieved full dominance on the North American continent.

15. The first five years of the war brought little but military disaster for Britain.

16. In 1760, having shattered the French navy earlier, the British took Montreal, and French America was no more.

17. In 1756–58 inept British generalship brought a succession of failures at Fort Oswego, Fort William Henry, and Fort Ticonderoga.

18. In that year William Pitt became First Minister in England, assuming virtual dictatorial powers.

Main thematic statement:

_____

_____

First paragraph:

_____

_____

_____

_____

_____

_____

_____

Second paragraph:

_____

_____

_____

_____

_____

_____

_____

Third paragraph:

_____

_____

_____

_____

_____

_____

_____

_____

Fourth paragraph:

_____

_____

_____

_____

_____

_____

_____

Summary statement: _____

_____

SET B
Exercise 1
(Optional)

Crucial to all effective organizing is the ability to subordinate lesser ideas to more general ones. In the spaces provided number the items from the most general to the most specific, using "1" for the most general and so on. In some cases the items are equal; in such cases use the same number.

a. Gen. Robert E. Lee _____
    Nineteenth-century America _____
    Southern military capability _____
    The Civil War _____
    Southern generalship _____

b. presidential nominating conventions _____
    Lyndon Johnson _____
    political parties _____
    defeated in 1968 _____
    Hubert Humphrey _____
    nominees of the '60s _____
    Democratic Party _____
    John F. Kennedy _____

c. *Roosevelt's New Deal: A History* _____
    the evidence of the past _____
    history-as-written _____
    A Survey History of the United States _____
    history-as-actuality _____

d. Irish monks became well-known for their missionary zeal and
their learning.   _____

Irish Christianity, isolated from the rest of Europe by pagan
England and Scotland, developed distinctive customs of
its own.   _____

They converted certain areas of Scotland and later extended
their activities to the European mainland.   _____

Organized around the monastery rather than the diocese, its
leaders were the abbots, not the bishops.   _____

Ireland had been converted to Christianity in the fifth century
by St. Patrick.   _____

e. Imprisonment in a concentration camp was an occasional
alternative to the death penalty.   _____

The definition of "treason" was expanded to include such
minor offenses as circulation of banned newspapers.   _____

Hitler made major changes in the German legal system.   _____

The death penalty, without the right of appeal, could be
invoked upon conviction for treason.   _____

The root principle of Hitler's new "justice" was
subordination of the individual to the state.   _____

**SET B
Exercise 2
(Optional)** Here we continue with another form of exercise aimed at enhancing the ability to subordinate specific ideas to more general ones. What follows is a scrambled paragraph; unscramble it, using numbers ("1" for the first sentence, "2" for the second, etc.) to indicate proper sentence order. Take special care in identifying the topic or lead sentence and keep aware of chronology.

_____ As they moved northward, the Boers had to fight both the British and native Africans but nonetheless succeeded in establishing two virtually independent South African states—the Transvaal and the Orange Free State.

_____ As Britishers emigrated to their new acquisition in increasing numbers, the older colonists, known in their own Dutch vernacular as Boers, became more and more discontented.

_____ In 1815 Britain acquired from the Netherlands a territory known as the Cape Colony at the southern tip of Africa.

_____ Well inland, these new but thinly populated states lived on for a time, scarcely noticed by the outside world.

_____ Between 1835 and 1837 several thousand Boers moved north in the "Great Trek," a heroic folk migration that still reverberates in nationalist South African feeling.

_____ The British established English as the official language, abolished slavery, attempted to protect the native blacks, and pursued other liberal legislative goals.

_____ Cape Colony was inhabited by a few thousand Dutch settlers who found the moderate climate comparable to that of their homeland.

_____ This British liberalism went against the grain of the stern-minded Boers, who were religiously and politically conservative.

Now read the sentences in order. Do they make sense?

**SET B
Exercise 3
(Optional)**

Here are two paragraphs mixed together. Separate and order them, using 1a, 1b, 1c, and so on for one of the paragraphs and 2a, 2b, 2c, and so on for the other. Pay close attention to chronology.

_____ His father was a passionate socialist who had been much influenced by the political writings of Bakunin.

_____ In the early '20s Mussolini moved to turn his premiership into a dictatorship.

_____ Back in Italy, he was imprisoned for his opposition to the war against Turkey (1911).

_____ He spent some time as an agitator among Italian laborers in Switzerland (1902–04) and in Austria (1909), but in the latter country was deported by the police.

_____ He created a Fascist militia of nearly 200,000 members who owed allegiance only to him.

_____ Mussolini was born in 1883, in the Romagna province of central Italy, an area long famous for its political extremists.

_____ Within a month after coming to office, he was able to obtain temporary dictatorial powers from Parliament, which feared economic chaos.

_____ In 1912 he assumed the editorship of the most important Italian socialist newspaper.

_____ Mussolini, a forceful youth, was already a militant socialist by the time he was eighteen.

_____ Before his dictatorial powers expired, he pressured Parliament to pass a law making certain that Fascists would dominate future parliaments.

_____ In addition, he enlarged the regular army, requiring its members to take an oath of personal loyalty to him.

**SET B
Exercise 4
(Optional)**

Again, one of the ways to secure good coherence within each paragraph is to remain conscious throughout its writing of the key word or words of the topic sentence. These words contain the controlling idea for the paragraph. In Exercises 2 and 3 you have worked up three paragraphs. Specify the key word or words of each.

Exercise 2 paragraph: _____

Exercise 3 paragraph: _____

Exercise 3 paragraph: _____

**SET B
Exercise 5
(Optional)**

In the following exercise there are eleven "pieces," that, when put together correctly, represent a simplified sentence outline for a short essay. Though much is missing, specifically included are a main thematic statement, three main points, six subpoints belonging somewhere under the main points, and a summary statement. Put all the pieces in their proper order (by number) in the form provided below.

1. By acquiring, in the 1890s, Cuba, Puerto Rico, and the Philippines, and by interventionist policies in Latin America, the United States had become a world power.

2. Concurrently with the consolidation of businesses had come a revolutionary change called "finance capitalism," making bankers the main owners of American industry.

3. During this ten-year period the American economic world was transformed.

4. Finally, the cultural predominance of rural America was severely weakened by the fact that through industrialization and immigration, cities were becoming the primary force in American life.

5. During a three-year period after January 1902, hundreds of union agitators were killed or injured and thousands were arrested.

6. During the years 1900–10 major economic, international, and population developments occurred that made America a different country than before.

7. Just as industry, finance, and labor had destroyed economic provincialism in the country, the imperialist, even more speedily, had brought a revolution in the nation's international position.

8. The transformation of America had become virtually an accomplished fact by 1910.

9. The movement toward business consolidation had progressed so far that by 1909, 1 percent of American manufacturers produced nearly half the nation's goods.

10. Paralleling the rise of "finance capitalism" was the development of a strong, though violence prone, labor movement.

11. Theodore Roosevelt underlined America's new international prominence by sending the U.S. Navy on a world tour.

I. Main Thematic Statement _____   C. Main point _____
   A. Main point _____   1. Subpoints _____
      1. Subpoints _____   2. _____
      2. _____   _____
         _____   D. Summary statement _____
         _____
         _____

   B. Main point _____
      1. Subpoints _____
      2. _____
         _____
         _____

**SET B
Exercise 6
(Optional)**

The final exercise requires something comparable to laying out a total essay that has both narrative and topical elements. The sentences that follow, when unscrambled, will describe the economic situation in Germany that led to the rise of Hitler. Your task is to put the numbered items into essay form, recognizing that, for the most part, paragraphs will be incomplete. In the spaces provided on the next page present the story in full sentence form, using all the items.

1. Hitler moved boldly and effectively in his first months in power to transform his chancellorship to a dictatorship.

2. They polled nearly 7 million votes in the national elections of July 1930, and more than doubled that vote two years later.

3. As a corporal in World War I he was decorated for bravery, deepening his already strong German nationalism, and after the war he decided to enter politics.

4. Many small businessmen, only now recovering from the runaway inflation of the early '20s, soon faced bankruptcy and destitution.

5. Brown-shirted Nazi storm troopers (SA) and black-uniformed SS elite corps supplemented police in an orgy of unlimited violence against all opponents of the new government.

6. The depression, which began in 1929, meant utter catastrophe for millions.

7. In 1923, while in prison, Hitler wrote *Mein Kampf*, a work that not only detailed his future plans, but also included a hodgepodge of national, social, and racial theories that had flourished in Germany and Austria since the mid-nineteenth century.

8. The rise of Hitler may be explained by noting that the despair of large numbers of Germans was so great as to induce them to accept almost any demagogue who promised to deliver them from confusion and fear.

9. The German masses were deeply affected, as within two years salaries fell by half, production by two-thirds, and the number of unemployed more than quintupled.

10. The early Nazis were a party of abnormal, unsavory types, such as Heinrich Himmler, Julius Streicher, Ernst Rohm, and Alfred Rosenberg, individuals later to be known for their casual attitude toward murder.

11. By July 1933 Hitler was able to declare all other parties dissolved and now Germany was a one-party state.

12. The headstrong child of highly emotional, uneducated parents, Hitler went to Vienna in 1909 at the age of twenty, picking up there the strong anti-Semitism that permeated the political atmosphere.

13. They were now the strongest party in the Reichstag and in early 1933 succeeded in making Hitler the new German Chancellor.

14. By 1932 great numbers of once law-abiding workers were looking for a solution to their problems; Adolf Hitler appeared to offer salvation.

15. He dissolved the Reichstag, calling for new elections; the newly elected Reichstag now voted a bill that practically abrogated the constitution, permitting the government to pass laws without parliamentary endorsement.

16. The transformation of Germany from a parliamentary state to a totalitarian dictatorship can be understood first by examining German turmoil during the depression years and second by considering Adolf Hitler's shrewd tactics.

17. The Communists were banned, the Social Democrats broken, the unions taken over and incorporated into a Nazi labor front, the separate state governments abolished, and the states totally integrated into the Reich, united under a central administration for the first time in German history.

18. Capitalizing on political and social unrest, the Nazis moved boldly forward in the early '30s.

19. In 1919 he joined the German Workers' Party (soon to be known as the Nazi party), a radical organization that emphasized racial purity, anticapitalism, and opposition to the punishing Treaty of Versailles of that year.

Main thematic statement:

_____

_____

First paragraph:

_____

_____

_____

_____

_____

_____

_____

_____

Second paragraph:

_____

_____

_____

_____

_____

_____

_____

Third paragraph:

_____

_____

_____

_____

_____

_____

_____

_____

Fourth paragraph:

_____

_____

_____

_____

_____

_____

_____

_____

Summary statement:

_____

_____

CHAPTER NINE

Continuity in Writing

One of the things that any writer must keep in mind at all times is that his or her eventual reader is often on unfamiliar ground. Whether the subject matter is a student paper, a scientific article, or a children's story, the reader is potentially "in trouble" because he must step out of his own concrete, here-and-now world into a symbolic world that the writer has created. However familiar that world is to a writer, it readily becomes a complicated one to the reader who must struggle with the twists and turns of language, the clash and mating of ideas, generally with the fleeting and insubstantial quality of all prose. The fact is that to most of us distractions come easily, and unless a writer leads us through the labyrinth of his world in a slowly paced and considerate way, we are apt to become lost and return to our own more comfortable private worlds.

All of this is said to emphasize the point that a writer can scarcely do enough to make himself or herself clear. One of the ways in which clarity is achieved, as we have seen in the preceding chapter, is to give strong organizational structure to the writing, so that all the parts can be seen to fit together. But even that is not enough. As a writer you must provide a continuing sense of *linkage* between the components of the world you are describing so that the reader isn't forced to stop and retreat to try to figure out on his own just what you are trying to say.

This sense of *linkage*, or continuity as it is often called, is especially strengthened by (1) effective use of transitional devices and (2) in the case of history writing, by usage of a "logic of narration."

Transitional devices are best described as the bridges that carry readers into new sentences and paragraphs. They show how each particular idea is related to that which immediately preceded it. One of the most common transitional devices is the expression *for example*. When readers see it they know that the following sentence will provide a specific illustration of the truth of the sentence preceding. Another frequently used transitional device is *as a result*, which tells readers that the sentence to follow will describe an effect of some causal influence that has just been discussed. In using such phrases an author takes his readers with him step by step, thus avoiding those abrupt shifts that can alienate even the most patient of them. In football parlance, by using transitional devices, a writer "calls signals" to the readers, enabling them to know where the next play is going.

There are several basic types of transitional expressions with which you should become very familiar. One way of classifying them is presented below. Note the sample phrases accompanying each category.

EXAMPLE: for example, as an illustration, for instance.

CONSEQUENCE: as a result, therefore, consequently, thus, because, accordingly, hence, for that reason, and so, then.

SIMILARITY: like, likewise, in like manner, similar, similarly.

ADDITION: and, furthermore, moreover, also, in addition, too, another.

CONTRAST: on the other hand, however, but, yet, nevertheless, in contrast to, even though, despite, conversely, although, unlike.

SEQUENCE: first, second, finally.

EMPHASIS: indeed, especially, in fact, certainly, truly.

TIME: then, now, next, afterward, gradually, immediately, at once, in the beginning, at first, up to this point, in (year), at the same time, as we shall see, later, eventually, meanwhile, when, briefly, soon, earlier, subsequently, at this point.

SUMMATION: in general, in summary, all in all, in conclusion, by and large, in short, all told.

PLACE: here, elsewhere, above, below, farther on, there, simultaneously, nearby, next to, outside, within, at.

RESTATEMENT: that is, put another way, in other words.

ATTITUDE: fortunately, unfortunately, in a sense, regrettably, undoubtedly.

The foregoing is by no means a complete list of phrases pertinent to each category, but they do give an idea of some of the more common "signals."

Aside from the usage of such phrases, another transitional technique followed by many writers is called "echo" transition—the repeating of an important word or phrase from one sentence or paragraph to another to let the reader know that the discussion is to continue along the same general line. When, for example, a writer is shifting to a new aspect of the same subject he had been discussing, he might present it as follows:

(*Last sentence of preceding paragraph*) "All in all, the economic burdens of the Depression weighed most heavily on the black American."

(*First sentence of following paragraph*) "The Depression brought a social climate that was, paradoxically, both wholesome and unhealthy."

Transitional devices go a long way toward "gluing" together a writer's ideas. An illustration of how they can help smooth the flow of thought is given in the paragraph below. First read it as it stands, and then note the difference as you read it eliminating the italicized phrases.

Until the spring of 1942 the Central Pacific fleet had to devote itself mostly to licking its wounds, but it did make a series of hit-and-run raids on Japanese-held islands. *Also* on April 19, sixteen AAF bombers under the command of Lt. Col. James Doolittle took off from a fleet carrier and bombed Tokyo. *Up to this point* the Japanese conquests had been so easy that the Japanese commanders were considering further expansion; *now* Doolittle's raid seems to have decided them. *Accordingly,* during the following months the Japanese pushed southward across New Guinea, down the Solomons, and toward Midway. *The result* was "strategic over-stretch," which was to be a vital element in weakening the Japanese perimeter and hastening their defeat.[1]

Effective use of transitional devices is a hallmark of all good writing. Yet it is not the whole solution to the problem of achieving continuity, especially in the field of history. Writing history presents a special problem, in that one undertakes to re-create a world of the past not in its full reality but "in sketch." Put in another way, the historian presents a world of the past reduced to the level of a mental picture, one with sufficient imagery to allow a reader to vicariously inhabit that former world. Perhaps the central point to be grasped here is that of *reduction*. What was at one time a full and concrete reality is reduced or changed to a sketchy and abstract account. But the reduction itself (the written account) must convey some idea of the complexity of that past reality.

No mean task this. What it requires is a "logic of narration" according to which the historian's account hangs together as a story and at the same time suggests the wholeness of that past world. The logic we speak of here is very much the logic of the storyteller whose tale has continuity (and charm) because he employs a bagful of narrative tricks, among which are (1) use of conventions, (2) emphasis upon conflict, and (3) presentation of a "moral" to the story.

1. Use of conventions. Many of the conventions that historians use to achieve a sense of organic wholeness were described in Chapter One, and, in fact, you were asked to do an exercise in order to identify them. One of the more important of them was *shift of scene*. Just as a film director will cut quickly from scene to scene to heighten suspense and tie the pieces of the story together, so too will the historian shift the focus of the narrative from place to place and person to person. After all, in real life many related activities are going on at once, but they cannot all be discussed at the same time. Another convention is *manipulation of time*, a crucial one because, by definition, history deals with change through time. Thus, in his narration, the historian reminds his readers of a tradition, or of some influential event occurring some time ago; sometimes he telescopes into a brief summary the actions of several days or even years, and at other times he takes his readers forward in time to show them an outcome. Still another important convention is that of the *characterization of individuals*. In focusing on the foibles, the quirks, the warmth, the orneriness, the heroism, and the villainy of various historical figures, he gives life and validity to the story. Finally, an understanding of a past is not possible without some kind of *description of prevailing conditions,* such as the mental fevers that were affecting elements of the population, the special lethargy of some aging bureaucracy, or the attitudes of profit-seekers in the society.

2. Emphasis upon conflict. Continuing an analogy made a moment ago, the historian, like the filmmaker, tends to highlight conflicts and disagreements rather than instances of social harmony. History is, among other things, concerned with change through time. And change is usually much more a product of conflict than consensus. Therefore, just as most good films dramatize human conflict, good narrative history explores the oppositions and conflicts that lie behind historical evolution. This distorts reality to some degree, for there

---

[1]Leland D. Baldwin, *The Stream of American History,* 4th ed. (New York: Van Nostrand Reinhold, 1969), p. 676.

is also much love, agreement, and cooperation in the world. But the distortion is necessary to maintain a sense of dramatic continuity. An excellent example of a historian's use of conflict is found in William Leuchtenburg's account of Republican Party problems in the presidential campaign of 1940. Note that Leuchtenburg also does a pretty fair job of characterization:

> Willkie [the Republican nominee] had a hard time finding a viable political position. Old Guard Republicans instinctively distrusted his mercurial temperament and resented the fact that he had been a Democrat such a short time before. "I don't mind the church converting a whore," former Indiana Senator Jim Watson told him bluntly at the G.O.P. convention, "but I don't like her to lead the choir the first night!" On the other hand, voters with harsh memories of Hoover and the Republican Party questioned the claims to liberalism of a utility tycoon. Democrats sneered that he was "Hobson's Choice"; that he had "an electric background, an electric personality and an electric campaign chest"; that he was, in Ickes' telling phrase, a "simple, barefoot Wall Street lawyer."[2]

Contrast this with a generalized, typically "textbook" account that fails to frame its oppositions sharply and fails even more in characterization:

> Yet there can be no doubt that in the summer of 1940 a large body of sentiment was by no means prepared for active participation in the European War. The presidential campaign reflected this fact. In essence, the President and Wendell Willkie were in agreement; they both wished to extend aid to the Allies. Willkie had difficulty in finding an appealing issue. He had endorsed a large part of the New Deal, and the third-term question interested only a fraction of the voters. If he criticized the Democrats for their slowness in building up national defense, there was a political danger that such criticism would imply more expenditures and more likelihood of conflict. Unemployment became a less useful issue as the preparedness movement created new jobs.[3]

3. Presentation of a "moral" to the story. Historians are not necessarily in the "morals" business, but the reader should recognize that the narrative historian, again like a good director, is not just a storyteller; he is also an interpreter. Therefore, scattered throughout any historical account but especially at its conclusion, one will usually find some sort of evaluation of the meaning of the events described or perhaps an analysis of the short- and long-term implications.

There are any number of analogies that one can use to emphasize the importance of continuity in all writing. Perhaps the best of them is to see it as comparable to home construction: thoughtful design (organization) + effective joining of members (continuity) = a sound edifice (historical account).

---

[2]Leuchtenburg, p. 319.
[3]Dexter Perkins and G. Van Deusen, *The United States of America, A History*, Vol. II (New York: Macmillan, 1968), pp. 605–6.

EXERCISES

SET A
Exercise 1

1. In the following excerpt, underline the transitional devices used to link the sentences and/or paragraphs together.

Although many pioneers moved several times during their lives, let us assume our first farmer remained wherever his farm was—Tennessee, western New York, western Pennsylvania, or eastern Ohio. But his sons, on attaining age twenty-one, headed for Indiana, for...Illinois, for Michigania (Michigan) or other areas to the west. Like their father they purchased their lands, at $1.25 an acre from the federal government, from a state government, from a land company, or from a neighborhood entrepreneur....Similar purchases were made by pioneers' sons below the Mason and Dixon line. Soon the young men were slashing and burning the pine barrens of Alabama and Mississippi just as their brethren in the Old Northwest were repeating the same backwoods patterns that their fathers had practiced before them. But there were differences....The initial purchase was probably larger than the father's had been farther east.

Moreover, the arrival of the young man and his bride in the new country was a little more propitious than the journey over the mountains that his parents had made with a couple of pack horses when he was a baby. This young man came in a farm wagon with a canvas cover over it....

2. As before, underline the transitional devices.

And so the Calvinists urged a life of rectitude, severity and, most important of all, diligence. In contrast to the Catholic theologians who tended to look upon worldly activity as vanity, the Calvinists sanctified and approved of endeavor as a kind of index of spiritual worth. Indeed, in Calvinist hands there grew up the idea of a man dedicated to his work: "called" to it, as it were. Hence the fervid pursuit of one's calling, far from evidencing a distraction from religious ends, came to be taken as evidence of a dedication to a religious life. The energetic merchant was, in Calvinist eyes, a *Godly* man, not an ungodly one; and from this identification of work and worth, it was not long before the notion grew up that the more successful a man, the more worthy he was. Calvinism thus provided a religious atmosphere which, in contrast to Catholicism, encouraged wealth seeking and the temper of a business-like world.

Perhaps even more important than its encouragement in seeking wealth was the influence of Calvinism on the use of wealth. By and large the prevailing attitude of the prosperous Catholic merchants had been....

3. In this paragraph insert appropriate transitional devices.

_____ he entered the presidential race, Goldwater was not assured that he would win. His candidacy, _____, could insure conservative power within the Republican party and strengthen the party's base in the South and Southwest. _____, the Goldwater campaign was not primarily concerned about popularity; not surprisingly, _____, Goldwater suffered major defeats in the New Hampshire and Oregon primaries among others. _____, the divisions among moderate Republicans, the hesitancy of anyone besides the controversial Nelson Rockefeller (then governor of New York and recently divorced and remarried) to contest Goldwater for the nomination, and Richard Nixon's strategy of equivocation in order to emerge as the convention's compromise choice further enhanced Goldwater's chances. . . .

_____ their major goal had been to reshape the Republican party, the Goldwater Republicans made a number of seemingly inept political decisions. _____ the convention, they made no concessions to Republican moderates concerning the platform. . . .

Sources

1. Richard A. Bartlett, *The New Country* (New York: Oxford University Press, 1975), p. 189.
2. Robert L. Heilbroner, *The Making of Economic Society*, 3rd ed. (Englewood Cliffs, N.J.: Prentice-Hall, 1970), p. 50.
3. Melvyn Dubofsky, Athan Theoharis, Daniel M. Smith, *The United States in the Twentieth Century* (Englewood Cliffs, N.J.: Prentice-Hall, 1978), p. 458.

**SET A
Exercise 2**

As the basis for this exercise we will use the passage by George Mowry, *The Era of Theodore Roosevelt,* found in Chapter Three, Set A (pages 47–51). Reread it, and then answer the following questions:

1. In nearly any episode of history an author will occasionally "cut away" from the basic narrative, using conventions as described earlier in this chapter. Specify two such "cuts" in the account you have just read:

_____

_____

_____

2. Describe briefly the basic oppositions that are given central emphasis in the account:

_____

_____

3. Are there any other oppositions, or perhaps other levels of opposition, that appear directly or indirectly in the account? Describe briefly:

_____

_____

4. Does the author appear in any way to line up with one side or another? If so, specify the particular passage or passages in which you see the author's leaning.

_____

_____

5. Specifically what does the author see as the meaning of the episode?

_____

_____

_____

SET B
Exercise 1
(Optional)

1. In the following excerpt, underline the transitional devices used to link the sentences and/or paragraphs together.

Hamilton also borrowed and manipulated mercantilist policies to create a strong state. But he was more narrowly driven by his own ambition, and his vision of the good society was far less balanced, democratic, or independent....

Jefferson, on the other hand, understood the comparative imbalance between England and America, and was in the last resort willing to accept the costs and the implications of modifying it. Hence he moved toward support for American shipping and manufactures. Whatever its short-run impact on the pro-English carrying trade, and even on the small merchant and consumer, his embargo was designed to preserve and extend America's economic independence. And it actually did function to create a composite political economy....

Unlike Jefferson, who was abroad as American minister to France, Hamilton, during the Constitutional Convention, candidly presented his views on the good society. But while his mind and logic were "damned sharp," as Robert Morris later remarked, the majority of the delegates had different ideas of the abstract good....

2. As before, underline the transitional devices.

Further, even if Dante's basic assumptions were mediaeval, his judgments frequently revealed a concern with humanity different from that found in traditional theology. In contrast to the *Summa* of St. Thomas, Dante's poem appeals more to the emotions than to the intellect. Where St. Thomas attempted to reconcile faith and reason, Dante evoked hope and fear, and stressed conduct more than belief, as shown by the presence of a controversial mediaeval prophet and a heretic in his *Paradise*. Thus Dante repeatedly veers away from the logical dogmatism found in scholastic philosophy toward the humane and ethical interest in man that was to characterize and illuminate the literature of the Renaissance. Finally, of course, Dante's style is so original and powerful that it left a lasting imprint on Italian as a literary language.

In the development of Italian literature, Dante is followed by Petrarch (1305–1374) and Boccaccio (1313–1375), who with him comprise the so-called "three crowns of Tuscany."

3. In this paragraph insert appropriate transitional devices.

There seemed four possible ways of disposing of the Philippine problem. The _____, returning the islands to Spain, found favor nowhere. The _____, selling or otherwise alienating the Philippines to some other power, seemed to invite a possible general European war; _____ it would hardly be more justified morally than remaining in possession ourselves. _____, we were being encouraged by England to remain in the Philippines, for American possession of those islands was much more palatable to England than possession by any other power. The _____ possibility, leaving the Philippines to themselves and giving them the independence Aguinaldo's men had been fighting for, was equivalent in most American minds to leaving them to anarchy. It _____ seemed to be another way of encouraging a scramble among other powers interested in the Far East. The _____ possibility was some form of American Possession, in the form of a protectorate or otherwise. _____ there was much sentiment for merely retaining a naval base and coaling station on the island of Luzon....

Sources

1. William Appleman Williams, *The Contours of American History* (New York: New Viewpoints, 1973), p. 155.

2. Robert E. Lerner, *The Age of Adversity* (Ithaca, N.Y.: Cornell University Press, 1968), p. 111.

3. Richard Hofstadter, "Manifest Destiny and the Philippines," *America in Crisis*, Daniel Aaron, ed. (New York: Knopf, 1952), pp. 186–7.

**SET B
Exercise 2
(Optional)**

As the basis for this exercise we will use the passage by William Leuchtenburg, *Franklin D. Roosevelt and the New Deal*, found in Chapter Three, Set B (Pages 52–56). Reread it, and then answer the following questions:

1. In nearly any episode of history an author will occasionally "cut away" from the basic narrative, using conventions as described earlier in this chapter. Specify two such "cuts" in the account you have just read:

_____

_____

_____

2. Describe briefly the basic oppositions that are given central emphasis in the account:

_____

_____

_____

_____

3. Are there any other oppositions, or perhaps other levels of opposition, that appear directly or indirectly in the account? Describe briefly:

_____

_____

_____

4. Does the author appear in any way to line up with one side or another? If so, specify the particular passage or passages in which you see the author's leaning.

_____

_____

_____

5. Specifically what does the author see as the meaning of the episode?

_____

_____

_____

Secondary Sources

Historians have long had a well-justified reputation for being bookworms. If an extraterrestrial civilization ever puts an earth historian in a zoo, the natural habitat should certainly be a used-book store or a cozy personal library with floor-to-ceiling books. One young historian, who collects books like an alcoholic empties wine bottles, was asked if he had read every book in his personal library. His response was: "Do you have a dictionary? Have you read every word?" Books were a passion that needed no further justification.

Books—secondary sources—are the historian's lifeblood. He reads them to keep up in his field, expand his knowledge, and share the ideas of other historians. Perhaps the greatest frustration for the historian, however, is the knowledge that books (even in his own narrow specialty) are being published far more rapidly than he can read them. Likewise, serious students often feel that they have too much to read in too short a time. It is not the purpose of this chapter to turn you into a speed reader with a photographic memory. But we will examine techniques that will allow you to get the most out of the reading you do.

SECONDARY SOURCES

Earlier we noted that secondary sources (books, articles, essays) are works of narration, explanation, and interpretation based on primary sources. [1] The key words here are *explanation* and *interpretation*. Many students hold the unfortunate (and wrong) opinion that history books are no more than dry collections of facts to be memorized. Of course, no student of history can ignore facts, for the study of history is ultimately based upon our knowledge of what actually happened in the past, that is, the facts. It is one of the historian's most important obligations to present the facts as clearly and as accurately as is humanly possible. But the presentation of the facts, important though it may be, is only one part of a larger whole. *The real objective of the historian is to offer an*

---

[1] In reality, very few books or articles are based *totally* on primary sources, because historians also consult a wide range of relevant secondary literature. Serious research studies, however, do tend to rely as much as possible on primary materials.

explanation and interpretation of how the relevant facts are related one to the other. It is the historian's job to explain *how and why* things happened as they did. Francis Parkman, the famous nineteenth-century American historian, put it well: "Facts may be detailed with the most minute exactness, and yet the narrative, taken as a whole, may be unmeaning or untrue."

Seen in this light, the facts *do not* "speak for themselves." They must be *interpreted* properly before they yield a true picture. For instance, a staple scenario of television detective shows is the story of an innocent bystander (usually with a criminal record) happening upon a murder victim and then running from the scene of the crime. The police (in this type of plot) jump to the conclusion that flight indicates guilt. The hero, however, usually a private detective of noble demeanor, saves the day by finding the real killer. The original suspect, it turns out, fled from fear, not guilt. The police had interpreted the "facts" one way; the private detective, on the basis of further inquiry, saw the facts in quite a different light. Historians, like the mythical detective, must be ever vigilant that their interpretations do full justice to the facts.

Many times the known facts will bear the weight of more than one interpretation. That is one of the reasons why historians keep writing and *rewriting* the history of a single event or period. They are not writing simply to regurgitate facts that have already been recorded in other books. They are writing to explore alternative interpretations (firmly based on the evidence) of why and how things happened the way they did, and perhaps to introduce new evidence not included in previous studies. Another reason for rewriting the histories of many events is that as our own historical situation changes, so too do our perspectives and interests change, and hence the sort of histories we read and write. It is not uncommon for new views of the past to grow out of contemporary passions and preoccupations; it was scarcely surprising that Americans became increasingly interested in the history of Southeast Asia during the Vietnam war. The study of history, therefore, involves not only learning the events of the past, but learning (from secondary sources) how others before you have tried to explain the interrelationships among those events. History, wrote Peter Geyl, "is an argument without end."

All good history is interpretation, but not all interpretation is good history. The fact that historical explanation involves an element of subjective judgment should not be taken to mean that "one opinion is as good as another." Interpretations based on shoddy scholarship or faulty reasoning should be exposed and rejected. It all boils down to this: There is room for much honest disagreement among historians, but in some cases it must be recognized that some interpretations fit the facts better than others. Hence all history, indeed all scholarship, must be judged with the critical eye of the skeptic. Reading history is not a passive task where one simply absorbs "knowledge"; it is a pursuit that requires the active intellectual participation of the reader.

HOW TO READ SECONDARY LITERATURE

How, you may ask yourself, can I actively participate in the books I read? As with anything worth doing, time and effort are essential. Unfortunately, no one has yet invented a labor-saving device to make learning effortless. You *can* save time and energy, though, if you know what you should be looking for when reading a work of nonfiction.

The basic point to remember is that when you read a secondary work (book or article) your main goal should be to understand the author's major *explanatory conclusions.* Of course, you will come across much new factual material, and you should master the most important of the new facts. But it is far more important to master the author's *interpretation of how the facts relate to one another and to understand the author's frame of reference or point of view.* It is common, as we all know, to forget facts relatively soon after we have learned them. There was once a noted expert on fish who became a college president. He vowed to memorize the name of every student on campus but soon abandoned the effort, complaining, "I found that every time I learned the name of a student, I forgot the name of a fish." Many of us share the college president's forgetfulness for facts. But we are much better able to remember neatly conceptualized generalizations. In the long run, then, it is easier and far more profitable to remember the overriding ideas and conclusions of the books you read.

THE THESIS

The first thing to look for is the author's *thesis* or central argument. When asked to state the thesis of a book or article, many students respond, "This book is about..." and proceed to tell the events the book describes. *This is wrong.* The *topic* of the book (the material the book covers) and the *thesis* (the interpretation applied to that material) are *not* one and the same. There are many examples of books that share the same general topic but differ markedly in thesis. In the late 1920s both Sidney Fay and Bernadotte Schmitt wrote lengthy studies on the origins of World War I.[2] Both authors had access to the same evidence, but each interpreted that evidence in a different way. Schmitt assigned to Germany most of the responsibility for starting the war, whereas Fay minimized German war guilt by distributing blame more widely among a number of countries. Thus the *topics* of the books were almost identical—that is, both books examined the events leading to the outbreak of hostilities in 1914. But the *theses* (interpretations) were radically different.

Usually the thesis of a book can be discovered quickly. If it can't, either the book is poorly constructed (not uncommon) or you are missing something somewhere. Many times the author states the thesis explicitly ("My thesis is..."); on other occasions you must do the work yourself. Most authors summarize their central arguments in a preface, introduction, or first chapter, and recapitulate the main points at the end of the book. *These are the sections of a book you should read first.* (In the case of an article, read the first few paragraphs and the last few in order to isolate the thesis.) Don't be afraid to read the last chapter before those in the middle; a history book is not a murder mystery where the reader needs to be kept in suspense until the end.

It is important to identify the thesis early so that as you read the rest of the book you need not read every detail with equal diligence. The facts in the book should support and illustrate the central unifying arguments. And if you have identified those unifying arguments from the beginning, you will be better able to concentrate on how the author builds his or her case rather than trying to

---

[2]Sidney B. Fay, *The Origins of the World War,* 2 vols. (New York: Macmillan, 1928); Bernadotte E. Schmitt, *The Coming of the War, 1914,* 2 vols. (New York: Scribners, 1930).

memorize a chaotic assortment of individual facts. As you become more and more familiar with a given topic, each new book you read on that topic can be mastered more efficiently. With the essential facts already at your command, you will be able to concentrate on the book's interpretation and how that interpretation differs from others you have read. You will be thinking creatively, not just absorbing masses of information.

Finally, although the thesis is the most important single element in a book, you should by no means ignore the rest of it. As you read you should take note of the important generalizations made in each chapter or subsection of the book. You should also make a mental (or preferably written) note of what factual material *is* covered. This is not the same as saying you should memorize all the facts. You should, however, have a clear idea of what the book does and does not contain. That way, if you need a specific piece of information in the future you will know where to find it.

Reading a secondary work is like mining for precious gems; the valuable stones must be separated from the worthless surrounding rocks. A valuable technique for "mining" secondary sources is *skimming*. After you have read carefully to establish the thesis, the rest of the book can be digested rapidly. A well-constructed book will contain regular patterns that can be used as shortcuts by the astute reader. For instance, an author's major points are usually summarized at the beginning or end (or both) of each chapter. Similarly, central ideas in individual paragraphs are often contained in a topic sentence, usually, but not always, the first sentence in the paragraph. Once you have established where a particular author tends to locate the ideas he or she considers most important, it is easy to concentrate on those key ideas and skim over much of the supportive or illustrative factual material. Note, however, that this technique is only valuable for books on *topics for which you already have a basic textbook knowledge*. Skimming is not so useful when reading a book on a totally new subject.[3]

THE AUTHOR'S FRAME OF REFERENCE: HIDDEN AGENDAS

"What I like in a good author," wrote Logan Pearsall Smith, "is not what he says, but what he whispers." Indeed, the "whispers" in a work of history are frequently as important as the uninhibited declarations. In every history book the author makes countless value judgments and decisions that are not explicitly identified, but nevertheless influence the tone, organization, point of view, and conclusions. It is important, therefore, for the reader to identify the author's underlying assumptions and values. There is no absolutely foolproof way of going about this. To some extent each book and each author is unique and the historian-detective must use any and all clues to penetrate below the surface. At a bare minimum the following questions should be asked of every book you read:

1. *Does the book reflect an identifiable political, national, religious, or ideological bias or point of view?* And if so, how might the author's bias or point

---

[3]The above discussion of thesis finding and skimming techniques is heavily indebted to Norman E. Cantor and Richard I. Schneider, *How to Study History* (New York: Thomas Y. Crowell, 1967), especially Chapter Five.

of view have influenced his or her choice of subject matter or conclusions? In many cases, for example, books on the religious upheavals of the Reformation era (the sixteenth century) written by Catholics treat the subject differently than those written by Protestants. Similarly, British accounts of the American Revolution often differ quite markedly from American accounts. Such a list could be lengthened almost without end.

2. *How does the author approach his or her subject?* Put another way, which of the varieties of history does the book represent? Earlier it was noted that most authors choose to emphasize some aspects of past experience more than others. A writer may concentrate on economic relationships (economic history), political issues (political-institutional history), the single individual (biography), the role of social groups (social history), the evolution of ideas (intellectual history), war (military history), diplomacy (diplomatic history), or any number of other facets of past life. In any event, the *approach* an author chooses in writing history reflects a conscious decision on his part. He *chose* to examine his subject from, say, an economic as opposed to a political perspective. You should always be conscious of this, and whenever you read a history book you should note the author's approach to the subject in question.

3. *How does the author organize the book?* The author also decided which mode of presentation would be most conducive to the clear communication of his material. Essentially there are two basic types of organization: *topical (i.e., analytical)* and *chronological.* In most cases the two forms are combined by alternating the narration of events in chronological order with periodic analyses of specific issues, problems, or topics. Taken as a whole, though, most books will conform to one organizational scheme. A look at the table of contents may help you determine whether a book is organized topically or chronologically. Usually, however, you have to dip into the work itself to get a firm sense of how the author has organized the material.

4. *What are the author's sources and how well are they used?* Here you are concerned with the author's research apparatus. Are there extensive footnotes? Few? None? Is the bibliography large? Small? Missing altogether? This sort of information can give you a clue as to the seriousness and perhaps the credibility of the book, although it would be a mistake to automatically equate extensive sources with quality. Also, a lack of such research apparatus does not necessarily mean that the book is worthless. It could have been the author's intention to write an introductory study intended for a nonprofessional audience.

You should also note what *type* of sources the author used. Are the sources appropriate to the subject matter? For instance, a history of American slavery using only material written by southern plantation owners would be highly suspect; likewise a history of the labor movement based only on the observations of the factory owners. Further, did the author use extensive primary sources, or was the book written on the basis of secondary literature? The answer to this question can help you discover whether the author was attempting to break new ground by examining primary sources or attempting to synthesize the research findings of a number of other historians.

5. *Who is the author?* To answer all the above questions it helps to know something about the author and his or her previous work. Is the author a scholar? Journalist? Politician? What is the author's political persuasion? Religion? Nationality? Is he or she a historian? Political scientist? Sociologist? Psychologist?

What kind of reputation does the author have in academic circles? Many times such information (or some of it) can be found on jacket covers or in a brief biographical sketch in the book itself. The reference librarian will also be able to guide you to pertinent biographical dictionaries.

6. *When was the book first published?* This piece of information can provide many clues to the quality and orientation of a book. A history of World War II, written in 1946, could be both less objective and less substantive than one written in 1970, although not necessarily. The 1970 author, though, would certainly have had access to far more evidence than the 1946 author.

A NOTE ON BOOK REVIEWS

The book review is one of the most common, and most commonly misunderstood, assignments in college. All too often students simply summarize the contents of a book. But from what we have said above it should be clear that a good book review should provide *critical commentary* on the author's thesis and major arguments, the organization and style of the book, the scholarly apparatus, and the author's values and assumptions. A good book review does, of course, indicate briefly what a book covers (the contents). But a good review should pay far more attention to *evaluating* the strengths and weaknesses of the book. The book review should ultimately answer the question: "Is this a good book that would be worth reading?"

The following checklist can serve as a guide for writing an intelligent critical book review. A good book review should answer the following questions:

1. What material does the book cover? (Should be noted in summary fashion.)
2. What is the author's thesis? How well does the author support his or her major conclusions?
3. How is the book organized? (Topical or chronological.)
4. How does the author approach the subject? That is, would you classify the work as political history? Economic history? Social history?
5. Who is the author? What are his or her underlying values and assumptions?
6. What are the literary qualities? Was the book well-written or did it read like a badly written insurance policy?
7. What did the book add to *your* understanding of the subject? Did you enjoy the book? Why or why not?
8. Finally, if you have read other books on the same general topic, how does this book compare? Most importantly, how does one interpretation (thesis) differ from the others?

The above questions need not be answered in any specific order, but all of them should be dealt with somewhere in the review. Further, a book review, like any piece of writing, should observe the basic requirements of literary discourse. There should be an introduction, followed by an extended discussion and conclusion; and the need for clarity and grammatical precision should be kept firmly in mind.

EXERCISES

**SET A
Exercise 1**
Above, a distinction was made between the *topic* of a book (what subject the book discusses) and the *thesis* of a book (the major argument or interpretation used by the author to tie together the events he or she discusses in a unified explanatory framework). In the thesis the author will usually identify those forces, individuals, and relationships that he or she considers most useful for explaining the events under consideration.

Below are a number of brief abstracts[4] of some recently published books in European history. These abstracts were written by the authors themselves or by editors and attempt to give a thumbnail description of the books. Some of the abstracts emphasize the material the book covers (the topic); others talk more about the author's interpretation of that material (the thesis); still others discuss both topic and thesis.

Identify those abstracts that primarily just summarize the contents of the book by placing a "C" in the appropriate space. Identify those that emphasize the author's interpretation, or thesis, by writing a "T." Note those passages that do both by recording a "CT." For those passages that you have marked "T" or "CT," underline the sentence (or sentences) that best represents the author's central thesis.

_____ **1.** *War in European History.* By Michael Howard. London, Oxford, and New York: Oxford University Press, 1976.

> This is a study of warfare as it has developed in Western Europe from the Dark Ages until the present day. In it I show not only how the techniques of warfare changed, but how they affected or were affected by social, economic, and technological developments in the societies that employed them. I trace the growth and decay of the feudal organization of Western Europe for war; the rise of mercenary troops and their development into professions as the framework of the state became strong enough to keep them permanently employed; the connection between war and the development of European trade overseas; and the impact of the French Revolution on the military system of the *ancien régime.* I go on to show how the development of industrial technology and the social tensions within industrial states culminated in the two world wars, and end by summarizing the military situation of a continent kept at peace by a balance of nuclear terror.

_____ **2.** *John Stuart Mill and Representative Government.* By Dennis F. Thompson. Princeton, N.J.: Princeton University Press, 1976.

> This book is the first major study of John Stuart Mill's *Considerations on Representative Government,* a work that Mill regarded as a mature statement of his theory of democracy. I analyze the structure of that theory, drawing on the whole corpus of the writings of Mill and his contemporaries. Contrary to most interpreters, I argue that Mill strikes a balance between participatory and elitist visions of democracy and that his theory is more coherent and systematic than has generally been assumed. At the same time, this study appraises Mill's arguments from the perspective of

[4]*The Journal of Modern History,* Vol. 49, Nos. 1 and 2 (March 1977, June 1977).

recent work in social science and democratic theory. The book has extensive footnotes and a twenty-five-page bibliography.

_____ **3.** *Colonial Self-Government: The British Experience, 1759–1856*. By John Manning Ward. Toronto: University of Toronto Press, 1976.

I offer a double reinterpretation of self-government in the British colonies, 1759–1856. (1) British ministers were usually willing, if imperial supremacy were maintained, that colonies should have a form of government resembling that in Britain, but the degree of resemblance permitted varied partly with the extent to which a colony was expected to reproduce English polity. Different forms of self-government were established at the same time. The possibilities varied further with changes in the constitution, politics, and attitudes of Britain to overseas colonies of settlement. (2) Imperial historians have misunderstood the British constitution, anachronistically assuming that "responsible" government (government by parliamentary ministers depending for office on the confidence of the Commons, not the sovereign) must have existed when Durham wrote his famous report. Colonial developments slightly affected British constitutional growth. The book treats principally Britain, Canada, Australia, and the West Indies, referring also to South Africa and New Zealand.

_____ **4.** *Britain's Imperial Century, 1815–1914: A Study of Empire and Expansion*. By Ronald Hyam. New York: Harper & Row; Barnes & Noble Import Division, 1976.

This study integrates the formal British empire and areas of informal influence such as China, Japan, and Latin America. The Victorian drives toward expansion—economic, strategic, diplomatic, and cultural—are considered, with Palmerston cast in a key role. Part 1 establishes an overall chronological framework for the whole century of cosmoplastic activity and analyzes the way the empire was run. Part 2 consists of seven regional chapters. Territorial acquisition is regarded as the result of an interlocking between two different levels of motive: a metropolitan level, concerned with high politics and prestige, and a local one, more concerned with selfish interests. At both levels the export of surplus sexual energy (often sublimated) is seen to be more important than the export of surplus capital; the private lives of empire builders are investigated. Other topics explored include relations with the United States, Asian and African resistance, sport, freemasonry, and the racial attitudes and educational theories of the British political elite. The book is based on close references to monographic material old and new, and for the period 1880–1914 (seen as "the search for stability") draws also on my own research.

_____ **5.** *Adolf Hitler*. By John Toland. Garden City, N.Y.: Doubleday & Co., 1976.

In an attempt to uncover the Hitler that lies behind the polemic cartoon-monster portrayals and present a realistic full-length biography, I conducted more than 250 interviews with those who knew Hitler intimately—with his inner circle, his doctors, his favorite architects, his military leaders, and the women he most admired.

Significant new documents, reports, and studies have also been utilized to unravel the mystery of Hitler: the dossiers of the U.S. Army Intelligence Command, including one agent's interview with the Fuhrer's sister Paula; documents in the National Archives such as a secret psychiatric report on Hitler in 1918; and unpublished diaries, notes, and memoirs including the revealing recollections of Hitler's youngest secretary. My book (the result of five and one-half years' work) has no thesis, and any conclusions to be found in it were reached only during the writing, perhaps the most meaningful being that Hitler was far more complex and contradictory than I had imagined.

_____ **6.** *The Origins of the Marshall Plan.* By John Gimbel. Stanford, Calif.: Stanford University Press, 1976.

Based on American and German primary sources, this study argues that the Marshall Plan is traceable to certain decisions on German recovery that George C. Marshall and Ernest Bevin made in April 1947, during the Moscow Council of Foreign Ministers. The larger European recovery program, called forth by Marshall on June 5, 1947, was an effort to gain political acceptance for those decisions in Europe and America. Current theories about the open door, multilateralism, and containment of Russia notwithstanding, the Marshall Plan was a series of pragmatic political and bureaucratic compromises to solve the economic problems of the German occupation. In the end, Americans provided economic aid—either directly or through Germany—to many of the nations that had expected to use German reparations and cheap German exports for their postwar recovery programs. As after the First World War, the United States helped Germany to settle its reparations obligations.

_____ **7.** *The Face of Battle.* By John Keegan. New York: Viking Press, 1976.

This book, an essay in military historiography, falls into three parts: a critique of conventional military historiography; an attempt to rewrite the history of three battles, Agincourt, Waterloo, and the Somme, in the light of that critique; and an effort to define the nature of battle and its present and future value. Briefly, I argue that traditional military historians have consistently underestimated the importance of the individual on battlefields and attempt to analyze his "motivation to combat." I perceive a growing divergence between social and battlefield experience over the last 500 years and believe that the divergence has become so great that future battlefields will prove uninhabitable.

**SET A
Exercise 2**

Often students pass over the preface or introduction to a book in order to get to the "meat." This is a mistake. Often the preface and/or introduction contain vital information that can make the mastery of the rest of the book far easier. The author will often state his or her purpose, thesis, point of view, and the like. There also might be clues to the author's value system. Even a brief preface can be a gold mine of information.

Read the preface below and in the spaces provided list what you see to be the important pieces of information contained therein. Be sure to note not only what the author claims the book will cover, but what he says it won't cover.

Bernard Porter, *The Lion's Share: A Short History of British Imperialism, 1850–1970* (New York: Longman, 1975), pp. x–xi. Reprinted by permission.

This book was written in order to fulfil a need, which was for a general descriptive and explanatory history of British colonialism since the middle of the nineteenth century. It differs from histories of the British *empire*, of which there are several, in concentrating on the processes and manifestations of real British power, influence and responsibility in the world; which disqualifies certain countries, like Canada and Australia, which figure large in histories of the empire but which almost never in our period were effectively ruled from Britain; and qualifies some other areas, notably the middle east and China, which were not colonies but were more affected by 'colonialism' than many countries that were. It also differs from histories of the British empire in being more Anglocentric in its perspective: not concerned at all with what happened in different parts of the empire unless and until it affected the policies and activities of Britain or Britons, and then only in so far as it affected them. The aim of the book is to explain Britain's relationship with the world outside Europe in the mid-nineteenth century, why she chose in the late nineteenth century in some areas to convert that relationship into a formal colonial one, how she and her agents ruled their empire all the way through, and how and why she gave it up.

Of course there are omissions, and biases. Some of the omissions are arbitrary—such as that of Ireland, which in many ways was treated and reacted like a colony, and has only been omitted on the (inadequate and inconsistent) ground that it was not called one. Others may be justified on the grounds that not everything can be included, but only those things relevant to the main concerns and main themes of the book: though even this blanket excuse will not cover all the gaps, some of which may be indefensible even by my own criteria. The subject as I have defined it is a broad and amorphous one, which renders any rules of selection highly fallible. It is also a subject bristling with controversies and—in many of the books which touch on it already—laden with biases. This book tries as far as possible to avoid bias, mainly by short-circuiting most of the controversies. The small controversies can be short-circuited usually because they do not really affect the broad issues. The big controversies are more difficult to avoid, and especially the biggest current one, which is about whether or not imperialism was an inevitable stage of capitalism. What I have tried to do on the latter issue is, at different points in the narrative, to describe and discuss some of the possible connexions between 'imperialism' and 'capitalism'. I believe that this discussion is constructive, but inconclusive on the main issue: which is for philosophers to pronounce on, and not historians, because it rests on general interpretations of causation and human motivation. This sounds agnostic: which on the whole the book is. It is agnostic especially so far as broad value-judgments are concerned, which on the phenomenon of 'imperialism' I believe to be as pointless as value-judgments on the industrial revolution, because it was just as little a matter of real choice. On smaller issues value-judgments abound in this book. But I believe them to be easily detectable, consequently easy to discount if required, and not affecting the main themes.

There are broad themes in the book. One is that 'imperialism', as the word is generally understood, was for Britain (it may not have been for other countries) a symptom and an effect of her decline in the world, and not of strength. Another theme is to do with the part the empire played in obscuring but at the same time aggravating a deep-seated malaise in the British national economy which set in around 1870. A third theme is that the empire was 'controlled' very much less by Britain than it controlled her; that all along she could only hold on to it by compromising her freedom of action considerably, and in the end could not even do that. My general impression of the empire over its last 100 years is that it was moulded far more by events than it moulded events: which perhaps diminishes its significance a little, but not its interest.

Important points from Preface:

1.
2.
3.
4.
5.

SET A
Exercise 3

It is vital for you to be able to translate the ideas of others (whether those of a lecturer or author) into your own words. This skill will help you take effective notes in class or useful review notes for books you have read. Effective summarizing techniques will also save you a good deal of time. If you can reduce lecture or written material into a brief summary you will avoid tedious verbatim copying. You will also (and this is important) be forced to think actively about what you have heard or read. If you find that you are unable to summarize something in your own words it may indicate that you did not fully understand it in the first place. All things considered, effective summarizing (note taking) skills are among the most useful a student can possess.

Now that you have read the preface in Exercise 2, summarize the major points in your own words. You may read the passage again, but try to write your summary without referring directly to the preface. That way you will be forced to put Porter's statements into your own words. Use no more than four or five sentences for your summary. You might wish to review the abstracts in Exercise 1 to get an idea of how some authors have summarized their own books.

Summary:

**SET A
Exercise 4:
Analysis of
Article**

Although most of our discussion on how to read secondary literature was focused on the reading of books, in this exercise you will be asked to analyze a brief *article* using the criteria described on pages 162–166. Remember, however, that books differ from articles only in length and depth of detail but not in their basic nature. Therefore, the same analytical principles can be applied to both.

For the articles reprinted at the end of the chapter you will be asked to describe in a few short sentences: (1) the topic, (2) the central thesis and major subpoints, (3) the dominant organizational scheme, (4) the author's approach or point of view, and (5) the nature and quality of the sources used. You will also be asked to respond to a number of specific short-answer questions.

Read Richard Etulain's article "Origins of the Western" (pages 175–179) and complete the questions below.

In the boxes provided supply the relevant information. You may refer back to the article as many times as necessary.

---

1. Topic of the article (i.e., subject matter):

---

2. Central thesis:

Indicate paragraph number(s) where the thesis is most clearly summarized.

---

3. Major subpoints (arguments/points supporting thesis):

Example: "About 1900 there was new interest in the historical novels."

_____

_____

_____

_____

_____

_____

_____

_____

_____

_____

4. Predominant mode of organization (topical/analytical of chronological/narrative):

5. Author's "approach" to the subject (i.e., emphasis in political history, intellectual history, cultural history, economic history, etc.):

Explain your choice:

6. Use of sources (discuss both type of sources used [primary vs. secondary] and the thoroughness of the documentation):

Without looking back at the article answer the following questions. These are items you should have taken mental note of as you read the article.

7.   What does the author do for a living?_____

_____

8.   Where does this author tend to place the topic sentence of each paragraph (i.e., the sentence that summarizes the major point of the paragraph)? For longer works, this information allows you to skim sections quickly and efficiently.

_____

9. Is there a bibliography? _____

Now check the article and see if you were right. Put the correct answer next to your first answer if a change is necessary.

10. Of all the reasons Professor Etulain cites for the emergence of the western novel, which does *he* consider most important? You may refer back to the article.

_____

_____

11. Did you detect bias in the article? If yes, explain.

_____

_____

_____

Richard Etulain, ORIGINS OF THE WESTERN*

¶ 1   In the first quarter of the present century, a new American literary type—the Western—arose. Because until recently historians and literary critics have paid scant attention to popular literature, the Western has received little notice. Those who have chosen to discuss this popular genre have usually dismissed it as literary trash or as a species of sub-literature.[2] This being the case, no one has undertaken a study of the origins of the Western. This paper is a very brief and tentative treatment of the rise of the Western and why it arose when it did.

¶ 2   Some students of popular culture contend that the roots of the Western can be traced back to Homer and other writers of the epic. Others suggest that it owes most of its ingredients to medieval romances and morality plays. And still others argue that Sir Walter Scott, Robert Louis Stevenson, and other writers of historical adventure influenced the shape and content of the Western more than any other source. Each of these arguments has its validity, but the major reasons for the rise of the Western are found in more recent trends in American cultural history. More than anything else the genre owes its appearance to the combined influence of a number of occurrences in the years surrounding 1900. Each of these events or cultural changes may have been largely independent of the rest, but all shared in giving rise to an indigenous literary type.[3]

¶ 3   The appearance of a new hero in American literature—the cowboy— offered distinctive experiences for the author of the Western to portray. As Warren French and Mody Boatright have pointed out, the cowboy appeared earlier in a few dime novels but nearly always as a minor figure

*From Richard Etulain, "Origins of the Western," *Journal of Popular Culture*, Vol. V, No. 4 (Spring, 1972), pp. 799–805. Reprinted by permission of the editor. (Professor Etulain is on the history faculty of Idaho State University, Pocatello.)

and frequently in an ungallant role. By 1890, however, the cowboy was beginning to move to the forefront as a western fictional hero. Commencing with the writings of Owen Wister, he received a new emphasis. This newly refurbished hero aided greatly the rise of the Western.[4]

¶ 4 Also, about 1900 there was a revival of interest in the historical novel—one of three such periods in American literary history. Americans turned to historical fiction as one possible formula for recapturing a past that they were reluctant to lose. Because the Western was to be historical or pseudo-historical, it benefited from the revival of interest in the historical novel.[5]

¶ 5 Moreover, there was an increased interest in the West during the last two decades of the nineteenth century. A series of critical economic problems brought to mind a sobering truth: the West was filling up; its wide open spaces would soon be gone. Tourists flocked west, and a number published their reactions to the region in such influential eastern magazines as *Outlook, Harper's, Scribner's,* and *Atlantic.* These same periodicals took more western fiction in the 1880's, and the western pieces became so popular by the middle 1890's that Henry Alden, an editor of *Harper's Monthly,* did his best to keep all of Owen Wister's work in his magazine. Several editors wanted Wister's fiction and only higher prices kept him in the *Harper's* fold.[6]

¶ 6 The era from 1890 to 1910 has frequently been termed "the strenuous age." The fiction of Jack London, Harold Bell Wright, Stewart Edward White, Rex Beach, and other writings of the rough, virile, and out-of-doors type speak for the age. It was the period of the Spanish American War generation, of Teddy Roosevelt, of militant Anglo-Saxonism. This spirit is found in the Western, particularly in its portrayal of the gallant hero who is always eager to combat any foe, regardless of the odds.

¶ 7 By the early 1890's interest in the dime novel was diminishing. Shortly after its inception during the Civil War, this popular type has turned to the West for several of its heroes—Buffalo Bill, Deadeye Dick, Old Scout, and other frontier worthies. As the dime novel began to disappear, the popularity of its hero fell rapidly. Readers undoubtedly were dissatisfied with a continuous line of heroes who fought off twenty Indians and rescued the heroine, even with one arm badly wounded. They wanted a gallant and strong protagonist but one that was, nonetheless, believable. Eventually, the hero of the Western satisfied both of these desires.[7]

¶ 8 The Western also continued an American melodramatic tradition that had appeared earlier in such sources as the writings of James Fenimore Cooper, the dime novel, and the works of the sentimental novelists. In the post-Civil War period western literature became a recognizable current in the stream of melodrama. The work of Bret Harte, the dime novelists, and the story paper writers firmly established the melodramatic tradition in the literature of the West. As one study of the western periodical literature of the late nineteenth century points out, western writers increasingly utilized vague western settings and general descriptions. And a nostalgic tone crept into western literature. It was as if those who had lived through the previous years were, by 1890 and afterward, looking back and trying to recapture some of their past glory.[8]

¶ 9   Finally, the most important reason for the rise of the Western is the most difficult to describe with precision. This factor is what historian Carl Becker calls the "climate of opinion" of an era. In this case, it is the predominant mentality of the progressive period in American history.

¶ 10   Several interpreters have described the Progressive Era as a watershed period in the American mind. From the 1890's until World War I a new urban industrial thrust in American society challenged the older mentality of a rural, agricultural America. For Americans who became Progressives, or who shared the moods and feelings of the Progressives, this conflict between the old and the new was a traumatic experience that was not easily resolved.

¶ 11   Many Progressives were forward-looking. Like Theodore Roosevelt, they accepted the new urban-industrial force and advocated a federal government strong enough to deal with the powerful forces that the cities and industrial capitalists had unleashed. These New Nationalists, as they were called, were optimistic reformers and called for strong, new leadership to deal with recent problems.

¶ 12   Another strain of the progressive mind that owed much to Populism is evident in the early ideas of Woodrow Wilson. He too thought that the rise of an urban-industrial America necessitated changes in the forms of government and society. But Wilson and his followers thought the necessary reform was that of breaking up large corporations and of returning to a pre-industrial America, of recapturing Jefferson's agrarian dream. If these advocates of New Freedom allowed themselves to do so, they easily slipped into a nostalgic longing for pre-Rockefeller, Carnegie, and Vanderbilt days.

¶ 13   The same nostalgia that was apparent among proponents of New Freedom was also evident among followers of New Nationalism. In several ways Roosevelt stands as a Janus figure: the venturesome technocrat and yet the advocate of individualism, the product of an eastern-Harvard gentility and yet the westerner and Rough Rider. Other Americans of the era shared Roosevelt's feelings: the desire to hold on to the fruits of industrialism without losing, at the same time, individual freedom. For these persons, the American West was the last frontier of freedom and individualism, and it had to be preserved as a sacred bulwark against profane industrialism.

¶ 14   And thus the West as a physical and spiritual frontier was an important symbol for Americans during the Progressive Era. To lose it or the idyllic existence that it represented was to lose part of their past and to bargain away their future. It is not difficult to perceive how this psychological necessity encouraged authors to devote more attention to the West in their writings. The need and mood were apparent, and writers who were a part of this identity crisis—or at lease sensed it—could assure themselves a larger audience if they portrayed the West romantically. So the conflict between industrial and agricultural America and the resultant nostalgia for the past were large encouragements for the rise of the Western.[9]

¶ 15   These trends were John the Baptists in preparing the way for the Western. Such writers as Owen Wister, Zane Grey, and Frederick Faust (Max Brand), sometimes working within the limits of these trends and sometimes pressured into new directions by them, did much to establish the dimensions of the Western. Wister, for example, utilized the new cowboy hero and the Wyoming past and blended them with the necessary ingredients of adventure fiction—love, action, and good versus evil—to produce the first Western in *The Virginian* (1902). He was, in short, the synthesizer of the elements that make up the Western. Following the pattern that Wister introduced, Grey and Brand, though men of lesser writing talents, turned out dozens of Westerns by the end of the 1920's. The roots of the Western, then, were nourished by cultural and intellectual currents that rippled through American experience between the end of the nineteenth century and the Depression.

¶ 16 Roderick Nash, who examines this era's need for wilderness symbols, expresses as well as anyone the cultural-intellectual matrix that helped spawn the Western. He says:

> America was ripe for the widespread appeal of the uncivilized. The cult had several facets. In the first place, there was a growing tendency to associate wilderness with America's frontier and pioneer past that was believed responsible for many unique and desirable national characteristics. Wilderness also acquired importance as a source of virility, toughness, and savagery—qualities that defined fitness in Darwinian terms. Finally, an increasing number of Americans invested wild places with aesthetic and ethical values, emphasizing the opportunity they afforded for contemplation and worship.[10]

What Nash points out—and this is a point that students of American popular culture must keep in mind—is that the origins of a new popular idea or genre are usually tied to specific occurrences in the mind and experience of the era that produces them. So it was with the beginnings of the Western.

NOTES

1. This essay is a portion of a paper presented at the meeting of the Popular Culture Association, East Lansing, Michigan, April 1971. I use the term *Western* in a narrower sense than most do who invoke the term. By a *Western*, I mean a novel about the West that follows a recognizable formula—most often that of action, romance, and stock characters. Thus, most of the novels of Zane Grey, Max Brand, Ernest Haycox, and Luke Short are Westerns; but the works of western writers like Willa Cather, John Steinbeck, and Walter Van Tilburg Clark are not.

2. For an example of this negative attitude: "It has been the fate of the American West to beget stereotypes that belong to pseudo art before it has yielded up the individual types that belong to art proper." Robert B. Heilman, "The Western Theme: Exploiters and Explorers," *Partisan Review*, XXVIII (March-April 1969), 286.

3. Four books have been especially helpful for the remarks in this paragraph and the paragraphs that follow: Henry Nash Smith, *Virgin Land: The American West as Symbol and Myth* (New York: Vintage Books, 1957), 88–137; E. Douglas Branch, *The Cowboy and His Interpreters* (New York: Cooper Square Publishers, 1960), 180–270; Joe B. Frantz and Julian E. Choate, *The American Cowboy: Myth and Reality* (London: Thames and Hudson, 1956), 140–79; and G. Edward White, *The Eastern Establishment and the Western Experience: The West of Frederic Remington, Theodore Roosevelt, and Owen Wister* (New Haven: Yale University Press, 1968), especially pp. 31–51. Since this essay was first written, Russel B. Nye's superb *The Unembarrassed Muse: The Popular Arts in America* (New York: Dial

Press, 1970) has appeared. The section in his book dealing with the rise of the Western agrees with several of my contentions and adds other helpful information on the nineteenth-century backgrounds of the Western. See pp. 280–304.

4. Warren French, "The Cowboy in the Dime Novel," *Texas Studies in English*, XXX (1951), 219–34; Mody C. Boatright, "The Beginning of Cowboy Fiction," *Southwest Review*, LI (Winter 1966), 11–28.

5. Willard Thorp, *American Writing in the Twentieth Century* (Cambridge: Harvard University Press, 1960), 1–11; Ernest E. Leisy, *The American Historical Novel* (Norman: University of Oklahoma Press, 1950), 9–17.

6. Earl Pomeroy, *In Search of the Golden West: The Tourist in Western America* (New York: Alfred A. Knopf, 1957), 73–111; L. J. Shaul, "Treatment of the West in Selected Magazine Fiction, 1870–1910—An Annotated Bibliography." Unpublished master's thesis, University of Wyoming, 1954, pp. 50–2. The Alden-Wister relationship and other details about readers' interest in western fiction published during the 1890's is exhibited in the Owen Wister Papers, Library of Congress.

7. Wallace Stegner, "Western Record and Romance," *Literary History of the United States*, ed. Robert Spiller and others (New York: The Macmillan Company, 1960), 862–4, 872. For the influences of Buffalo Bill and his Wild West shows, see Don Russell, *The Lives and Legends of Buffalo Bill* (Norman: University of Oklahoma Press, 1960); and Joseph Schwartz, "The Wild West Show: 'Everything Genuine,'" *Journal of Popular Culture*, III (Spring 1970), 656–66.

8. Smith, *Virgin Land*, 88–137; Mary Noel, *Villains Galore* (New York: The Macmillan Company, 1954), 131–2, 149–59; Shaul, "Treatment of the West," 51–2.

9. The previous paragraphs are a product of several sources. The split between past and present that plagued many Progressives is abundantly documented in important books on this era by such writers as Richard Hofstadter, George Mowry, and Arthur Link. I am also indebted to W. H. Hutchinson for suggesting to me several years ago the close relationship between the rise of the Western and the traumas of the progressive period. More recently, this relationship is dealt with in White's *The Eastern Establishment and the Western Experience*; and in David Noble's several books on the Progressives, particularly in his latest book, *The Progressive Mind, 1890–1917* (Chicago: Rand McNally, 1970); Peter Schmitt adds another dimension in his stimulating monograph *Back to Nature: The Arcadian Myth in Urban America* (New York: Oxford University Press, 1969). Finally, Roderick Nash and John William Ward suggest that the clash between past and present was a pivotal tension in the twenties. See Nash's *The Nervous Generation: American Thought, 1917–1930* (Chicago: Rand McNally, 1970); and Ward's "The Meaning of Lindbergh's Flight," *American Quarterly*, X (Spring 1958), 3–16.

10. Roderick Nash, *Wilderness and the American Mind* (New Haven: Yale University Press, 1967), p. 145.

**SET B
Analysis of
Article
(Optional)**

Read Edmund S. Morgan's article, "The Puritans and Sex," (pages 183–193) and complete the questions below:

In the boxes provided below supply the relevant information. You may refer back to the article as many times as necessary.

1.

Topic of the article (i.e., subject matter):

2. **Central thesis:**

Indicate paragraph number(s) where the thesis is most clearly summarized.

3. **Major subpoints (arguments/points supporting thesis):**

_____

_____

_____

_____

_____

_____

_____

_____

_____

_____

_____

_____

_____

_____

4. **Predominant mode of organization (topical/analytical or chronological/narrative):**

5. Author's "approach" to the subject (i.e., emphasis in political history, intellectual history, cultural history, economic history, etc.):

Explain your choice:

6. Use of sources (discuss both the type of sources used [primary vs. secondary] and the thoroughness of the documentation):

7. Which article—Etulain's or Morgan's—is better history? Why?

8. Option: Write a brief (200–300 word) review of the Morgan article. Write as if your review were to be published in the book-review section of your local newspaper and read by a group of educated but non-specialist readers. You may wish to reread the book-review notes on page 166.

Edmund S. Morgan, THE PURITANS AND SEX*

¶ 1 Henry Adams once observed that Americans have "ostentatiously ignored" sex. He could think of only two American writers who touched upon the subject with any degree of boldness—Walt Whitman and Bret Harte. Since the time when Adams made this penetrating observation, American writers have been making up for lost time in a way that would make Bret Harte, if not Whitman, blush. And yet there is still more truth than falsehood in Adams's statement. Americans, by comparison with Europeans or Asiatics, are squeamish when confronted with the facts of life. My purpose is not to account for this squeamishness, but simply to point out that the Puritans, those bogeymen of the modern intellectual, are not responsible for it.

¶ 2 At the outset, consider the Puritan's attitude toward marriage and the role of sex in marriage. The popular assumption might be that the Puritans frowned on marriage and tried to hush up the physical aspect of it as much as possible, but listen to what they themselves had to say. Samuel Willard, minister of the Old South Church in the latter part of the seventeenth century and author of the most complete textbook of Puritan divinity, more than once expressed his horror at "that Popish conceit of the Excellency of Virginity."[1] Another minister, John Cotton, wrote that

> Women are Creatures without which there is no comfortable Living for man: it is true of them what is wont to be said of Governments, *That bad ones are better than none:* They are a sort of Blasphemers then who dispise and decry them, and call them a *necessary Evil,* for they are a *necessary Good.*[2]

These sentiments did not arise from an interpretation of marriage as a spiritual partnership, in which sexual intercourse was a minor or incidental matter. Cotton gave his opinion of "Platonic love" when he recalled the case of

> one who immediately upon marriage, without ever approaching the *Nuptial Bed,* indented with the *Bride,* that by mutual consent they might both live such a life, and according did sequestring themselves according to the custom of those times, from the rest of mankind, and afterwards from one another too, in their retired Cells, giving themselves up to a Contemplative life; and this is recorded as an instance of no little or ordinary Vertue; but I must be pardoned in it, if I can account it no other than an effort of blind zeal, for they are the dictates of a blind mind they follow therein, and not of that Holy Spirit, which saith *It is not good that man should be alone.*[3]

¶ 3 Here is as healthy an attitude as one could hope to find anywhere. Cotton certainly cannot be accused of ignoring human nature. Nor was he an isolated example among the Puritans. Another minister stated plainly that "the Use of the Marriage Bed" is "founded in mans Nature," and that

---

*From Edmund S. Morgan, "The Puritans and Sex," *The New England Quarterly,* Vol. XV, No. 4 (December 1942), pp. 591–607. Reprinted by permission.

consequently any withdrawal from sexual intercourse upon the part of husband or wife "Denies all relief in Wedlock vnto Human necessity: and sends it for supply vnto Beastiality when God gives not the gift of Continency."[4] In other words, sexual intercourse was a human necessity and marriage the only proper supply for it. These were the views of the New England clergy, the acknowledged leaders of the community, the most Puritanical of the Puritans. As proof that their congregations concurred with them, one may cite the case in which the members of the First Church of Boston expelled James Mattock because, among other offenses, "he denied Coniugall fellowship vnto his wife for the space of 2 years together vpon pretense of taking Revenge upon himself for his abusing of her before marryage."[5] So strongly did the Puritans insist upon the sexual character of marriage that one New Englander considered himself slandered when it was reported, "that he Brock his deceased wife's hart with Greife, that he wold be absent from her 3 weeks together when he was at home, and wold never come nere her, and such Like."[6]

¶ 4   There was just one limitation which the Puritans placed upon sexual relations in marriage; sex must not interfere with religion. Man's chief end was to glorify God, and all earthly delights must promote that end, not hinder it. Love for a wife was carried too far when it led a man to neglect his God:

> ...sometimes a man hath a good affection to Religion, but the love of his wife carries him away, a man may bee so transported to his wife, that hee dare not bee forward in Religion, lest hee displease his wife, and so the wife, lest shee displease her husband, and this is an inordinate love, when it exceeds measure.[7]

Sexual pleasures, in this respect, were treated like other kinds of pleasure. On a day of fast, when all comforts were supposed to be foregone in behalf of religious contemplation, not only were tasty food and drink to be abandoned but sexual intercourse, too. On other occasions, when food, drink, and recreation were allowable, sexual intercourse was allowable too, though of course only between persons who were married to each other. The Puritans were not ascetics; they never wished to prevent the enjoyment of earthly delights. They merely demanded that the pleasures of the flesh be subordinated to the greater glory of God: husband and wife must not become "so transported with affection, that they look at no higher end than marriage it self." "Let such as have wives," said the ministers, "look at them not for their own ends, but to be fitted for Gods service, and bring them nearer to God."[8]

¶ 5   Toward sexual intercourse outside marriage the Puritans were as frankly hostile as they were favorable to it in marriage. They passed laws to punish adultery with death, and fornication with whipping. Yet they had no misconceptions as to the capacity of human beings to obey such laws. Although the laws were commands of God, it was only natural—since the fall of Adam—for human beings to break them. Breaches must be punished lest the community suffer the wrath of God, but no offense, sexual or otherwise, could be occasion for surprise or for hushed tones of voice.

How calmly the inhabitants of seventeenth-century New England could Contemplate rape or attempted rape is evident in the following testimony offered before the Middlesex County Court of Massachusetts:

> The examination of Edward Wire taken the 7th of october and alsoe Zachery Johnson, who sayeth that Edward Wires mayd being sent into the towne about busenes meeting with a man that dogd hir from about Joseph Kettles house to goody marches. She came into William Johnsones and desired Zachery Johnson to goe home with her for that the man dogd hir. accordingly he went with her and being then as far as Samuell Phips his house the man over tooke them. which man caled himselfe by the name of peter grant would have led the mayd but she oposed itt three times: and coming to Edward Wires house the said grant would have kist hir but she refused itt: wire being at prayer grant dragd the mayd between the said wiers and Nathanill frothinghams house. hee then flung the mayd downe in the streete and got atop hir; Johnson seeing it hee caled vppon the fellow to be sivill and not abuse the mayd then Edward wire came forth and ran to the said grant and took hold of him asking him what he did to his mayd, the said grant asked whether she was his wife for he did nothing to his wife: the said grant swearing he would be the death of the said wire. when he came of the mayd; he swore he would bring ten men to pul down his house and soe ran away and they followed him as far as good[y] phipses house where they mett with John Terry and George Chin with clubs in there hands and soe they went away together. Zachy Johnson going to Constable Heamans, and wire going home. there came John Terry to his house to ask for beer and grant was in the streete but afterward departed into the towne, both Johnson and Wire both aferme that when grant was vppon the mayd she cryed out severall times.
>
> Deborah hadlocke being examined sayth that she mett with the man that cals himselfe peeter grant about good prichards that he dogd hir and followed hir to hir masters and there threw hir downe and lay vppon hir but had not the use of hir body but swore several othes that he would ly with hir and gett hir with child before she got home.
>
> Grant being present denys all saying he was drunk and did not know what he did.[9]

¶ 6 The Puritans became inured to sexual offenses, because there were so many. The impression which one gets from reading the records of seventeenth-century New England courts is that illicit sexual intercourse was fairly common. The testimony given in cases of fornication and adultery—by far the most numerous class of criminal cases in the records—suggests that many of the early New Englanders possessed a high degree of virility and very few inhibitions. Besides the case of Peter Grant, take the testimony of Elizabeth Knight about the manner of Richard Nevars's advances toward her:

> The last publique day of Thanksgiving (in the year 1674) in the evening as I was milking Richard Nevars came to me, and offered me abuse in putting his hand, under my coates, but I turning aside with much adoe,

saved my self, and when I was settled to milking he agen took me by the shoulder and pulled me backward almost, but I clapped one hand on the Ground and held fast the Cows teatt with the other hand, and cryed out, and then came to mee Jonathan Abbot one of my Masters Servants, whome the said Never asked wherefore he came, the said Abbot said to look after you, what you doe unto the Maid, but the said Never bid Abbot goe about his businesse but I bade the lad to stay.[10]

¶ 7 One reason for the abundance of sexual offenses was the number of men in the colonies who were unable to gratify their sexual desires in marriage.[11] Many of the first settlers had wives in England. They had come to the new world to make a fortune, expecting either to bring their families after them or to return to England with some of the riches of America. Although these men left their wives behind, they brought their sexual appetites with them; and in spite of laws which required them to return to their families, they continued to stay, and more continued to arrive, as indictments against them throughout the seventeenth century clearly indicate.

Servants formed another group of men, and of women too, who could not ordinarily find supply for human necessity within the bounds of marriage. Most servants lived in the homes of their masters and could not marry without their consent, a consent which was not likely to be given unless the prospective husband or wife also belonged to the master's household. This situation will be better understood if it is recalled that most servants at this time were engaged by contract for a stated period. They were, in the language of the time, "covenant servants," who had agreed to stay with their masters for a number of years in return for a specified recompense, such as transportation to New England or education in some trade (the latter, of course, were known more specifically as apprentices). Even hired servants who worked for wages were usually single, for as soon as a man had enough money to buy or build a house of his own and to get married, he would set up in farming or trade for himself. It must be emphasized, however, that anyone who was not in business for himself was necessarily a servant. The economic organization of seventeenth-century New England had no place for the independent proletarian workman with a family of his own. All production was carried on in the household by the master of the family and his servants, so that most men were either servants or masters of servants; and the former, of course, were more numerous than the latter. Probably most of the inhabitants of Puritan New England could remember a time when they had been servants.

¶ 8 Theoretically no servant had a right to a private life. His time, day or night, belonged to his master, and both religion and law required that he obey his master scrupulously.[12] But neither religion nor law could restrain the sexual impulses of youth, and if those impulses could not be expressed in marriage, they had to be given vent outside marriage. Servants had little difficulty in finding the occasions. Though they might be kept at work all day, it was easy enough to slip away at night. Once out of the house, there were several ways of meeting with a maid. The simplest way was to go to her bed-chamber, if she was so fortunate as to have a private one of her own. Thus Jock, Mr. Solomon Phipps's Negro man, confessed in court

> that on the sixteenth day of May 1682, in the morning, betweene 12 and one of the clock, he did force open the back doores of the House of Laurence Hammond in Charlestowne, and came in to the House, and went up into the garret to Marie the Negro.
>
> He doth likewise acknowledge that one night the last week he forced into the House the same way, and went up to the Negro Woman Marie and that the like he hath done at severall other times before.[13]

Joshua Fletcher took a more romantic way of visiting his lady:

> Joshua Fletcher...doth confesse and acknowledge that three severall nights after bedtime, he went into Mr Fiskes Dwelling house at Chelmsford, at an open window by a ladder that he brought with him. the said windo opening into a chamber, whose was the lodging place of Gresill Juell servant to mr. Fiske. and there he kept company with the said mayd. she sometimes having her cloathes on, and one time he found her in her bed.[14]

Sometimes a maidservant might entertain callers in the parlor while the family were sleeping upstairs. John Knight described what was perhaps a common experience for masters. The crying of his child awakened him in the middle of the night, and he called to his maid, one Sarah Crouch, who was supposed to be sleeping with the child. Receiving no answer, he arose and

> went down the stayres, and at the stair foot, the latch of doore was pulled in. I called severall times and at the last said if shee would not open the dore, I would breake it open, and when shee opened the doore shee was all undressed and Sarah Largin with her undressed, also the said Sarah went out of doores and Dropped some of her clothes as shee went out. I enquired of Sarah Crouch what men they were, which was with them. Shee made mee no answer for some space of time, but at last shee told me Peeter Brigs was with them, I asked her whether Thomas Jones was not there, but shee would give mee no answer.[15]

In the temperate climate of New England it was not always necessary to seek out a maid at her home. Rachel Smith was seduced in an open field "about nine of the clock at night, being darke, neither moone nor starrs shineing." She was walking through the field when she met a man who

> asked her where shee lived, and what her name was and shee told him, and then shee asked his name, and he told her Saijing that he was old Good-man Shepards man. Also shee saith he gave her strong liquors, and told her that it was not the first time he had been with maydes after his master was in bed.[16]

¶ 9 Sometimes, of course, it was not necessary for a servant to go outside his master's house in order to satisfy his sexual urges. Many cases of fornication are on record between servants living in the same house. Even where servants had no private bedroom, even where the whole family slept in a single room, it was not impossible to make love. In fact many love affairs must have had their consummation upon a bed in which other people were sleeping. Take for example the case of Sarah Lepingwell. When Sarah was brought into court for having an illegitimate child, she related that one night when her master's brother, Thomas Hawes, was visiting the family, she went to bed early. Later, after Hawes had gone to bed, he called to her to get him a pipe of tobacco. After refusing for some time,

> at the last I arose and did lite his pipe and cam and lay doune one my one bead and smoaked about half the pip and siting vp in my bead to guie him his pip my bead being a trundell bead at the sid of his bead he reached beyond the pip and Cauth me by the wrist and pulled me on the side of his bead but I biding him let me goe he bid me hold my peas the folks wold here me and if it be replyed come why did you not call out I Ansar I was posesed with fear of my master least my master should think I did it only to bring a scandall on his brothar and thinking thay wold all beare witnes agaynst me but the thing is true that he did then begete me with child at that tim and the Child is Thomas Hauses and noe mans but his.

In his defense Hawes offered the testimony of another man who was sleeping "on the same side of the bed," but the jury nevertheless accepted Sarah's story.[17]

¶ 10 The fact that Sarah was intimidated by her master's brother suggests that maidservants may have been subject to sexual abuse by their masters. The records show that sometimes masters did take advantage of their position to force unwanted attentions upon their female servants. The case of Elizabeth Dickerman is a good example. She complained to the Middlesex County Court,

> against her master John Harris senior for profiring abus to her by way of forsing her to be naught with him: ... he has tould her that if she tould her dame: what cariag he did show to her shee had as good be hanged and shee replyed then shee would run away and he sayd run the way is befor you: ... she says if she should liwe ther shee shall be in fear of her lif.[18]

The court accepted Elizabeth's complaint and ordered her master to be whipped twenty stripes.

¶ 11 So numerous did cases of fornication and adultery become in seventeenth-century New England that the problem of caring for the children of extramarital unions was a serious one. The Puritans solved it, but in such a way as to increase rather than decrease the temptation to sin. In 1668, the General Court of Massachusetts ordered:

> that where any man is legally convicted to be the Father of a Bastard childe, he shall be at the care and charge to maintain and bring up the same, by such assistance of the Mother as nature requireth, and as the Court from time to time (according to circumstances) shall see meet to Order: and in case the Father of a Bastard, by confession or other manifest proof, upon trial of the case, do not appear to the Courts satisfac-

tion, then the Man charged by the Woman to be the Father, shee holding constant in it, (especially being put upon the real discovery of the truth of it in the time of her Travail) shall be the reputed Father, and accordingly be liable to the charge of maintenance as aforesaid (though not to other punishment) notwithstanding his denial, unless the circumstances of the case and pleas be such, on the behalf of the man charged, as that the Court that have the cognizance thereon shall see reason to acquit him, and otherwise dispose of the Childe and education thereof.[19]

As a result of this law a girl could give way to temptation without the fear of having to care for an illegitimate child by herself. Furthermore, she could, by a little simple lying, spare her lover the expense of supporting the child. When Elizabeth Wells bore a child, less than a year after this statute was passed, she laid it to James Tufts, her master's son. Goodman Tufts affirmed that Andrew Robinson, servant to Goodman Dexter, was the real father, and he brought the following testimony as evidence:

> Wee Elizabeth Jefts aged 15 ears and Mary tufts aged 14 ears doe testy-fie that their being one at our hous sumtime the last winter who sayed that thear was a new law made concerning bastards that If aney man wear aqused with a bastard and the woman which had aqused him did stand vnto it in her labor that he should bee the reputed father of it and should mayntaine it Elizabeth Wells hearing of the sayd law she sayed vnto vs that If shee should bee with Child shee would bee sure to lay it vn to won who was rich enough abell to mayntayne it wheather it wear his or no and shee farder sayed Elizabeth Jefts would not you doe so likewise If it weare your case and I sayed no by no means for right must tacke place: and the sayd Elizabeth wells sayed If it wear my Caus I think I should doe so.[20]

A tragic unsigned letter that somehow found its way into the files of the Middlesex County Court gives more direct evidence of the practice which Elizabeth Wells professed:

> der loue i remember my loue to you hoping your welfar and i hop to imbras the but now i rit to you to let you nowe that i am a child by you and i wil ether kil it or lay it to an other and you shal have no blame at al for I haue had many children and none have none of them.... [i.e., none of their fathers is supporting any of them.][21]

¶ 12 In face of the wholesale violation of the sexual codes to which all these cases give testimony, the Puritans could not maintain the severe penalties which their laws provided. Although cases of adultery occurred every year, the death penalty is not known to have been applied more than three times. The usual punishment was a whipping or a fine, or both, and perhaps a branding, combined with a symbolical execution in the form of standing on the gallows for an hour with a rope about the neck. Fornication met with a lighter whipping or a lighter fine, while rape was treated in the same way as adultery. Though the Puritans established a code of laws which demanded perfection—which demanded, in other words, strict obedience to the will of God, they nevertheless knew that frail human beings could never live up to the code. When fornication, adultery, rape, or even buggery and sodomy appeared, they were not surprised, nor were they so severe with the offenders as their codes of law would lead one to believe. Sodomy, to be sure, they usually punished with death; but rape, adultery, and fornication they regarded as pardonable human weaknesses, all the more likely to appear in a religious community, where the normal course of sin was stopped by wholesome laws. Governor Bradford in recounting the details of an epidemic of sexual misdemeanors in Plymouth, wrote resignedly:

> it may be in this case as it is with waters when their streames are stopped or damned up, when they gett passage they flow with more violence, and make more noys and disturbance, then when they are suffered to rune quietly in their owne chanels. So wickednes being here more stopped by strict laws, and the same more nerly looked unto, so as it cannot rune in a comone road of liberty as it would, and is inclined, it searches every wher, and at last breaks out wher it getts vente.[22]

¶ 13 The estimate of human capacities here expressed led the Puritans not only to deal leniently with sexual offenses but also to take every precaution to prevent such offenses, rather than wait for the necessity of punishment. One precaution was to see that children got married as soon as possible. The wrong way to promote virtue, the Puritans thought, was to "ensnare" children in vows of virginity, as the Catholics did. As a result of such vows, children, "not being able to contain," would be guilty of "unnatural pollutions, and other filthy practices in secret: and too oft of horrid Murthers of the fruit of their bodies," said Thomas Cobbett.[23] The way to avoid fornication and perversion was for parents to provide suitable husbands and wives for their children:

> Lot was to blame that looked not out seasonably for some fit matches for his two daughters, which had formerly minded marriage (witness the contract between them and two men in *Sodom*, called therfore for his Sons in Law, which had married his daughters, Gen. 19. 14.) for they seeing no man like to come into them in a conjugall way...then they plotted that incestuous course, whereby their Father was so highly dishonoured....[24]

¶ 14 As marriage was the way to prevent fornication, successful marriage was the way to prevent adultery. The Puritans did not wait for adultery to appear; instead, they took every means possible to make husbands and wives live together and respect each other. If a husband deserted his wife and remained within the jurisdiction of a Puritan government, he was promptly sent back to her. Where the wife had been left in England, the offense did not always come to light until the wayward husband had committed fornication or bigamy, and of course there must have been many offenses which never came to light. But where both husband and wife lived in New England, neither had much chance of leaving the other without being returned by order of the county court at its next sitting. When John Smith of Medfield left his wife and went to live with Patience Rawlins, he was sent home poorer by ten pounds and richer by thirty stripes. Similarly Mary Drury, who deserted her husband on the pretense that he was impotent, failed to convince the court that he actually was so, and had to return to him as well as to pay a fine of five pounds. The wife of Phillip Pointing received lighter treatment: when the court thought that she had overstayed her leave in Boston, they simply ordered her "to depart the Towne and goe to Tanton to her husband." The courts, moreover, were not satisfied with mere cohabitation; they insisted that it be peaceful cohabitation. Husbands and wives were forbidden by law to strike one another, and the law was enforced on numerous occasions. But the courts did not stop there. Henry Flood was required to give bond for good behavior because he had abused his wife simply by "ill words calling her whore and cursing of her." The wife of Christopher Collins was presented for railing at her husband and calling him "Gurley gutted divill." Apparently in this case the court thought that Mistress Collins was right, for although the fact was proved by two witnesses, she was discharged. On another occasion the court favored the husband: Jacob Pudeator, fined for striking and kicking his wife, had the sentence moderated when the court was informed that she was a woman "of great provocation."[25]

¶ 15 Wherever there was strong suspicion that an illicit relation might arise between two persons, the authorities removed the temptation by forbidding the two to come together. As early as November, 1630, the Court of Assistants of Massachusetts prohibited a Mr. Clark from "cohabitacion and frequent keepeing company with Mrs. Freeman, vnder paine of such punishment as the Court shall thinke meete to inflict." Mr. Clark and Mr. Freeman were both bound "in XX £ apeece that Mr. Clearke shall make his personall appearance att the nexte Court to be holden in March nexte, and in the meane tyme to carry himselfe in good behaviour towards all people and espetially towards Mrs. Freeman, concerneing whome there is stronge suspicion of incontinency." Forty-five years later the Suffolk County Court took the same kind of measure to protect the husbands of Dorchester from the temptations offered by the daughter of Robert Spurr. Spurr was presented by the grand jury

> for entertaining persons at his house at unseasonable times both by day and night to the greife of theire wives and Relations &c The Court having heard what was alleaged and testified against him do Sentence him to bee admonish't and to pay Fees of Court and charge him upon his perill not to entertain any married men to keepe company with his daughter especially James Minott and Joseph Belcher.

In like manner Walter Hickson was forbidden to keep company with Mary Bedwell, "And if at any time hereafter hee bee taken in company of the saide Mary Bedwell without other company to bee forthwith apprehended by the Constable and to be whip't with ten stripes." Elizabeth Wheeler and Joanna Peirce were admonished "for theire disorderly carriage in the house of Thomas Watts being married women and founde sitting in other mens Laps with theire Armes about theire Necks." How little confidence the Puritans had in human nature is even more clearly displayed by another case, in which Edmund Maddock and his wife were brought to court "to answere to all such matters as shalbe objected against them concerning Haarkwoody and Ezekiell Euerells being at their house at unseasonable tyme of the night and her being up with them after her husband was gone to bed." Haarkwoody and Everell had been found "by the Constable Henry Bridghame about tenn of the Clock at night sitting by the fyre at the house of Edmond Maddocks with his wyfe a suspicious weoman her husband being on sleepe [sic] on the bedd." A similar distrust of human ability to resist temptation is evident in the following order of the Connecticut Particular Court:

> James Hallett is to returne from the Correction house to his master Barclyt, who is to keepe him to hard labor, and course dyet during the pleasure of the Court provided that Barclet is first to remove his daughter from his family, before the sayd James enter therein.

These precautions, as we have already seen, did not eliminate fornication, adultery, or other sexual offenses, but they doubtless reduced the number from what it would otherwise have been.[26]

¶ 16 In sum, the Puritan attitude toward sex, though directed by a belief in absolute, God-given moral values, never neglected human nature. The rules of conduct which the Puritans regarded as divinely ordained had been formulated for men, not for angels and not for beasts. God had created mankind in two sexes; He had ordained marriage as desirable for all, and sexual intercourse as essential to marriage. On the other hand, He had forbidden sexual intercourse outside of marriage. These were the moral principles which the Puritans sought to enforce in New England. But in their enforcement they took cognizance of human nature. They knew well enough that human beings since the fall of Adam were incapable of obeying perfectly the laws of God. Consequently, in the endeavor to enforce those laws they treated offenders with patience and understanding, and concentrated their efforts on prevention more than on punishment. The result was not a society in which most of us would care to live, for the methods of prevention often caused serious interference with personal liberty. It must nevertheless be admitted that in matters of sex the Puritans showed none of the blind zeal or narrow-minded bigotry which is too often supposed to have been characteristic of them. The more one learns about these people, the less do they appear to have resembled the sad and sour portraits which their modern critics have drawn of them.

Notes

1. Samuel Willard, *A Compleat Body of Divinity* (Boston, 1726), 125 and 608–613.
2. John Cotton, *A Meet Help* (Boston, 1699), 14–15.
3. *A Meet Help,* 16.
4. Edward Taylor, Commonplace Book (manuscript in the library of the Massachusetts Historical Society).
5. Records of the First Church in Boston (manuscript copy in the library of the Massachusetts Historical Society), 12.

6. Middlesex County Court Files, folder 42.

7. John Cotton, *A Practical Commentary...upon the First Epistle Generall of John* (London, 1656), 126.

8. *A Practical Commentary*, 126.

9. Middlesex Files, folder 48.

10. Middlesex Files, folder 71.

11. Another reason was suggested by Charles Francis Adams in his scholarly article, "Some Phases of Sexual Morality and Church Discipline in Colonial New England," *Proceedings* of the Massachusetts Historical Society, XXVI, 477–516.

12. On the position of servants in early New England see *More Books*, XVII (September, 1942), 311–328.

13. Middlesex Files, folder 99.

14. Middlesex Files, folder 47.

15. Middlesex Files, folder 52.

16. Middlesex Files, folder 44.

17. Middlesex Files, folder 47.

18. Middlesex Files, folder 94.

19. William H. Whitmore, editor, *The Colonial Laws of Massachusetts. Reprinted from the Edition of 1660* (Boston, 1889), 257.

20. Middlesex Files, folder 52.

21. Middlesex Files, folder 30.

22. William Bradford, *History of Plymouth Plantation* (Boston, 1912), II, 309.

23. Thomas Cobbett, *A Fruitfull and Usefull Discourse touching the Honour due from Children to Parents and the Duty of Parents toward their Children* (London, 1656), 174.

24. Cobbett, 177.

25. Samuel E. Morison and Zechariah Chafee, editors, *Records of the Suffolk County Court, 1671–1680, Publications* of the Colonial Society of Massachusetts, XXIX and XXX, 121, 410, 524, 837–841, and 1158; George F. Dow, editor, *Records and Files of the Quarterly Courts of Essex County, Massachusetts* (Salem, 1911–1921), I, 274; and V, 377.

26. *Records of the Suffolk County Court*, 422–443 and 676; John Noble, editor, *Records of the Court of Assistants of the Colony of Massachusetts Bay* (Boston, 1901–1928), II, 8; *Records of the Particular Court of Connecticut, Collections* of the Connecticut Historical Society, XXII, 20; and a photostat in the library of the Massachusetts Historical Society, dated March 29, 1653.

Historiography

A university professor once berated a young graduate student for what he termed "stale historiography." A fellow student later commented that this sounded something akin to bad breath. What the professor meant, of course, was that the student in question was not familiar with the most recent scholarly interpretations in a particular subfield of history.

"Historiography" is not a word that one normally confronts in a program of casual reading; nevertheless, the *concept* behind the word should be familiar to every student of history. In fact, you probably already know the concept even if the word itself is unfamiliar. Literally the word means "the writing of history." In modern usage, however, the word refers to the *study of the way history has been and is written—the history of historical writing, if you will.* To study the history of historical writing is to study not the events of the past directly, but the *interpretations* of those events in the works of individual historians. To acquaint oneself, for example, with the variety of ways historians have tried to explain the coming of the American Civil War is to become familiar with the "historiography" of that subject.[1] Graduate students in history must spend years mastering the major interpretations in their particular specialties, including the most recent scholarship. Hence the sin of "stale historiography."

In this chapter it is not our intention to recruit fledgling graduate students, but, by examining a few of the most important historiographical trends, to help you read history more intelligently. Before beginning, though, a few cautions are necessary.

Trying to summarize even a few historiographical trends in capsule form is a sin only slightly less serious than omitting the subject altogether. Not only is the topic immense, but any secondhand summary of another historian's work should be viewed with the utmost suspicion. If you want to know what a given historian says about a subject, you should read that historian's work directly.

Furthermore, every historian's work is to some extent unique, since personal

---

[1]Some historians see that war as a conflict between an agrarian economy (the South) and an industrializing economy (the North); others emphasize slavery as the key issue; still others see states' rights versus federal sovereignity as the basic pattern.

values, assumptions, biases, and angle of vision color all historical writing. Yet below we will discuss historiography in terms of exceedingly broad trends and generalized characteristics. That is, we will suggest a number of "patterns" that seem to be reflected in a great number of historical works. And, because all such patterns are to some extent subjective (see Chapter Seven), you should keep in mind (1) that other historians writing such a book as this could legitimately emphasize wholly different patterns and (2) that no work of history will fit any pattern exactly. Again, the only way to study historiography properly is to read a lot of history.

HISTORY: THE BEGINNINGS

The Western tradition of historical writing began with the ancient Hebrews and Greeks. The Jews, in their long struggle for freedom and autonomy, developed the belief that their people were special in the eyes of God (Yahweh) and that their historical experiences reflected God's will. Conscious of their special role as God's "chosen people," the Jews wrote history as a chronicle of their continuing and evolving relationship with the Creator. Essentially the books of the Old Testament comprise a written history of the Jewish people and Hebrew nation. In summary, Jewish historical writing was very "God-centered" and would, as will be seen, have an immense influence on the Western historical tradition, especially during the Christian Middle Ages.

If Jewish historical writing was "God-centered," it was the ancient Greeks who first wrote history in self-consciously *human* terms. At first the Greeks saw both their own past and the workings of the physical universe as the products of supernatural forces and the intervention of the gods. Later, in the sixth century B.C. , a number of Greek philosophers began to reject supernatural explanations in favor of natural ones. Nature was seen to function according to concrete "natural" laws that could be comprehended through human reason. The past, long explained through myths and legends, came to be explained as the product of human actions and decisions.

Herodotus (fifth century B.C.), the so-called Father of History, wrote the first systematic historical work based on personal observations and the examination of witnesses and surviving records. In his account of the Greek wars against the Persians he did include much unsubstantiated legend, but essentially his was a history of human actions told in *human* terms. Thucydides, who, a generation later, wrote a justly famous account of the Peloponnesian Wars (431–404), was even more scrupulous in his use and analysis of evidence. He insisted that his history include only relevant, verifiable facts, and that it explain events only in ways that could be substantiated by the evidence. Thus in Thucydides we first see what moderns would call a true historical spirit.[2]

There was little change in the nature of written history when the glory that was Greece succumbed to the power that was Rome. During the European Middle Ages (ca. A.D. 500–1300), however, a change of some magnitude took place. With the triumph of Christianity, history writing again became more concerned with the relationship of human history to what was seen to be God's eternal plan.

---

[2]The English word "history," it might be noted, comes from the Greek word for "research."

Christian historiography mirrored that of the Hebrews, not that of the Greeks and Romans, although Greek and Roman influences were much in evidence. To Christian writers in the Middle Ages, human experiences on earth were but a minor part of a larger design. It was the job of history, therefore, to find and reveal the transcendent design of God hidden in the chaos of day-to-day events. That is why many histories written in the Middle Ages began with the biblical story of creation and incorporated that part of the Jewish Old Testament tradition that fit the redemptive message of Christianity. The proper concern of written history was *not* the earthly fate of a particular state or people, but the universal story of the pilgrimage of the human race toward salvation.

Only in the Renaissance (fifteenth and sixteenth centuries) did historians again turn to the more secular, humanistic style of the Greeks. Especially important were a number of fifteenth-century Italian historians, Niccolo Machiavelli (1469–1540) and Francesco Guicciardini (1483–1527) being the best known. To these writers, Christians though they were, the function of history was not, as in the Middle Ages, to reveal God's designs in the affairs of men, but simply to narrate the experiences of particular states and individuals without reference to a divine plan. The Renaissance also saw the gradual emergence of new critical standards for collecting, reading, and interpreting evidence. History was not yet a recognized independent field of study (like theology or law), but the path was now clearly marked. Progress, though, would be slow.

In spite of the long tradition of history writing in the West, the *discipline of history* as we know it is relatively young. Indeed, history emerged as a formal academic study only in the early nineteenth century. To be sure, many pre-nineteenth-century historians produced works of great power and sophistication, as any reader of Thucydides or Gibbon can attest. Yet, generally, such works were few and far between, for history still lacked a coherent and workable critical methodology. Much history was written, but seldom did the historians consider the question: "What are the criteria for writing good history?" Many pre-nineteenth-century historians handled evidence with a casual disregard for critical standards. Often they cited no sources whatever; on other occasions they accepted myth, legend, and gossip as fact; on yet others, they read or interpreted records with too much credulity and too little skepticism.

In another way, the pre-nineteenth century historians had a blind spot. They did not fully understand that in some respects past ages differed from their own; they had difficulty realizing that styles, habits, and values changed over time. We find many Renaissance paintings, for example, in which biblical scenes are portrayed with figures dressed in "modern"—that is, fifteenth-century—garb and surrounded by the latest architectural styles. The equivalent today would be a painting that depicted George Washington dressed in a Brooks Brothers suit and standing in front of a Frank Lloyd Wright house.

Conversely, when many of the early historians *did* perceive differences between their age and another, their response was not to try to *understand* that which was different, but to denounce it. Thus did Voltaire, in the eighteenth century, dismiss the Middle Ages as unworthy of study because medieval men and women were not "enlightened," as he felt himself to be. In a word, such an attitude is unhistorical. (See Chapter Five, Context.)

LEOPOLD VON RANKE AND THE RISE OF MODERN HISTORY

Historical studies came into their own following the immense political and social upheavals that accompanied the French Revolution (1789–1815). The Revolution represented a massive break with the past and, accordingly, made men much more "history-conscious" than ever before. Thus, it was in the nineteenth century that history became the "Queen of the Sciences" and earned a permanent place in the academy.

The man most responsible for elevating the study of history to a new plateau was the German historian *Leopold von Ranke* (1795–1886). Ranke was the George Washington of academic history—the founding father of the modern discipline as we know it. Ranke's contributions were threefold: (1) He played a leading role in establishing history as a respected discipline in the universities, (2) he firmly established the notion that all sound history must be based on primary sources and rigorous "scientific" method, and (3) he reflected the broader nineteenth-century attempt to define the concept of "historical mindedness." Of these, the latter two points require further elaboration.

Ranke and Historical Method. Before Ranke, as we have seen, much history was written, but "there was no systematic use of sources and no accepted methodological principles."[3] Many pre-Rankean historians relied heavily on the work of other authors (secondary sources) rather than going to the original documents, or primary sources. Ranke, on the other hand, stressed the importance of basing any historical narrative firmly on the reading of primary sources. Furthermore, he insisted that the historian constantly inform the reader of the specific sources upon which a given point was based. Hence the central importance after Ranke of thorough footnotes and bibliographies. (Now you know whom to blame.) In a word, Ranke popularized the idea that history could be "scientific" not in the sense that history could discover general laws of behavior, but that historical writing should be based on rigorous critical standards.

Ranke and Historical Mindedness. Ranke also contributed to the rise of the conviction that one should not study a past age in terms of one's *own* values and culture but in terms of the values and realities of the age itself. According to Ranke, one should not make moral judgments on past individuals and past cultures but try to understand them in their own terms. To Ranke, every age and individual was "immediate to God" (did not need to be justified) and worthy of our sympathy and understanding. Ranke appreciated the fact that things *do* change over time, and as we have seen, this basic insight is central to the whole process of historical thinking.

Ranke, then, and many other eminent scholars, established the study of history on a firm methodological foundation. But what sorts of things did these pioneers write about? Space forbids a detailed chronicle of history and historians in the nineteenth century, but two general points can be made:

1. Most nineteenth-century history was political, legal, or diplomatic in emphasis. Historians began to get access to government archives that had hitherto been closed to researchers. Naturally, their work tended to reflect the

---

[3]Arthur Marwick, *What History Is and Why It Is Important* (Bletchley, England: The Open University Press, 1970) p. 42.

character of the documents they were working with. Center stage were the actions of kings, parliaments, law courts, armies, navies, and diplomats—"drum and trumpet" history as it came to be known.

2. Nineteenth-century history, especially in Europe, tended to be *national* in focus—more in the sense of "nationality" than "nation." During that era a number of "new" nations, or ethnic groups, perceiving their cultural and historical uniqueness, began to explore their own historical roots with great vigor. Even history coming out of the more established nations, such as England and France, reflected this compulsion to probe the depths of their national experience. Much the same could be said of the histories produced in nineteenth-century America. Across the board, historiography during during this period tended to be ethnocentric, nationalistic, and frequently chauvinistic.

KARL MARX AND HISTORY

If Ranke and his contemporaries saw only politics and diplomacy as worthy of the historian's attention, it was the German economist and revolutionary philosopher Karl Marx who opened historians' eyes to the importance of social and economic forces in human affairs. Marx (1818–1883) is widely recognized as one of the most influential thinkers of the last one hundred years. Much modern scholarship in history, economics, political theory, sociology, and philosophy cannot be fully appreciated without some understanding of Karl Marx's ideas.

This is not the place to discuss Marx's system in detail, but a few words concerning his impact on the discipline of history are in order. It should be noted from the start, however, that a consideration of Marx the historian can be effectively divorced from consideration of Marx the prophet of socialism. In the latter guise Marx, and his collaborator, Friedrich Engels, postulated a broadly "progressive" theory of history, which held that human societies would evolve through a number of stages culminating in the establishment (through revolution) of a "dictatorship of the proletariat" and, eventually, a classless society. This was a secular version of the story of the movement of the human race toward a "preordained goal." The validity of this vision is best left to the philosophers, since historical evidence can never confirm or deny such all-encompassing metaphysical theories.

More important for our purposes is the fact that Marx opened new intellectual vistas by breaking out of the political-diplomatic straitjacket that had bound most historical investigations before his time. Marx, notes one American historian, "became the first to formulate, in explicit fashion, the economic interpretation of history."[4] Marx (and Engels) argued that, at any given point in time, the mode of economic production determined, to a great extent, the character of the entire society—its ideas, values, political structure, and social relations. To some of Marx's more dogmatic followers, this insight was converted into a thoroughgoing economic determinism. That is, economic forces were seen to *totally determine* the nature of society, and changes in the economic structure were considered the *sole* engine of historical change. Marx himself never went so far; late in life he even commented: "I am not a Marxist." Marx and Engels did not

---

[4]Allan Nevins, *The Gateway to History* (Chicago: Quadrangle Books, 1963), p. 268.

deny that noneconomic factors could be contributing causes of events. They simply asserted that economic factors were of primary importance.

Within this general framework, the history of economic and social *classes* was more relevant than the history of great men or ruling elites. "The history of all hitherto existing society," wrote Marx and Engels in one of their more famous lines, "is the history of class struggle." This, of course, is a very debatable conclusion. Of significance though is the fact that Marx and Engels saw class interests as a vital element in any historical equation.

Marx's impact on politics and political thought has been immense and requires no further comment. But what of Marx's impact on the writing of history?

In communist countries, of course, where Marxism in some form or another is an official ideology, historical writing is "Marxist" in the extreme. And, quite frankly, much of it is not very good history. Evidence is chosen, organized, analyzed, and interpreted more with an eye to validating the ideology than establishing the best true story about the past. Much official communist history written in Russia, the eastern European countries, and elsewhere suffers from this defect. In fairness, we should also note that any time scholarship is subordinated to the dictates of an ideology—Marxist or non-Marxist—it is truth that suffers.

In the non-communist West the influence of Marx, while great, has been much less direct. In the broadest sense Marx is significant because, by emphasizing the importance of economic factors in history, he opened the door to a new approach to the past. Few historians today, whatever their political orientation, would deny the validity of exploring the role of classes, economic interests, and modes of production in the historical process. Economic interpretations have, in fact, become a staple of American historiography. A famous (if not totally respected) example would be Charles A. Beard's *An Economic Interpretation of the Constitution of the United States* published in 1913. In that work Beard examined the economic interests of the framers of the Constitution and concluded that the Constitution was designed more to protect property rights than political rights. Whatever the accuracy of this interpretation (and it has been vigorously challenged), the important thing to note is the explicitly economic focus of the work. Beard was no Marxist, but he acknowledged a debt to Marx just the same. Few historians have gone as far as Beard in emphasizing economic factors so single-mindedly, but even fewer would deny that the economic "question" is one that must be asked in order to understand any given segment of the past.[5]

THE TWENTIETH CENTURY

The twentieth century, especially in the decades since 1945, has witnessed a "knowledge explosion" of sorts. Books, articles, reports, and the like have been

---

[5]It should be noted that for some Western scholars the Marxian message has been more direct. There are many scholars, historians among them, who consciously call themselves "Marxists," and they have adopted an explicitly Marxian (class-oriented) approach to the study of history and society. Within the ranks of historians, such scholars are a distinct minority. Yet certain Marxist historians have produced solid, scholarly works, which have greatly enriched our understanding of many historical events. The thing to remember is that the test of good history is not the author's ideology, but the thoroughness and accuracy of the work he or she produces.

pouring off the presses with ever-increasing velocity. The "explosion" has been most visible in the sciences, but the generalization is applicable to history as well. It is safe to say that more history has been written and published in the twentieth century than in all the previous centuries combined. Moreover, recent historical writing has displayed such kaleidoscopic diversity that history is a more exciting field than ever before. Unfortunately, the mass and diversity of recent historical scholarship also makes it impossible to summarize neatly even the most prominent trends in twentieth-century historiography. What follows, therefore, is a very selective and idiosyncratic sampling of what we see to be some of the defining characteristics of recent historiography—especially American historiography.

THE "NEW" SOCIAL HISTORY

There is nothing especially "new" about social history. Social history, simply put, is the history of life in the broadest sense; the history of the everyday experience of the "average" man and woman. It is the history of occupations, life-styles, leisure activities, family structures, eating habits, sexual practices, reading preferences, beliefs, and values; it is "grass roots" history; it is, in the memorable words of G. M. Trevelyan, "history with the politics left out." Historians have been writing social history for some time. Even today, one of the most frequently cited examples of brilliant social history is T. B. Macaulay's famous third chapter in his *History of England*. Macaulay, of course, wrote in the middle years of the nineteenth century.

Although social history has long been with us, only in recent decades has it become a central concern of the historical profession. In the nineteenth century social history was strictly subordinated to the more important priority of telling the story of political, constitutional, and military affairs. Social history was used to "set the scene" or provide a pleasant interlude in the narrative. Today, however, social history is taught and studied as a field of inherent interest and importance. To this extent social history is "new."

Social history is new in another sense—it is much more "scientific" and less anecdotal than had previously been the case. Social history is one area where the application of statistical methods and computer analysis has been especially productive. Much social history today is, in effect, *historical demography* (see Chapter Two, Set B, Exercise 2) where historians systematically analyze large-scale population trends and calculate such things as average family sizes, death rates, marriage ages, and average incomes. The more literary tradition of social history has by no means been abandoned, but statistical methods have given the social historian another arrow in his quiver.

The most fruitful contribution of the social historians has been to cast the spotlight on groups that have typically been ignored in traditional history—workers, farmers, peasants, women, children, ethnic minorities, and the aged. In fact, the popularity and vitality of social history is in part a reflection of the increasing sense of identity among various ethnic subcultures. Witness the proliferation of books on black history, Chicano history, native American (Indian) history, and the like. The feminist movement has likewise inspired a great many valuable studies, which highlight the role of women in history, not to mention histories of family life, child-rearing practices, and sexuality. In sum, the "new" social history has brought to life the experiences of countless groups previously bypassed by the mainstream historical surveys.

PSYCHOHISTORY

Psychohistory is another growing and popular subfield within Clio's ranks,[6] but still somewhat of a black sheep in the eyes of traditionalists. In the late nineteenth century a number of writers, of whom Sigmund Freud (1856–1939) was the most influential, began to draw attention to the importance of the unconscious mind and irrational impulses in human behavior. Just as Marx had emphasized the importance of economics in human affairs, Freud's many trailblazing studies underscored the role played by hidden psychological drives. Freud's message was reinforced by the senseless slaughter of World War I (1914–18), which dramatized for a complacent Europe how easily irrationality and animal brutality could triumph over intellect and reason. In the years after the war psychiatry and psychoanalysis came into their own; and, after the next world war, the insights of psychiatry were applied to figures of historical import, both alive and dead. Psychohistory was born.

Perhaps the best known of the psychohistories is Erik Erikson's masterful study, *Young Man Luther* (1958). Since the publication of Erikson's book, many other historians and psychologists have attempted to apply psychological and/or psychoanalytic theories to the study of past individuals and events—sometimes successfully and sometimes not. Nevertheless, psychohistory seems here to stay. Even the more traditional historians are paying closer attention to the psychological dimensions of the events and individuals that they study.

COMPUTERS AND QUANTIFICATION

Another distinctly twentieth-century phenomenon is the growing use of computers and statistical methods in history. These techniques have been especially productive (as noted above) in the realms of economic and social history. Historical studies of voting behavior have also benefited from the application of well-thought-out computer programs to historical evidence. There is, however, a problem with this type of history. Most historical questions cannot be answered with computers, however sophisticated the machines or their programs. Too often scholars become so hypnotized by the attractions of new statistical methodologies that they end up letting the methodology dictate the type of research they do. This, in the words of one political scientist, is akin to buying a leash and then looking for a dog to attach to it. Quantification has a place in historical studies, but the limitations of "mere numeration" must ever be kept in mind.

POPULAR HISTORY

The twentieth century, especially since the advent of the cheap paperback and television, has been the age of popularized history par excellence. There has

---

[6]Clio is the Muse of History.

been a tremendous growth in the amount of history written for the viewing or reading enjoyment of a mass audience. In the final analysis this is a good thing, for unless historians communicate their findings to a larger audience, they are serving no useful function in the society. On the other hand, popular history (whether presented in books or on television) can also be a dangerous thing. Too frequently good entertainment is bad history, for to emphasize the dramatic and sensational is often to distort the truth. More than ever must the reading and viewing public be able to discriminate between good history and bad history.

Moreover, so insatiable is the public appetite for the "inside story" of this event or that disaster that "instant" histories have become commonplace. Almost before events have run their course popular histories are on the drugstore reading racks. Whether the subject is the Kennedy assassination, the Manson murder case, the latest terrorist outrage, the death of a rock star, or the mass suicides in Guyana, paperback "histories" are available almost before the dust has settled. The dangers inherent in such books should be apparent. They are put together in haste on the basis of evidence that is far from complete, and public passions may still be fully aroused. The authors, in many cases, are not trained historians or even trained journalists. In sum, such books should be read with a very critical eye.

Even more does this advice apply to television shows that purport to document "real" events through a dramatic re-creation. Many such shows in recent years (a number of BBC historical dramatizations come to mind) have been excellent as history as well as very entertaining. Others, however, have obscured the line between truth and fiction so much that their value as history is limited. In any case, it is obvious that it is more important than ever to have a historically literate population if for no other reason than to judge critically the mass of popularized and instant histories that bombard us daily.

If one can perceive a trend over time, it is this: Historical writing in the West has become broader in geographic scope, casting its beam on civilizations and cultures hitherto ignored; it has become more eclectic, with few aspects of life escaping critical attention; and it has become ever more rigorous and imaginative in its use of evidence, our comments on "instant" history notwithstanding. History as a discipline, therefore, is alive and growing, telling its story of change, but telling also of how tenaciously the past survives in the present.

EXERCISES

Exercise 1 Match the items in List A with those in List B. Put the proper letters from List B next to the most appropriate item in List A. Try to do this exercise from memory before you refer back to the text of the chapter.

List A

_____ **1.** Psychohistory

_____ **2.** God-centered history

_____ **3.** Economic interpretation of the framing of the U.S. Constitution

_____ **4.** Earliest "critical" historian

_____ **5.** Historical demography

_____ **6.** Concern with the history of "particular individuals and states"

_____ **7.** Proponent of rigorous use of primary sources

_____ **8.** History seen as the history of class struggle

_____ **9.** Psychoanalysis

_____ **10.** The history of history

List B

A. Machiavelli

B. Karl Marx

C. Medieval history

D. Thucydides

E. Leopold von Ranke

F. T. B. Macaulay

G. Erik Erikson

H. Historiography

I. The "new" social history

J. Charles Beard

K. Sigmund Freud

SET Exercise 2 In this chapter we have discussed historiography—the history of historical writing—in exceedingly general terms. Quite frequently, students will benefit most by studying the historical interpretations associated with a *specific concrete historical problem or event*—the origins of the American Civil War, the reasons for the fall of the Roman Empire, the nature of the Puritan Revolution in England, and so on. It is on this level—concrete, particular events—that the dynamics of historical interpretation and reinterpretation can best be studied.

Rather than providing a "canned" exercise at this point, we suggest that students study, individually or as a class, some of the major interpretations surrounding a specific event or problem. There are numerous edited collections that bring together excerpts representing a variety of interpretations of famous events. The instructor can provide suggestions and guidance.

The Uses
of History

On May 20, 1927, a foolhardy young mail pilot began a perilous journey. Charles A. Lindbergh set out to be the first to fly a plane nonstop from New York to Paris. Defying the elements, more than 3,000 miles of ocean, and his own desire to sleep, "Lucky Lindy" made the trip in just over thirty-three hours. Overnight Lindbergh became a hero, and he and his silver monoplane, the Spirit of St. Louis, became symbols of the fledgling air age.

It had taken mankind countless generations to conquer the air, but it took only a few short decades to take the next step: the conquest of space. Thirty years after Charles Lindbergh vaulted the Atlantic, the Soviet Union launched the first space satellite; a mere twelve years later (1969) American astronauts walked for the first time on the surface of the moon. Within less than a single lifetime the air age had given way to the space age. This technological and scientific leap symbolizes a central reality of the modern period: in many areas of life—in science and technology, government, economic organization, and social relations—the pace of change seems to be accelerating. Tomorrow often seems to be here before today has been fully comprehended.

In such an environment, where events of even a decade ago appear (to some) to occupy a very remote past, one might begin to question the validity of studying history. How, after all, can the experiences of imperial Rome, Elizabethan England, or colonial America have any relevance for the "Pepsi Generation"? How can history teach anything to a society that is experiencing such rapid technological and demographic transformations? Such questions are heard often these days, but they miss the mark by a considerable distance. Significant changes have occurred, but in countless areas of life organic connections with the past have not been broken. The legacies and burdens of the past, the long-term continuities, are with us still. The study of history, moreover, has hardly become irrelevant. In fact, one could argue that precisely *because* change has been rapid in our time, the need for good history has actually increased. There is much truth in the aphorism "the more things change, the more they stay the same." Without historical perspective we are in danger of falling into the prideful, naïve (and mistaken) notion that the problems we face and the solutions we propose are unprecedented and bear no relationship to human problems of the past. Just one of the contributions history can make is to serve as a useful antidote to such narrow present-mindedness.

HISTORY, IDENTITY, AND THE MODERN WORLD

Even the rapid change we see around us should not hide the basic reality that all that we do, all that we think, indeed all that we are is the cumulative result of past experiences. The future is an abstraction; the "present" is but a fleeting moment; all else is history. The past and judgments about the past are inescapable. Every moment of our lives we make statements or act according to some perception of past events. Our perceptions of the past may be incomplete or fallacious, but we are thinking historically nevertheless. You may choose a school course because you like a given teacher; vote Democratic or Republican because of your assessment of the record of the party in question; or reject a date with someone who "isn't your type." All of these decisions are historical judgments based on an analysis of past experience. And every time you make such an analysis of the past you are functioning as a historian.

Not only is it impossible to escape history, it would be catastrophic to try. Imagine for a moment what life would be like if you totally lost your memory. You would, in a very real sense, have no sense of belonging—no family, no friends, no home, no memories to guide your behavior; in a word, no identity. Clearly your sense of personal identity is not so much a function of what you *are* at the moment, but what you *have been* for your entire life. In more subtle ways your personal identity is a product of the lives of countless others and their forebears—people whose activities have created the social and political environment in which you live. The same can be said of society as a whole. A society's identity is the product of the myriad individuals, forces, and events that constitute that society's past. History, the study of the past, is society's collective memory. Without that collective memory society would be as rootless and adrift as an individual with amnesia. In the words of George Santayana, "A country without a memory is a country of madmen."

Of the many legitimate reasons for studying history, this seems to us to be one of the most compelling. Individually and collectively *what we are* is the product of *what we have been*. Our sense of personal and social identity is a direct outgrowth of our history, and to study that history is to discover a "means of access to ourselves." The immense success of Alex Haley's family history, *Roots*, reflects the deep human need to know where one comes from and where one fits into the grand scheme.

THE PAST AS PROLOGUE

A close corollary of this notion that history is a road to self-knowledge is summed up by the cliche: to comprehend the present, study the past. Not only is history necessary for establishing a sense of cultural and personal identity, it is vital for understanding the issues and problems that presently confront the United States and the world. This is *not* to say that history can provide clear and unambiguous solutions to present-day problems. To some extent all historical events are unique because history never exactly "repeats itself." Even the study of close historical parallels will not yield specific concrete solutions to current problems. But to try to cope with current problems without first knowing the relevant historical background is highly dangerous, to say nothing of naïve. A knowledge of the pertinent historical background may not tell you how to solve a given problem, but it will provide a more meaningful understanding of the complexities involved and even perhaps indicate, in a general way, what types of solution may or may not be feasible.

For example, a more thorough knowledge of the history of Southeast Asia might have helped American policy-makers avoid the worst agonies of Vietnam. The U.S. intervention in Vietnam was designed to "contain" communism within the boundaries of China. The containment of China herself (as distinct from the ideology of communism) was also a central concern. The triumph of communism in Vietnam, so the reasoning went, would represent a victory for Chinese imperialism. A study of East Asian history, however, would have revealed that the Vietnamese had for centuries resisted Chinese encroachments, and that a communist Vietnam would probably not be a puppet of the Chinese. Lack of historical understanding, therefore, was one of the factors that lay behind the American policy in Vietnam. Examples could be multiplied endlessly, but all of them would simply underscore the sentiments of Oscar Wilde: "He to whom the present is the only thing that is present knows nothing of the age in which he lives."

The idea that knowledge of the past is essential for understanding the present is scarcely debatable. Yet a caution is in order here. Nothing is easier to abuse than the historical analogy or historical parallel. Time and again politicians, journalists, and the man or woman on the street will be heard to declare that "history proves" this or "history shows" that. With solemn conviction they will assert that history somehow supports their position on some contemporary issue. The problem is that the historical record is so rich and varied that one can always find examples that seem to support one's case. (History, in this sense, is much like the Bible. If one reads selectively, biblical passages can be found to support just about any notion under the sun.) Unfortunately, "history" in the abstract, "proves" or "shows" nothing in an absolute sense. Parallels between past and present circumstances are never exact because there are elements in every situation that are unique to that situation. Hence it is wise to distrust those who claim too much for the historical parallel or analogy. In fact, history makes one of its most useful contributions when it exposes the *inapplicability* of many inaccurate or misleading analogies.

HISTORY AND THE HUMAN CONDITION

The relevance of history is not confined to a specific set of contemporary preoccupations. In a much broader sense, the study of the past, even the remote past, can pay real dividends. If experience is a good teacher, then history, the study of all past experience, is a good teacher as well. True, history never repeats itself precisely, but human nature seems, nevertheless, to have remained much the same over the centuries. To learn how men and women in all ages and places have acted, loved, played, negotiated, worked, and fought; to study the social, political, and economic dynamics of other cultures; to share the thoughts and passions of fellow human beings is to better understand *all* human behavior, past and present.

The study of geographic areas and historical periods other than one's own is especially valuable. It helps one realize the incredible diversity of the human experience and is an excellent antidote for cultural ethnocentrism. As the French philosopher Descartes put it: "It is good to know something of the customs of different peoples in order to judge more sanely of our own." Too often we all fall into the trap of believing that the way things are done here and now is the only way or the "best" way. History allows us to step out of our own cultural circumstances and taste the infinite variety of life-styles and organizational structures that mankind has created over the millennia. History also helps us develop a tolerance and appreciation of cultures, customs, and ideas other than our own. An open mind can be one of history's finest products.

HISTORICAL COMPETENCIES AND THE MARKETPLACE

If the above arguments seem too abstract, there are more bread-and-butter reasons for studying history. First, history is perhaps the most comprehensive of the academic disciplines in that *all* human experience is the object of study. As such, history provides an indispensable background for all other disciplines, especially those in the humanities and social sciences. For the student who is unsure of his or her precise career direction, history is an ideal beginning point because it provides the necessary background and skills for so many other areas of study.

In addition, training in history develops many skills necessary for survival in the economic marketplace. A basic feature of our society is the central importance of the research report. Countless occupations in the areas of business, law, government, education, and journalism involve information gathering and report writing, and, in the words of historians Barzun and Graff, "the attitude and technique of the report-writer are derived in a straight line" from the discipline of history.[1] The historian must learn to ferret out information, evaluate it, organize it, interpret it, and report on it. Obviously the skills history develops in research, analysis, writing, and oral communication have applicability far beyond the study of history per se.

HISTORY AS ENJOYMENT

History has often been dismissed as "mere storytelling." We disagree. But even if history were "mere storytelling," it would be well worth reading and studying. In the first place, much historical writing is literarily and stylistically superb. To read many of the great historians is as esthetically and intellectually exciting as reading a renowned novelist or poet. Moreover, the stories the historian tells are often more bizarre and interesting than many a piece of imaginative fiction. The story of Watergate could never have been told by a novelist—the plot would not have been believable. The true story of the lives of Czar Nicholas II of Russia, his wife Alexandra, and the religious visionary Rasputin would strain the will to believe of a jaded soap-opera fan. Truth, as the saying goes, *is* often stranger than fiction.

In short, history can be both artistically edifying and *fun*. It may seem trivial to assert this, but necessary. Those who equate history with the material in a plodding, dry, introductory textbook simply don't know what they are missing.

---

[1] Jacques Barzun and Henry F. Graff, *The Modern Researcher*, rev. ed. (New York: Harcourt, Brace, 1970), p. 5.

EXERCISES

Exercise 1 In the commentary above a number of justifications were given for the study of history. In brief they were

1. History provides a source of personal and social identity.

2. History helps us understand the problems of the present.

3. History—good history—is a corrective for misleading analogies, parallels, and "lessons" of the past.

4. History can help one develop tolerance and open-mindedness.

5. History helps us better understand all human behavior and all aspects of the human condition.

6. History provides a basic background for many other disciplines.

7. Historical study develops many cognitive skills.

8. Some works of history are worth reading as literature.

9. History is fun.

Which of the above do you agree with? Disagree with? Why? Do not be afraid to disagree. Remember, the above list in many ways reflects the personal opinions and leanings of the authors.

> **Discussion:**
> Why do you think most historians reject the notion that history should be studied to enable us to better predict the future?

Exercise 2 Below are some comments on the utility of history by a number of well-known writers and thinkers. Which statements would you agree with? Disagree with? Explain your decision.

1. "[History is] a useless heap of facts." (Lord Chesterfield)

2. "History, by appraising . . . [students] of the past, will enable them to judge of the future." (Thomas Jefferson)

3. "If history teaches any lesson at all, it is that there are no historical lessons." (Lucien Febvre)

4. "The value of history . . . is that it teaches us what man has done and thus what man is." (R. G. Collingwood)

5. "History is a means of access to ourselves." (Lynn White, Jr.)

6. Everything is the sum of its past and nothing is comprehensible except through its history." (Pierre Teilhard de Chardin)

7. "Whoever wishes to foresee the future must consult the past; for human events ever resemble those of preceding times. This arises from the fact that they are produced by men who ever have been, and ever shall be, animated by the same passions, and thus they necessarily have the same results." (Niccolo Machiavelli)

Question: Which one of the above justifications for the study of history do you see as *most* defensible? *Least* defensible? Why?

Exercise 3 Which of the "justifications" for the study of history listed in Exercise 1 does each of the following statements represent? Indicate your choice by placing the proper number (1 through 9) next to the passage in question. If more than one seems appropriate, please so indicate. If none of the given justifications seems to fit, record a "0." You will find the numbered list on page 211.

_____ **1.** If history is correctly taught and studied, it allows for a new level of self-discovery and a new degree of empathy with other people.

_____ **2.** A man who ignores history will still make the historical assumptions which are implicit in most language and in all political judgments, but he will not know he is making them and so will be unable to criticise them or reconsider the evidence on which they are based.

_____ **3.** There is much to be said for the view that the greatest function of historical study is as an addition to experience, tending to an appreciation of the existence in the past of the race of many confrontations with problems similar to our own.

_____ **4.** The study of history is in the truest sense an education and a training for political life. . . . The most instructive, or rather the only, method of learning to bear with dignity the vicissitudes of fortune is to recall the catastrophes of others.

_____ **5.** The second thesis of this book is that policy-makers ordinarily use history badly. When resorting to an analogy, they tend to seize upon the first that comes to mind. They do not search fitness or even ask in what ways it might be misleading. . . . The third thesis, corollary to the second, is that policy-makers can, if they will, use history more discriminatingly. They can seek alternative analogies and parallels and in doing so reflect on whether a moral seen in one case is a principle exemplified in many.

_____ **6.** In reality, what more agreeable entertainment to the mind, than to be transported into the remotest ages of the world, and to observe human society, in its infancy, making the first faint essays towards the arts and sciences; . . . What amusement, either of the sense or imagination, can be compared with it.

_____ **7.** Everything has a history. At least part of the answer to any question about the contemporary world can come from studying the circumstances that led up to it.

_____ **8.** History is worth studying because it is a creative act. It not only allows for but demands serious application and industry, the exercise of a creative imagination and high qualities of literary exposition.

_____ **9.** History can help us shake off the shackles of excessive ethnocentrism and the debilitating bias of cultural and racial purity.... History helps to illuminate the human condition. Far from making us "unpatriotic," history helps us to know why we hold particular loyalties; it promotes in us the greatest kind of loyalty—a commitment to freedom of critical inquiry.

_____ **10.** History enables bewildered bodies of human beings to grasp their relationship with their past, and helps them chart on general lines their immediate forward course. And it does more than this. By giving peoples a sense of continuity in all their efforts, red-flagging error, and chronicling immortal worth, it confers on them a consciousness of unity, a realization of the value of individual achievement, and a comprehension of the importance of planned effort as contrasted with aimless drifting.

Sources

1. Cantor and Schneider, p. 3.
2. G. Kitson Clark, *The Critical Historian* (London: Heinemann, 1967), p. 8.
3. Shafer, ed., p. 9.
4. Polybius, *Histories*, in C. VanDoren and M. Adler, eds., *Great Treasury of Western Thought* (New York: Bowker, 1977), p. 958.
5. Ernest R. May, *"Lessons" of the Past* (New York: Oxford University Press, 1975), pp. xi–xii.
6. David Hume, *Of the Study of History* in VanDoren and Adler, eds., *op. cit.*, p. 962.
7. Jules Benjamine, *A Student's Guide to History* (New York: St. Martin's, 1975), p. 2.
8. N. Cantor and R. Schneider, *op. cit.*, p. 3.
9. Lester D. Stephens, *Probing the Past* (Boston: Allyn and Bacon, 1974), p. 123.
10. Nevins, p. 14.

How to Use
a Library

Today's students are more technologically sophisticated than ever before. Many are totally at home with computers, hand calculators, videotape cameras, cassette recorders, microfilm readers, and other magical machines. Yet all too many students never master (some never attempt to master) the largest and most complex piece of "equipment" that colleges possess—the library. This is a shame; the library is the most important educational resource on the campus. The library not only houses the books, journals, films, and documents that serve as the lifeblood of learning, it is often a pleasant (and increasingly colorful) place to browse, study, and think. Its potential for providing a companion for the Saturday-night party should also not be overlooked.

Historically, libraries were simply places to store books. Access was difficult and often limited to members of ruling aristocracies. In recent decades, however, this picture has changed radically. The storage of books has taken a back seat to providing services for people. The library exists for human beings, not just books, and if it is not used it serves no real useful purpose. On the other side of the coin, the student who fails to take good advantage of the library is depriving himself or herself of one of the most fruitful lessons a college education can provide.

It is not the purpose of this section to make you experts on library usage. One can no more learn to use a library by reading about it than one can learn to ride a bicycle from reading an article about bike racing. *The only way to learn how to use a library properly is experience.* Consequently, it is the modest aim of this chapter to help you get enough of a toehold to function as an educated beginner.

There are three basic things one must know to begin—once one has located the library in the first place, that is. You should know:

1. How your library is laid out and how books are classified therein.
2. How to initiate a search for the information you need.
3. Whom to ask for help if you reach a dead end.

LAYOUT OF THE LIBRARY

Your first task is to play the role of a tourist in your own library. Wander around and note where certain important items are located. One scholar insists that pinpointing the rest rooms should be the first priority. One must not denigrate such a practical suggestion, but ultimately it is more important to locate the following:

1. The card catalogue
2. The main desk
3. The reference room or reference area along with the general placement of the major indexes and encyclopedias
4. The book stacks
5. The reserve book room or shelves

When you have finished your tour (or even before you begin), ask for any informational guides or pamphlets that might be available.

As overwhelming as a library may seem at first glance, the thing to remember is that everything in it is classified according to a system. Those who understand the system ultimately understand how to make the library work for them. You should, therefore, find out what classification system your library uses and endeavor to master its basic features.

The two dominant systems of classification are: (1) The Dewey Decimal System and (2) the Library of Congress system. The *Dewey Decimal System* is based on numbers divisible by ten (hence "decimal"). There are ten general categories numbered with hundreds (100, 200, 300, etc.), nine subcategories for each general category (110, 120, 130, etc.), and yet nine further sub-subcategories for each of these (111, 112, 113, etc.). When further subcategories are needed, they are designated by the addition of one, two, or sometimes three numbers following a decimal point (e.g., 909.6, 909.7, 909.8). Much of this is irrelevant to anyone but a librarian, but a knowledge of the "hundreds" will give you an immediate overview of the major branches of knowledge and where they are located in the library. They are:

000s	General Works	500s	Pure Sciences
100s	Philosophy	600s	Applied Sciences
200s	Religion	700s	Arts and Recreation
300s	Social Sciences	800s	Literature
400s	Linguistics	900s	History, Geography

In history the major subcategories are as follows:

910	Geography	960	African History
920	Biography	970	North American History
930	Ancient World History	980	South American History
940	European History	990	History of Oceana
950	History of Asia		

The *Library of Congress system* is a broader-based and hence preferred by many large university research libraries. Even many smaller libraries already use, or are converting to, the Library of Congress system. In this system twenty-one letters of the alphabet are assigned to general categories.

A.	General Works	D.	Universal History
B.	Philosophy/Religion	E–F.	American History
C.	Auxiliary Sciences of History	G.	Geography/Anthropology

H.	Social Sciences	Q.	Science
J.	Political Science	R.	Medicine
K.	Law	S.	Agriculture
L.	Education	T.	Technology
M.	Music	U.	Military Science
N.	Fine Arts	V.	Naval Science
P.	Language & Literature	Z.	Bibliography—Library Science

Innumerable subcategories can be created by adding a second letter to the general designation.

It is, of course, totally unnecessary to memorize either system; but it is a good idea to know the classification numbers for your own field of study. Also do not ignore the pleasures and benefits that can accrue from simply browsing at random through the stacks. Not only does browsing make the "system" more comprehensible, it is an emotionally and intellectually rewarding activity for anyone who finds bookstores a congenial place to shop.

THE CARD CATALOGUE: INITIATING THE SEARCH

Understanding your library's classification system will help you locate the relevant book collections, but to find specific works on specific topics you will have to turn to the *card catalogue*. The card catalogue is the most important research tool in the library. It is essentially a complete, cross-indexed, bibliography of all the materials in the library. *The card catalogue is arranged alphabetically and each book is listed at least three times—on an author card, a title card, and a subject card.* Thus you can find a book even if you are lacking a vital piece of information, such as the name of the author.

Looking up the works of a given author or a specific title is relatively easy. Finding all the relevant books on a given subject or topic, however, is not always so simple. The problem arises when your idea of what a proper subject heading should be differs from the subject headings actually in use in the catalogue. For instance, books on the history of England are not found under "England" but under "Great Britain." Even more perplexingly, library materials on Revenue Sharing will be found under the subject heading "Intergovernmental Fiscal Relations"—a category that neither logic nor imagination could supply. If you run into a dead end, consult the publication entitled *Library of Congress Subject Headings.* This massive work will guide you to one or more proper categories. Finally, do not hesitate to ask the librarian for help—not even the most sophisticated library users know all the tricks of card-catalogue use.

Another error, related to that above, is not searching for *additional* subject headings that might yield results. In other words, do not end your catalogue search if you have consulted just one or two subject categories. For instance, if you are interested in the history of witchcraft, it is not enough to look under "witchcraft"; additional works might be found under such headings as "magic," "occult sciences," "demonology," "Inquisition," "sorcery," "Salem," and so on. Likewise, the catalogue cards on medieval and early modern history should not be overlooked. Often the catalogue itself will include cards that refer you to other potentially useful subject headings.

Finally, do not overlook the cards themselves as useful sources of information.

Each card contains a wealth of data. In addition to the classification number, the card will tell you the number of pages in a book, whether the book is illustrated, the date of publication, and, often, some of the topics covered. A typical author card is reproduced below.

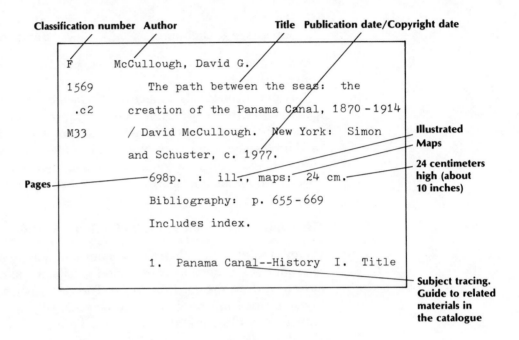

Although the card catalogue is *the* place to begin a search for book titles, there are still many other avenues that might be traveled. There are literally hundreds of indexes and printed bibliographies that can help students locate books and articles.[1] As Montaigne noted, without much exaggeration, "There are more books upon books than upon all other subjects."

The only bound indexes that merit special mention at this point are the periodical indexes, which do for journal (magazine) literature what the card catalogue does for books. For the student of history and politics the most important are the *Readers' Guide to Periodical Literature* and the publication known variously as the *International Index* (to 1965), the *Social Sciences and Humanities Index* (to 1974), and now separately as the *Social Sciences Index* and the *Humanities Index*.

The *Readers' Guide* and similar indexes list articles alphabetically by author and under one or more subject headings. The abbreviations used to save space in these mammoth volumes are confusing at first, but easily comprehended after a brief look at the key in the front. Reference books and indexes always have a preface that explains their use. And the system will be well worth your time to master because these indexes are invaluable resources for countless topics. The more current information you seek, the more will you find it necessary to consult such indexes and the periodical articles they list.

---

[1] Remember, even though your card catalogue lists all the books in *your library*, your library (in most cases) will not have all the possible books on a topic. Printed catalogues and bibliographies will acquaint you with sources you may wish to order through interlibrary loan or seek in another library.

THE REFERENCE ROOM AND THE REFERENCE LIBRARIAN

The above guides, indexes, and bibliographies are usually found in a special reference room or reference area. This is a section of the library you should get to know well. It would take literally hundreds of pages simply to list the materials that might be found in the larger reference collections. (Note: Reference materials are those that usually cannot be checked out of the library.) Even small libraries often house an impressive array of reference works—dictionaries, encyclopedias, indexes, bibliographies, statistical compilations, and the like. We won't bore you with even a short list of potentially valuable sources. Simply remember that somewhere in your reference collection there is a book(s) that contains the answer to just about any question you might have. For instance, just in the category of dictionaries there are historical dictionaries, pronunciation dictionaries, slang dictionaries, and rhyming dictionaries. There are dictionaries of forgotten words, new words, common words, foreign words, technical words, crossword-puzzle words, uncouth words, and even criminal words.[2] And even then the list is not exhausted.

Faced with such overwhelming diversity you may well ask, "How do I begin?" Of course the card catalogue will list all the reference works in your library. Browsing through the reference collection is even a better way to get a feel for the scope and diversity of the holdings. Perhaps the best way to get started, however, is to ask the reference librarian for help. Usually reference librarians will bend over backward to aid the student in need. But do not expect them to do your work for you. Seek guidance, not ready-made answers.

One manual on library usage lists the following rules for seeking help from reference librarians.

Rule 1. Don't be afraid to approach a reference librarian; that's what he's there for. In fact, if not enough people use his services, he'll be out of a job.

Rule 2. Not every employee of a large library is a reference librarian, so don't be surprised or annoyed if you get sent to another desk.

Rule 3. Don't expect the reference librarian to answer your research questions for you. He may be able to do so if they are simple ones, but his function is primarily to lead you to likely sources, not to do your research for you.

Rule 4. Be specific in your questions and requests. Don't say, "I want to find out something about China" when what you mean is, "I want to find out how the Chinese cook rice." You'll find what you want a lot more rapidly if you make your request as specific as possible.

Rule 5. Don't be afraid to come back if you don't find what you want in the first source the librarian recommends....If you miss the first time round, he'll probably know of other sources for you to investigate.[3]

In summary, remember, the only way to learn to use the library is to *use the library*. Happy hunting.

---

[2] A good example of how specialized some dictionaries can be is Eric Partridge's, *A Dictionary of the Underworld*. It is subtitled: "Being the vocabularies of crooks, criminals, racketeers, beggars and tramps, convicts, the commercial underworld, the drug traffic, the white slave traffic, [and] spivs." The dictionary is 886 pages long! If you want to know what a "spiv" is, look it up in this dictionary.

[3] The five rules were drawn from Robert W. Murphey, *How and Where to Look It Up* (New Yo[rk]: McGraw-Hill, 1958), p. 29. In addition, the library layout and card catalogue sections drew some i[deas] from William Coyle, *Research Papers*, 2nd ed. (Indianapolis, Ind.: Odyssey Press, 1965), pp[.]

EXERCISES

**SET A
Exercise 1**

Using a diagram and/or words, note the location of the following in your library:

The card catalogue	The U.S. history collection
The main desk	The European history collection
The reference room/area	The *Readers' Guide*
The reserve room/area	The encyclopedia sets
The periodical room/area	The audio-visual section (if applicable)

**SET A
Exercise 2[4]**

Answer the following questions about your college library:

1. What are the regular opening and closing hours on weekdays?

2. Who is the chief reference librarian?

3. Who is the head librarian?

---

[4]For the concept of Exercises 2 and 3 (and some of the questions in Exercise 2) the authors are indebted to Coyle, *ibid.*, pp. 103–06.

4. Is the library open on Sunday?

5. Where can you find out which periodicals the library subscribes to?

6. What is the policy for checking out books?

SET A Exercise 3 Using the reference collection, answer the following questions and list the source(s) you used. *Try to avoid general encyclopedias for this exercise*—the object is to acquaint you with as wide a variety of sources as possible.

Note: We have purposely not listed specific reference works because of space considerations. But keep in mind that there are numbers of possible sources in each of the following categories:

Atlases (maps plus much more useful geographic information)
Dictionaries (word origins, word histories, word meanings)
Dictionaries of Famous Quotations
Biographical Dictionaries (biographies of the famous and near famous)
Book Review Indexes (abstracts of reviews of important books)
Periodical Indexes (the *Readers' Guide, Humanities Index,* etc.)
Guides to Government Publications
Almanacs and Yearbooks (information on the year just past plus many statistics)
Encyclopedias (a little bit, and sometimes a lot, on almost everything)
Works of special value to historians, such as:
    Guide to Historical Literature (American Historical Association)
    An Encyclopedia of World History (ed. William L. Langer)
    Encyclopedia of American History (ed. Richard B. Morris)
    Various dictionaries of dates

QUESTIONS 1. Locate a book review of David McCullough's *The Path Between the Seas* (1977). Simply provide the citation for the magazine or journal in which the review appeared, including the author of the review and the date.

_____

Source: _____

2. What mountain is the highest in Colorado? _____

Source: _____

3. Which baseball team won the National League pennant in 1933?_____

Source: _____

4. On what date was President Theodore Roosevelt born? _____

Source: _____

5. Locate a magazine article (author, date, periodical) about President Jimmy Carter written in 1977.

_____

_____

Source: _____

6. Who wrote: "A good book is the precious lifeblood of a master spirit"?

_____

Source: _____

7. When and where was the Battle of the Bulge fought?_____

_____

_____

_____

Source: _____

8. What is Julia Ward Howe famous for? _____

_____

Source: _____

9. How many plays has Arthur Miller written? _____

_____

Source: _____

10. What or whom is a "cony catcher"? _____

_____

Source: _____

11. What is the classification number for Winston Churchill's _The Gathering Storm?_

_____

Source: _____

12. When was Benjamin Disraeli prime minister of Britain? _____

_____

Source: _____

13. Which schools in your state have graduate programs in history? _____

_____

Source: _____

SET B
(Optional)

1. What is the longest river in France? _____

_____

Source: _____

2. On what date did Charles Dickens die? _____

_____

Source: _____

3. Who wrote: "Power tends to corrupt and absolute power corrupts absolutely"?

_____

Source: _____

4. Who was the women's 100-meter-run champion in the 1968 Olympics?_____

_____

Source: _____

5. Locate an article on American slavery written after 1970 and appearing in a historical journal. Cite the title of the article, the author, the journal, and the date.

_____

Source: _____

6. When did Nigeria become an independent nation?_____

_____

Source: _____

7. When was Georg Leo von Caprivi chancellor of Germany? _____

_____

Source: _____

8. Locate, and provide the citation for, a book review of Betty Friedan's *The Feminine Mystique.*

_____

_____

_____

_____

Source: _____

9. What was the population of Great Britain (England, Scotland, Wales) in 1861? 1961?

_____

Source: _____

10. What are the dates of the Tokugawa Shogunate in Japan? _____

_____

Source: _____

Suggestions for Further Reading

The Nature of History—Philosophy of History

Becker, Carl. *Everyman His Own Historian.* New York: Appleton-Century-Crofts, 1935.

Bloch, Marc. *The Historian's Craft.* New York: Knopf, 1961.

Butterfield, Herbert. *The Historical Novel.* Cambridge: Cambridge University Press, 1924.

_____. *History and Human Relations.* London: Collins, 1951.

_____. *Man on His Past.* Cambridge: Cambridge University Press, 1955.

_____. *The Whig Interpretation of History.* London: G. Bell, 1931.

Carr, E. H. *What Is History?* New York: Knopf, 1962.

Collingwood, R. G. *The Idea of History.* Oxford: Clarendon Press, 1946.

Commager, Henry Steele. *The Nature and Study of History.* Columbus, Ohio: Charles E. Merrill Books, 1965.

Dray, William H. *Philosophy of History.* Englewood Cliffs, N.J.: Prentice-Hall, 1964.

Fischer, David Hackett. *Historians' Fallacies: Toward a Logic of Historical Thought.* New York: Harper & Row, 1970.

Gardiner, Patrick L. *The Nature of Historical Explanation.* New York: Oxford University Press, 1952.

_____, ed. *Theories of History.* New York: Free Press, 1959.

Gottschalk, Louis. *Understanding History.* New York: Knopf, 1950.

Gustavson, Carl G. *The Mansion of History.* New York: McGraw-Hill, 1976.

_____. *A Preface to History.* New York: McGraw-Hill, 1955.

Hexter, J. H. *The History Primer.* New York: Basic Books, 1971.

Hughes, H. Stuart. *History as Art and as Science.* New York: Harper & Row, 1964.

Kitson Clark, George. *The Critical Historian.* London: Heinemann, 1967.

Marwick, Arthur. *The Nature of History.* London: Macmillan, 1970.

Meyerhoff, Hans, ed. *The Philosophy of History in Our Time.* New York: Doubleday, 1959.

Nash, Ronald H., ed. *Ideas of History.* 2 vols. New York: E. P. Dutton, 1969.

Nevins, Allan. *The Gateway to History.* Chicago: Quadrangle Books, 1963.

Norling, Bernard. *Timeless Problems in History.* Notre Dame, Ind.: University of Notre Dame Press, 1970.

_____. *Toward a Better Understanding of History.* Notre Dame, Ind.: University of Notre Dame Press, 1960.

Rowse, A. L. *The Use of History.* Rev. ed. London: English Universities Press, 1963.

Smith, Page. *The Historian and History.* New York: Knopf, 1964.

Tholfsen, Trygve R. *Historical Thinking.* New York: Harper & Row, 1967.

Trevelyan, G. M. *An Autobiography and Other Essays.* London: Longmans, Green, 1949.
_____. *Clio, A Muse and Other Essays.* New ed. London: Longmans, Green, 1930.
Walsh, W. H. *An Introduction to Philosophy of History.* 3rd ed. rev. London: Hutchinson University Library, 1967.

Historical Methodology

Altick, Richard D. *The Scholar Adventurers.* New York: Macmillan, 1950.
Aydelotte, William O. *Quantification in History.* Reading, Mass.: Addison-Wesley, 1971.
Barzun, Jacques. *Clio and the Doctors: Psycho-history, Quanto-history and History.* Chicago: Chicago University Press, 1974.
_____, and Henry F. Graff. *The Modern Researcher.* Rev. ed. New York: Harcourt, Brace, 1970.
Cantor, Norman F., and Richard I. Schneider. *How to Study History.* New York: Thomas Y. Crowell, 1967.
Daniels, Robert V. *Studying History: How and Why.* 2nd ed. Englewood Cliffs, N.J.: Prentice-Hall, 1972.
Elton, G. R. *The Practice of History.* London: Sydney University Press, 1967.
Gawronski, Donald V. *History Meaning and Method.* 3rd ed. Glenview, Ill.: Scott, Foresman, 1975.
Gray, Wood, et al. *Historian's Handbook: A Key to the Study and Writing of History.* 2nd ed. Boston: Houghton Mifflin, 1964.
The History Teacher. Long Beach, Calif.: The Society for History Education. Published Quarterly.
Marwick, Arthur. *What History Is and Why It Is Important; Primary Sources; Basic Problems of Writing History; Common Pitfalls in Historical Writing.* Bletchley, England: The Open University Press, 1970.
Neugent, Walter T. K. *Creative History.* Philadelphia: Lippincott, 1967.
Renier, G. J. *History: Its Purpose and Method.* New York: Harper & Row, 1965 (1950).
Shafer, Robert Jones, ed. *A Guide to Historical Method.* Rev. ed. Homewood, Ill.: Dorsey, 1974.
Shorter, Edward. *The Historian and the Computer.* Englewood Cliffs, N.J.: Prentice-Hall, 1971.
Stephens, Lester D. *Probing the Past: A Guide to the Study and Teaching of History.* Boston: Allyn and Bacon, 1974.
Winks, Robin W., ed. *The Historian as Detective: Essays on Evidence.* New York: Harper & Row, 1968.

Historiography

Barnes, Harry E. *A History of Historical Writing.* 2nd rev. ed. New York: Dover, 1963.
Gay, Peter, and Gerald J. Cavanaugh, eds. *Historians at Work.* 2 vols. New York: Harper & Row, 1972.
Geyl, Pieter. *Debates with Historians.* New York: Meridian Books, 1958.
Gilbert, Felix, and Stephen R. Graubard, eds. *Historical Studies Today.* New York: Norton, 1972.
Gooch, George Peabody. *History and Historians in the Nineteenth Century.* Rev. ed. London: Longmans, Green, 1952.
Halperin, S. William, ed. *Some Twentieth-Century Historians.* Chicago: University of Chicago Press, 1961.
Higham, John, Leonard Krieger, and Felix Gilbert. *History: The Development of Historical Studies in the United States.* Englewood Cliffs, N.J.: Prentice-Hall, 1964.

Kraus, Michael. *The Writing of American History.* Norman, Okla.: University of Oklahoma Press, 1953.

Kren, George M., and Leon H. Rappoport, eds. *Varieties of Psychohistory.* New York: Springer, 1976.

Stephens, Lester D. *Historiography: A Bibliography.* Metuchen, N.J.: Scarecrow Press, 1975.

Stern, Fritz, ed. *The Varieties of History from Voltaire to the Present.* Cleveland: World, 1956.

Thompson, James Westfall. *A History of Historical Writing.* 2 vols. New York: Macmillan, 1942.

Wolman, Benjamin B., ed. *The Psychoanalytic Interpretation of History.* New York: Harper & Row, 1971.